Cover: Nathan Love, Erwin Madrid

mheducation.com/prek-12

Send all inquiries to:
McGraw-Hill Education
Two Penn Plaza
New York, NY 10121

ISBN: 978-0-07-901819-9
MHID: 0-07-901819-X

Printed in the United States of America.

5 6 7 8 9 LWI 25 24 23 22 21

D

Program Authors

Diane August

Donald R. Bear

Kathy R. Bumgardner

Jana Echevarria

Douglas Fisher

David J. Francis

Vicki Gibson

Jan Hasbrouck

Timothy Shanahan

Josefina V. Tinajero

Growing and Learning

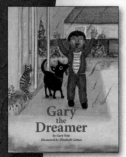

UNIT
2

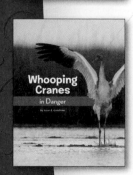

Figure It Out

One of a Kind

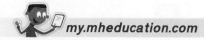

Meet the Challenge

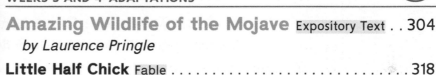

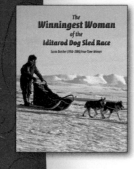

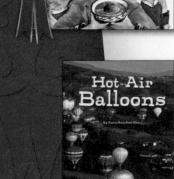

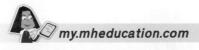

Take Action

Think It Over

Essential Question

How do people from different cultures contribute to a community?

Read about the poet and author Gary Soto. Find out about Gary's culture and his community.

 Go Digital!

Gary the Dreamer

by Gary Soto
illustrated by Elizabeth Gómez

I was born in April, a month when it rains and rains. Maybe this is why when I was three years old I liked to open my mouth and taste rain! Also, April is when flowers bloom. Bees arrive out of nowhere.

I lived in a small white house. My dog's name was Blackie. My cat's name was Boots. I had a canary just bigger than a big person's thumb. But my bird flew away when the little door of its cage was left open. So sorry, little canary, but I think it was me who left it open!

I remember my high chair. I remember watching my parents and older brother at the dinner table. When I got a little bigger, I got to sit with them. Most mornings, I ate oatmeal sprinkled with brown sugar. The sugar was like rocket energy. I blasted out of the house ready to play.

I played tag with the neighbor kids. I played hide-and-seek. I played catch with oranges. In our backyard, we had an orange tree. We also had plum, lemon, and apple trees. Lucky me! Anytime I was hungry for a snack, I just went outside and picked a fruit!

I didn't have many toys. My army men were pinto beans and pebbles. I played with them in the dirt. I got dirty from playing hard. It seemed like a giant pepper shaker had sprinkled me with dust!

My favorite fruit was watermelon. After I ate a slice of watermelon, I ended up with seeds in my mouth. These seeds were my ammo to spit at my older brother. He would spit some back at me. It was sort of like a fun war. The seeds flew all over the place.

14

In kindergarten, I learned my colors. I learned to tie my shoes and to be nice. I liked to sing, too. My brother said he could hear me from the next classroom.

I made my first friend, Darrell. I made another friend, José. At recess, we went on the slide. It was like a big shiny spoon, and slippery! Then we went on the swings. It was scary but fun going high and jumping out. Then we went on the monkey bars. If I fell, I never got hurt.

In first grade, I **practiced** writing the alphabet. The letters were big and blocky. I wrote my name: G A R Y.

Some days my nice teacher would have to tell me, "Gary, sit still." I wiggled a lot in my chair. I dreamed a lot. I was busy looking at the floor, or my hands, or out the window—wow, could that be my canary in the tree?

I couldn't **pronounce** some words. I couldn't say "sandwich." I would say "sammie." I knew that two plus two was four. But what was five plus seven? I counted out my answer on my fingers, sticky from the peanut butter and jam inside my "sammie."

STOP AND CHECK

Ask and Answer Questions
Why does Gary like recess? Reread page 15 to find the answer.

In second grade, we collected money to help children in Africa. They didn't have anything to eat. I collected pennies, lots of pennies. I noticed that the pennies were the same as me. You see, I was naturally brown, and even browner from running in the sun. I felt like I was giving poor Africa a piece of me.

My **classmates** got taller. But I seemed to stay the same size. I still liked playing at recess. I liked dodge ball, kickball, and foursquare. I would **tumble** when I played soccer. I was quick. I **admire** people who are quick, and who play fair.

STOP AND CHECK

Ask and Answer Questions How does Gary feel about collecting pennies? Reread to find the answer.

16

By third grade, I was a good reader. I loved picture books. The pages were bright and colorful as toucans, those tropical birds with long beaks. Every week I went to the public library. I checked out mountains of books.

I was still a dreamer. Sometimes I watched ants going in and out of their holes. Or I would watch water racing in the curb. The river of water carried matchsticks, leaves, gum wrappers, and those poor little ants! I rescued some of those ants. I put them carefully on my finger and set them on the cement curb. They lay for a while, like weak little shadows. Then they woke up and staggered away.

It was fun in third grade. I still stayed small, like those ants I guess. I was **scared** of math—poor me! But reading was what I really liked. I read on the couch. I read in bed with carrot sticks like pencils in my hands.

STOP AND CHECK

Visualize How does Gary feel about reading? Use the words in the story to picture what is happening.

I liked to read in my favorite tree. Once, when Boots came by, I tossed a piece of bark at him. He looked around and meowed. I giggled. I tossed another piece of bark at him. This time Boots saw me and climbed up the tree. We sat on a fat limb, the two of us. I read him a story about a bird. He licked his paws. The engine inside him began to purr. I guess Boots liked reading, too.

On weekends, my family went to Chinatown.
We bought groceries there at the Mexican store.
I remember mariachis roving the street. Their
sombreros were huge. You couldn't see their eyes,
only their hanging mustaches. Their trumpets
blared. The guitars strummed. Their violins seemed
to weep. The *guitarrón* thumped deeply.

One time, I saw a dog dance to the mariachi
music. The dog went back and forth, back and
forth, like he was doing the cha-cha.

Every night I took a bubble bath in our deep tub. The water roared from the faucet as I climbed in. The bubbles rose like mountains, no, like really pretty clouds. I scooped up the bubbles and patted them onto my face. I pretended that I had a beard. I placed some of the bubbles on my head. Oh, a sombrero!

I was a dreamer. I was sometimes in another world.

In bed, I covered myself with two blankets. I thought about the day before I fell asleep, so tired. My legs kicked, as I dreamed I was running for a touchdown and the whole school was watching me!

Gary Soto grew up to be an author. He dreamed up ideas for more than forty books for children and grown-ups. He shares his Mexican-American culture through his poems and stories.

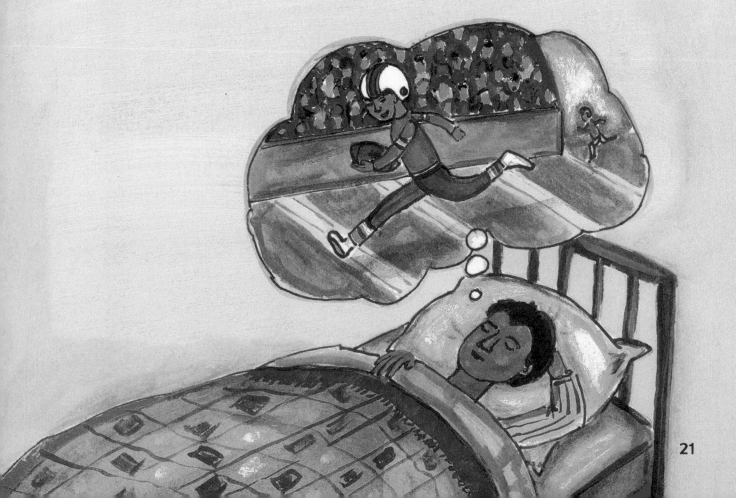

About the Author and Illustrator

Gary Soto may be a dreamer, but he is also a reader. He says, "I don't have much of a life because my nose is often stuck in a book. But I discovered that reading builds a life inside the mind. I enjoy biographies and novels and reading in Spanish." He also likes theater, sports, and traveling. Gary is an award-winning author of more than forty books for children and grown-ups.

Elizabeth Gómez is a well-known painter and book illustrator. Her dreamy paintings shine with lovely colors. "In everything I paint," she says, "there are always people, animals, plants, and beauty." Elizabeth also helps people paint murals on school walls. She says that she loves to see a plain wall become a little gem.

Author's Purpose
Why do you think the author called himself a dreamer?

Respond to the Text

Summarize

Think about the sequence of events in *Gary the Dreamer*. Summarize what you learned about Gary's life. Use your Sequence Chart to help you.

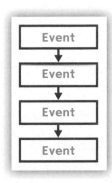

Write

How does Gary Soto show how his dreams helped him become a writer? Use these sentence frames to organize your text evidence.

> Gary describes his childhood by . . .
> He shares his dreams to help me understand . . .
> At the end, Gary writes . . .

Make Connections

What did young Gary learn from his community? **ESSENTIAL QUESTION**

How do authors and writers share their cultures? **TEXT TO WORLD**

Compare Texts
Read about how two people share their cultures.

Sharing Cultures

Pat Mora is an author. Kadir Nelson is an artist. Their stories and paintings help others learn about different cultures.

Pat Mora Loves Books

Pat Mora has a special word for how she feels about books. She calls it *bookjoy.* Born in El Paso, Texas, in 1942, Pat learned to love books and reading from her mother. Books are magic to Pat.

"I wouldn't be me without books," she says.

Pat grew up in a bilingual home. That means she and her family spoke both English and Spanish. Pat is proud of her culture. She has written more than 36 children's books. Many of them are written in both English and Spanish.

Pat Mora grew up in a town on the border of America and Mexico.

Pat uses her stories and poems to share her culture. She works hard to share her love of books with all children. Every year in April, many libraries and schools in America celebrate Día. Día is the nickname for Children's Day, Book Day. *Día* means "day" in Spanish. Children get together at libraries, schools, and parks to celebrate. It's like a big book fiesta, or party.

Heroes and History

Kadir Nelson was born in Washington, DC, in 1974. When he was three years old, he picked up a pencil and started drawing. Then, when he turned eleven, he spent the summer with his uncle. His uncle was an artist and teacher. Kadir says that summer changed his life.

Kadir Nelson has also illustrated many children's books. His art has been on magazine covers.

Kadir is inspired by brave and honest leaders. He sometimes paints African American heroes he admires, such as Martin Luther King Jr. He also paints great athletes and everyday heroes, such as dads taking their children to the beach.

Kadir wants people to feel good when they look at his art. His paintings are colorful and real. They burst with action. Kadir says he has always been an artist. Sharing how he sees the world is part of who he is.

Inspired by Cultures

Pat's books and Kadir's paintings are inspired by their cultures. Their stories and paintings **contribute** to how other people see the world. That's inspiring!

Make Connections

How do people help others learn about different cultures? ESSENTIAL QUESTION

How can artists and authors contribute to their communities? TEXT TO TEXT

Essential Question

What can traditions teach you about cultures?

Read about Yoon. Find out what a tradition taught her.

Go Digital!

Yoon and the Jade Bracelet

By **Helen Recorvits**
Pictures by **Gabi Swiatkowska**

My name is Yoon. I came here from Korea, a country far away.

Soon after we settled in America, it was time to **celebrate** my birthday. I was hoping for a very special present—a jump rope. I watched the girls in my school yard turning such a rope and jumping and singing happy songs. I wanted so much to jump and sing with them, but I was still the new girl. I had not been invited yet.

On my birthday, my mother called to me.
"Little Yoon, come! I have a present for you!"
I clapped my hands and ran to her.
She handed me something thin and flat wrapped in pretty paper. "Happy birthday!" she said.
Jump ropes are not thin and flat, I thought. I tried not to show my **disappointment**. "Thank you, Mother," I said, smiling.

My mother watched excitedly as I opened the present. It was a Korean storybook about a little girl who was tricked by a tiger. I knew the story, and I laughed at the silly girl.

"The pictures are colorful," I said.

"Yes, they **remind** me of the pictures you draw, Yoon."

I liked the book, but my heart still longed for a jump rope.

"And here is another surprise," my mother said as she handed me a lovely box.

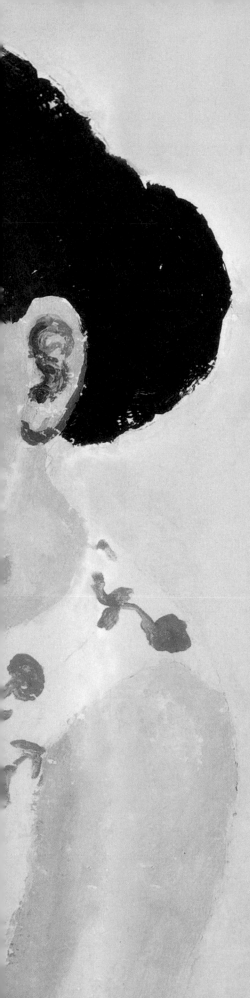

Inside was a pale green bracelet. I held its cool smoothness in my hand.

"A jade bracelet, Yoon," my mother said. "When I was a young girl, my own mother gave me this very bracelet. Now I am giving it to you."

"It is a wonderful present," I said. It was so wonderful I felt afraid to take it from her.

"Look, Yoon," she said. "Here is your Korean name now etched inside." She showed me the dancing **symbols** that meant Shining Wisdom.

Then she told me the story of jade. "Jade is a stone from the earth, but it is called the gem of the heavens. Green is the color of happiness and hope, and it is said that wearing jade will bring you good luck. It is the symbol of truth and friendship. A **precious** gem for a precious daughter." My mother slipped the bracelet onto my wrist.

At lunchtime the next day at school, I sat at the end of the table. An older girl from another class sat down beside me.

"Oh, look," she said, "you are wearing such a pretty bracelet!"

"Thank you," I said.

"You are alone today. I will be your friend. Would you like to play jump rope with me?" the older girl asked.

Jump rope? "Yes, yes!" I answered.

"Good! I will teach you. We will have fun!"

"Yes!" I said, smiling at my new friend. Jump rope!

After lunch we ran outside to play awhile. The
older girl tied one end of the rope to the fence.
Then she gave me the other end to turn, turn. She
jumped and sang while I turned faster, slower,
faster. I turned and turned. My arm grew tired. I
had learned the rope part very well, but I really
wanted to learn the jump part.

"When will *I* jump?" I asked.

"Tomorrow," the older girl said. The bell rang.
It was time to go inside, and she took the rope
from me.

"I really like your bracelet," she said. "In
America, friends share things. If we are going to be
friends, you should share your bracelet with me.
You should let me wear it—just for today."

My birthday bracelet? Oh, no, no, no. I could not
share that. My mother's own mother had given it to
her, and now it was mine. No, no, I shook my head.

STOP AND CHECK

Visualize Visualize Yoon and
the older girl jumping rope.
How does Yoon feel?

"Well ... then how can we be friends?" the older girl asked. "I thought you wanted to learn how to jump rope?"

I slipped the jade bracelet off and held it in my hand. My mother said it would bring me good luck and good friends. But sharing it did not seem right.

Quickly the older girl grabbed the bracelet from me and twisted it onto her own wrist. "Do not worry," she said. "I will give it back tomorrow."

When I got home from school, I went straight to my room. My mother came in to check on me. As I sat on my bed reading my new Korean storybook, she reached for my arm and gasped.

"Where is your bracelet, Yoon?"

I shrugged with shame, not trusting myself to speak.

"Oh, I see a sad face. Did you lose it at school, Yoon?"

I shrugged again.

"Maybe it rolled away and is hiding somewhere here," she said with teary eyes. And she kneeled to look under my bed.

"Mother," I said, tugging her sleeve, "I left it at school. I will get it tomorrow."

STOP AND CHECK

Visualize How does Yoon's mother feel about the missing bracelet? What words help you visualize what is happening on this page?

The next morning I waited in the school yard for the older girl. She was still wearing my jade bracelet.

"It is time to give back my bracelet," I said.

"I will give it to you later," she said, rushing past me.

All morning my heart was heavy with worry. I could not remember how to spell "cat" or how to add two plus two.

After lunch, when the children ran outside, I found the older girl again. "You have my bracelet and I want it back," I said.

"Stop bothering me! Do not be a pest!" She pushed me away and laughed.

I was just like the silly girl in my storybook. I had been tricked by a tiger.

Back in my classroom, I laid my head on my desk.

"What is wrong, Yoon?" my teacher asked.

I told my teacher about the older girl, and she sent for her.

"Do you have something that belongs to Yoon?" my teacher asked her. "Is that her bracelet you are wearing?"

"Oh, no!" the older girl said with her trickster tongue. "It is mine!"

"No! It is my birthday bracelet!" I said.

The children in my class gathered around us.

"Yoon was wearing it yesterday," the ponytail girl said.

"Yes," said the freckle boy. "I saw it, too."

"Can you tell me something about this bracelet, Yoon?" my teacher asked.

"My mother gave it to me," I answered, looking into the tiger girl's face. "This bracelet is a symbol of kindness and **courage**. It is a symbol of jade friendship—true friendship."

"Now *you* tell me about this bracelet," my teacher said to the older girl.

"Well ... it is smooth and green," she answered in a sure voice.

I worried I would never get my bracelet back. I did not feel like Shining Wisdom. My mother should have named me Shining Fool instead.

Then I had a very good idea. I whispered something into my teacher's ear.

"So tell me about the inside of this bracelet," she asked the older girl.

"Well ... it is smooth and green," she repeated.

The teacher told her to take it off, and the girl struggled to get it over her hand. My teacher looked inside and saw the dancing Korean symbols.

"Do you know what this says?" she asked the girl.

"No," the older girl said. "Well ... I thought it was my bracelet. I used to have one just like it. Maybe this one does belong to Yoon."

My teacher's eyes said Older-girl-you-are-in-trouble.

Then my teacher slid the jade bracelet easily over my hand. "Here is your name bracelet, Shining Wisdom."

And it fit. Perfectly.

My mother saw the bracelet on my wrist after school. She clapped her hands. "Aha! It *was* at school!"

"Mother," I asked, "does wearing jade make wishes come true?"

STOP AND CHECK

Visualize How does Yoon's mother feel when she sees the bracelet again? Visualize or picture in your mind what is happening in the story.

42

"Yes," she said. "It is known to happen." She smiled. "And what are your wishes?"

So I told her about my jump rope wish and my wish for true friends.

And I told her a story about a wise girl who tricked a tiger.

About the Author and Illustrator

Helen Recorvits has an early memory of her mother reading to her. Her favorite story then was Cinderella. When she was eight years old, Helen began writing her own stories. She shared them with her cousins. She wrote a weekly newspaper column when she was a teenager. Today she lives in Rhode Island. She teaches second grade.

Author's Purpose
Why do you think the author wrote about a girl and her bracelet?

Gabi Swiatkowska was born in Poland. Her first memory is of the crows that gathered in front of her house. She wrote stories and drew pictures, mostly of princesses. She studied art at the Lyceum of Art in Poland. Gabi also studied at the Cooper Union School of Art in New York. She lives in Brooklyn, New York.

Respond to the Text

Summarize

Think about the important details from *Yoon and the Jade Bracelet*. Summarize what you learned about the characters, setting, and story structure. Details from your Story Map may help you.

Characters

Setting

Beginning

↓

Middle

↓

End

Write

How does Yoon change from the beginning of the story to the end? Use these sentence frames to organize your text evidence.

At the beginning, Yoon wants . . .
The author helps me see that . . .
At the end, Yoon . . .

Make Connections

What did you learn about traditions in Yoon's culture? ESSENTIAL QUESTION

Why is learning about traditions and cultures important? TEXT TO WORLD

Compare Texts
Read about different traditions
that families celebrate.

Family Traditions

Many different people live in the United States.
Some come from other countries. Some groups have
been here a long time. Each group has its special
culture and **traditions**. People want to keep traditions
alive. They share them with their families. You can
learn about people by looking at their traditions.

Celebrating a New Year

Chinese families celebrate Lunar New Year.
Lunar New Year happens in January or February.
It lasts about two weeks. The holiday means that
winter is ending. Spring is on the way!

The traditions for Lunar New Year are very old.
Adults give children bright red envelopes. Red stands
for good luck and happiness. The envelopes are full
of good luck money.

Families wear colorful costumes to celebrate Lunar New Year.

This holiday is also a time for feasts. Chinese families share sweet, smooth, rice cakes. Some families eat a whole cooked fish. They give oranges as presents. They eat noodles, too. These foods are symbols for a happy year and long life.

In most big cities families watch the Lunar New Year parade. Dragon dancers glide down the street. Lion dancers wear costumes in red, yellow, and green. Bands march by in rows. Their drums beat out happy tunes. People in traditional costumes go by on floats. They wave to the crowd. BANG! Watch out for firecrackers! They are part of the tradition, too. Loud sounds are symbols of a joyful time of year.

Families Get Together

Summer is a time for family reunions. Many American families enjoy this tradition. Aunts, uncles, and cousins travel from far away. Family members play games together. They tell family stories. They share traditional foods, such as barbecue and homemade sweets. Sometimes there's a talent show. Family members often wear special T-shirts to show their **pride**.

Reunions can last for three days. People feel sad when the reunion ends. Then planning begins for the next one!

This family enjoys traditional foods at their reunion.

Larry Dale Gordon/The Image Bank/Getty Images

48

Storytelling and Dance

Many Native American cultures have traditions of storytelling and dance. The stories are from long ago. Older people tell the stories to their children and grandchildren. They may use the culture's native language. The stories explain things in nature. They tell about the courage of early people.

Some Native American groups get together in the summer. They meet at big pow wows. These festivals celebrate culture through dance and music. Storytellers bring the old tales to life. The soft notes of a flute may help tell a story. The firm beat of a drum adds power. People from other cultures can watch and listen. Everyone enjoys the stories and learns about the traditions.

Traditions Are Everywhere

Traditions are a kind of glue. They hold families together. They make a culture strong. And traditions help us know the many people in the United States.

Native American storytellers pass down tales from long ago.

Make Connections

What can you learn about families through their traditions? ESSENTIAL QUESTION

Tell about some other family traditions you have read about. TEXT TO TEXT

Protecting Our Parks

Essential Question

How do landmarks help us understand our country's story?

Read two different arguments about protecting our national parks and monuments.

Go Digital!

In 1872, Yellowstone National Park became America's first **national** park. This happened thanks to a group of explorers who saw how beautiful the land was. They wanted to protect it. So they went to Washington, DC, to write a law to protect nature. This **grand** act helped to create many more parks.

The National Park Service was started in 1916. It takes care of parks and national **monuments** in the United States. Many parks contain the last **traces** of some plants and animals. Protecting these lands is an important job.

STOP AND CHECK

Ask and Answer Questions
What kinds of problems can overcrowding at parks cause? Reread to find the answer.

Too Many Visitors

The park service must protect a **massive** amount of land. No one knew that millions of people would want to visit. There were no clues. Now more than 275 million visitors come to the parks and monuments each year!

The park service wants people to visit. But overcrowding, or too many people, can create problems. There are often long waits to enter a park. Too many cars pollute the air. People drop litter on the hiking trails. Some people have even **carved** their names into cliffs. This makes the parks less enjoyable to visit.

People who work at the parks and **landmarks** are looking for new ways to control crowds. Other people disagree about what should be done.

Allow All Access

The National Park Service thinks that people should be able to visit America's parks and landmarks. Their mission is to protect land so that it can be enjoyed by everyone. They want families to hike the trails, observe the animals, and learn about our country's history. But visitors need bathrooms, parking lots, and places to eat. The park service can make changes. They can create rules to handle crowds. They could spend money to fix damage to the parks. They could build more parking lots, restaurants, and bathrooms.

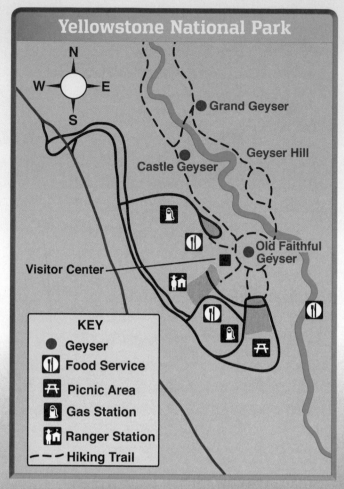

Yellowstone National Park

Grand Geyser

Geyser Hill

Castle Geyser

Old Faithful Geyser

Visitor Center

KEY
- ● Geyser
- Food Service
- Picnic Area
- Gas Station
- Ranger Station
- - - - Hiking Trail

In addition to places to eat and rest, Yellowstone National Park also has shops, museums, and cabins.

Neal Herbert, NPS

Protect Our Parks

Overcrowding is a problem at national parks. It can lead to pollution, litter, and noise. Many people think that national parks should be kept natural. They suggest only letting a certain number of people visit each day. They think that adding more parking lots and bathrooms will harm the plants and animals.

A Path Forward

America's national park system was not built to handle millions of visitors. If changes aren't made, overcrowding could damage the land and harm plants and animals. Everyone should have the chance to enjoy nature.

A Meaningful Symbol

Each element of the National Park Service's symbol represents something that the agency protects.

- The bison represents wildlife.
- The tree represents plants.
- The mountain represents geology.
- The lake represents natural resources such as water and air.
- The arrowhead represents the history of our country.

Source: National Park Service

Respond to the Text

Use important details from the selection to summarize. SUMMARIZE

Why is *Protecting Our Parks* a good title for this selection? WRITE

Why do so many people visit parks and monuments? TEXT TO WORLD

Compare Texts

Read what the manager of the National Park Service's youth programs thinks about visiting parks.

5 Questions

For George McDonald

The National Park Service recently celebrated its 100th anniversary. George McDonald is the park service's youth programs manager. He spoke with TFK's Elizabeth Winchester.

You were raised in New York City. How did you experience national parks when you were a kid?
I used to climb trees around Grant's Tomb and attend concerts there. I also have memories of visiting the Statue of Liberty.

What are you doing to achieve your goal to give more people access to national parks and sites?
I work on the development of new sites that target minority groups, like the African Burial Ground [in New York City] and the Tuskegee Airmen National Historic Site [in Alabama].

The Find Your Park program encourages families to visit parks and share their experiences. Why?
It is important for young people and their families to identify with these magnificent places because they belong to everyone. Find Your Park encourages more people to appreciate our country's valuable resources, and to also protect them.

Kids get free admission to national parks. The Every Kid in a Park program gives free admission to the families of fourth graders. Why?
Reaching kids at this age increases their chances for academic success. I visited the national monuments in Washington, DC, when I was in the fourth grade, and it led to lifetime dedication to studying history. Our goal is to continue the Every Kid in a Park program. We want to have a lasting positive impact.

What is your favorite park, and how can kids celebrate the park service?
Yosemite is my favorite. It is so beautiful. To celebrate, go out to a park and have fun!

Yosemite National Park is in California. It covers 1,200 square miles.

Michal Jastrzebski/Shutterstock.com

Places to Visit

Yosemite National Park is just one of many **landmarks** and monuments in the United States. Here is a look at some others. What do you think you can learn from each one?

Statue of Liberty National Monument
Location: New York City, New York
Date Created: 1886
Why It's Important: The statue is a symbol of freedom and liberty. France gave it to the United States as a gift of friendship. It stands in New York Harbor.

Great Smoky Mountains National Park
Location: Tennessee and North Carolina
Date Created: 1934
Why It's Important: The park is one of the last large hardwood forests in the country. It's a safe place for many animals. There are about 1,500 black bears in the park today.

John F. Kennedy Space Center
Location: Cape Canaveral, Florida
Date Created: 1965
Why It's Important: The first men to walk on the Moon blasted off from the Kennedy Space Center in 1969. Since then, NASA has launched more than 135 missions from here.

Martin Luther King, Jr. Memorial
Location: Washington, DC
Date Created: 2011
Why It's Important: Martin Luther King, Jr. wanted all people to have the same rights. He inspired people to fight for the rights of African Americans.

Make Connections

What can you learn from visiting landmarks?
ESSENTIAL QUESTION

How are these landmarks and monuments like others you have read about? **TEXT TO TEXT**

ALL ABOARD!

ELIJAH McCOY'S STEAM ENGINE

By Monica Kulling
Illustrated by Bill Slavin

Essential Question

How can problem solving lead to new ideas?

Read about Elijah McCoy's idea. Find out how it made train travel safer and faster.

Go Digital!

SUMMER DAYS were mowing days in Colchester, Ontario. Elijah McCoy watched his father cut the tall grass. He was waiting for the machine to break. When it did, he jumped for joy. Elijah was only six, but already he was good at tinkering with tools.

From All Aboard! Elijah McCoy's Steam Engine by Monica Kulling, illustrated by Bill Slavin. © 2010 published by Tundra Books.

Elijah McCoy was born in 1844. His parents had come to Canada on the Underground Railroad. They didn't talk much about the slave days. Elijah and his eleven brothers and sisters kept them busy.

Elijah's mother and father saved every penny they could to send Elijah to school. At sixteen, he crossed the ocean to study in Scotland. Elijah had a dream: he wanted to work with machines. He wanted to become a mechanical engineer.

In 1866, Elijah finished school in Scotland. His family now lived in Michigan. One day, a locomotive rolled into the station with Elijah on board. His mind was crackling with ideas. In Michigan, he was going to be an engineer!

Elijah went looking for work at the Michigan Central Railroad.

"It takes learnin' to be an engineer," said the boss, spitting at Elijah's feet. "I got ashcat work if you wannit. Ain't hard. You bail it in. You grease the pig."

"Excuse me?" said Elijah.

"You shovel coal into the firebox," replied the boss, slowly. "You oil the wheels. You oil the bearings. It's not hard."

What a letdown! Elijah knew engines inside out. He knew how to **design** them. He knew how to build them. He also knew the boss didn't think much of him because he was Black. But Elijah needed work, so he took the job.

The steam locomotive was exciting. People called it the Iron Horse. It was a fire-breathing monster. When it had a head of steam, it was faster than a horse and buggy!

Feeding coal into the firebox was hot, hard work. It was also tricky. The fire boiled the water. The boiling water made steam. The steam worked the machinery. If the fire got too hot, the boiler might explode. If it wasn't hot enough, the train wouldn't move. Or it couldn't climb the smallest hill.

Elijah went to work in old clothes. An ashcat's job was a dirty one. Soon Elijah was covered in soot and cinders.

STOP AND CHECK

Ask and Answer Questions
How did Elijah feel about his job as an ashcat? Reread pages 62 and 63 to find the answer.

A boy was under the train. His clothes smelled of oil.

"That's your grease monkey," said the boss. "He'll oil the places you can't get to."

A grease monkey was paid pennies a day. At night he slept on the train's grimy floor. The work was dangerous, and boys often got hurt. Or worse.

There has to be a safer way, thought Elijah.

Elijah baled in the coal as fast as he could. Sweat poured down his face. His hands were raw. The water in the boiler took time to heat up. While Elijah baled, the grease monkey clambered around, oiling. Finally, the train was tanked up, ready for its run.

The engine huffed and puffed. Smoke billowed from its stack. The wheels clacked. The locomotive chugged along for about half an hour. *Chug! Chug! Chug!*

Suddenly, *screeeeech!* The train stopped cold. The boy hopped down and crawled under the wheels. Elijah hopped down with his oil can. The passengers stayed put. They waited. And waited some more.

"All aboard!" cried the conductor.
The pig was greased and ready to go.
Chug! Chug! Chug!

The passengers looked out at the passing farms.
They talked. They ate. They laughed.

Half an hour later—*screeeeech!*

Time to grease the pig again.

What a job! Elijah didn't know which part he hated
more—feeding the firebox or oiling the engine.

STOP AND CHECK

Ask and Answer Questions
Why was early train travel so slow? Reread pages 66 and 67 to find the answer.

The train's metal parts needed oil to work smoothly. Without oil, the parts would stick and wear down. The train would stop.

While Elijah scooped coal, his mind sparked with ideas. Could he invent an oil cup that oiled the engine while the train was running? Every night after work, Elijah made drawings. Finally, he had a drawing of an oil cup he knew would work.

It took two years for Elijah to make a model of his oil cup. In 1872, he applied for a patent to protect his invention. Then he took the metal cup to work.

"There's a hole here to let the oil drip out," Elijah told the boss. "It drips oil when oil is needed. It drips it *where* it's needed. It's **simple**. Why not give it a try?"

Surprisingly, the boss agreed. Elijah attached the cup to the engine.

"Just for the Kalamazoo run," added the boss gruffly.

The train rumbled off, heading for Kalamazoo, Michigan. The engine huffed and puffed. Smoke billowed from its stack. The wheels clacked. The train chugged along for half an hour. *Chug! Chug! Chug!*

Everyone wondered when the train would stop. But it didn't. It chugged along for another half hour. And another.

STOP AND CHECK

Visualize What do you think the train ride was like? Use the descriptions to visualize the ride.

Elijah McCoy's oil cup worked! It oiled the engine while the train was running. The train reached Kalamazoo in record time. The grease monkey was safe. Elijah was happy.

Elijah McCoy's oil cup made train travel faster and safer. Elijah worked on engine inventions all his life. He followed his dream. When Elijah got older, he **encouraged** children to stay in school and to follow their dreams too.

THE REAL MCCOY!

Have you ever heard someone say they want the "real McCoy"? It means they want the real thing—no knockoffs, no **substitutes**. Other inventors copied Elijah McCoy's oil cup, but their drip cups didn't work as well. When engineers wanted to make sure they got the best oil cup, they asked for the real McCoy.

Was Elijah McCoy a one-hit wonder? No way. He was an inventing marvel. During his lifetime, he filed 57 patents—more than any other Black inventor. Most of his inventions had to do with engines, but several did not. Elijah invented a portable ironing board, a lawn sprinkler, and even a better rubber heel for shoes. Want the best **quality**? Ask for the real McCoy!

ABOUT THE AUTHOR AND ILLUSTRATOR

MONICA KULLING

was born in Vancouver, British Columbia. As a girl, she loved the outdoors. She climbed trees, played baseball, and rode her bike. She liked to read comic books, too. She began to read and write poetry when she was in high school. When she was in college, she fell in love with children's literature. Then it was full steam ahead. She's been writing children's books since then.

BILL SLAVIN

has illustrated more than seventy children's books including *The Big Book of Canada*. He has won many awards for his illustrations. Now he is working on a new series called *Elephants Never Forget*. He lives in Ontario, Canada with his wife, Esperança Melo.

AUTHOR'S PURPOSE
Why do you think the author wrote about Elijah McCoy's life?

Respond to the Text

Summarize

Think about the important details from *All Aboard!* Summarize what you learned about how problem solving led to new ideas. Your Cause and Effect Chart may help you.

Cause	→	Effect
First	→	
Next	→	
Then	→	
Finally	→	

Write

How does the author help you understand what it takes to invent something important? Use these sentence frames to organize your text evidence.

> Monica Kulling writes about how Elijah . . .
> She uses descriptive language to tell about . . .
> This helps me understand that . . .

Make Connections

What did you learn about solving problems from Elijah McCoy?
ESSENTIAL QUESTION

Think of an invention that people use every day. Describe how it helps people. **TEXT TO WORLD**

Compare Texts

Read about how Thomas Edison's inventions made the world a better place to live.

Lighting the World

A Bright Idea

In 1878, Thomas Alva Edison started an **investigation.** It would light up the world. Back then, homes and streets were lit by gas. People wanted to use electricity to light their homes. No one had found a good way to do it.

Edison and his helpers tried to make an electric light bulb. In an electric light bulb, a strip of material gets hot and glows. However, the strip burned up too quickly.

Edison **examined** many materials. None of them worked. He even tried beard hair. Then he tried bamboo. A strip of bamboo glowed for a long time inside the bulb. Edison's idea for the light bulb was a success.

Edison's **solutions** went beyond the light bulb. He designed power plants to make electricity. He designed a system to bring electricity into homes. Because of Edison, most people have light and electricity today.

Edison changed the world with his many inventions.

(bkgd) Don Farrall/Photodisc/Getty Images (inset) Boyer/Roger Viollet/Getty Images

It's Electric!

Thomas Edison did many experiments with electricity. You can do an experiment with electricity, too. Investigate static electricity. Static electricity is an electric charge. It can build up when objects are rubbed together. Static electricity can pull objects together or push them apart.

Static Electricity Experiment

1. Cut several small pieces of tissue paper.

2. Place the pieces of paper on a table.

3. Hold the comb over the papers. What happens?

4. Now rub the comb on the wool about 10 times.

5. Hold the comb over the paper.

Materials
- scissors
- plastic comb
- wool scarf or sweater
- tissue paper

What happens to the paper?
What causes the paper to stick to the comb? Talk about your investigation with a partner.

Make Connections
How did Thomas Edison solve a problem with a new idea? **ESSENTIAL QUESTION**

What other inventors have you read about? How are they alike? **TEXT TO TEXT**

Essential Question

What can stories teach you?

Read about how stories help a wolf make new friends.

Go Digital!

WOLF!

By Becky Bloom

Illustrated by Pascal Biet

After walking for many days, a wolf wandered into a quiet little town. He was tired and hungry, his feet **ached**, and he had only a little money that he .. kept for emergencies.

Then he remembered. There's a farm outside this village, he thought. I'll find some food there ...
As he peered over the farm fence, he saw a pig, a duck, and a cow reading in the sun.

The wolf had never seen animals read before. "I'm so hungry that my eyes are playing tricks on me," he said to himself. But he really was very hungry and didn't stop to think about it for long.

The wolf stood up tall, took a deep breath ... and leaped at the animals with a howl—

"AaaOOOOOooo!"

Chickens and rabbits ran for their lives, but the duck, the pig, and the cow didn't budge.

"What is that awful noise?" complained the cow. "I can't **concentrate** on my book."

STOP AND CHECK

Visualize Which words help you visualize the wolf's actions?

"Just ignore it," said the duck.

The wolf did not like to be ignored.

"What's wrong with you?" growled the wolf. "Can't you see I'm a big and dangerous wolf?"

"I'm sure you are," replied the pig. "But couldn't you be big and dangerous somewhere else? We're trying to read. This is a farm for **educated** animals. Now be a good wolf and go away," said the pig, giving him a push.

The wolf had never been treated like this before.

"Educated animals ... educated animals!" the wolf repeated to himself. "This is something new. Well then! I'll learn how to read too." And off he went to school.

The children found it strange to have a wolf in their class, but since he didn't try to eat anyone, they soon got used to him. The wolf was serious and hardworking, and after much **effort** he learned to read and write. Soon he became the best in the class.

Feeling quite **satisfied**, the wolf went back to the farm and jumped over the fence. I'll show them, he thought.

He opened his book and began to read:

"Run, wolf! Run!
See wolf run."

"You've got a long way to go," said the duck, without even bothering to look up. And the pig, the duck, and the cow went on reading their own books, not the least impressed.

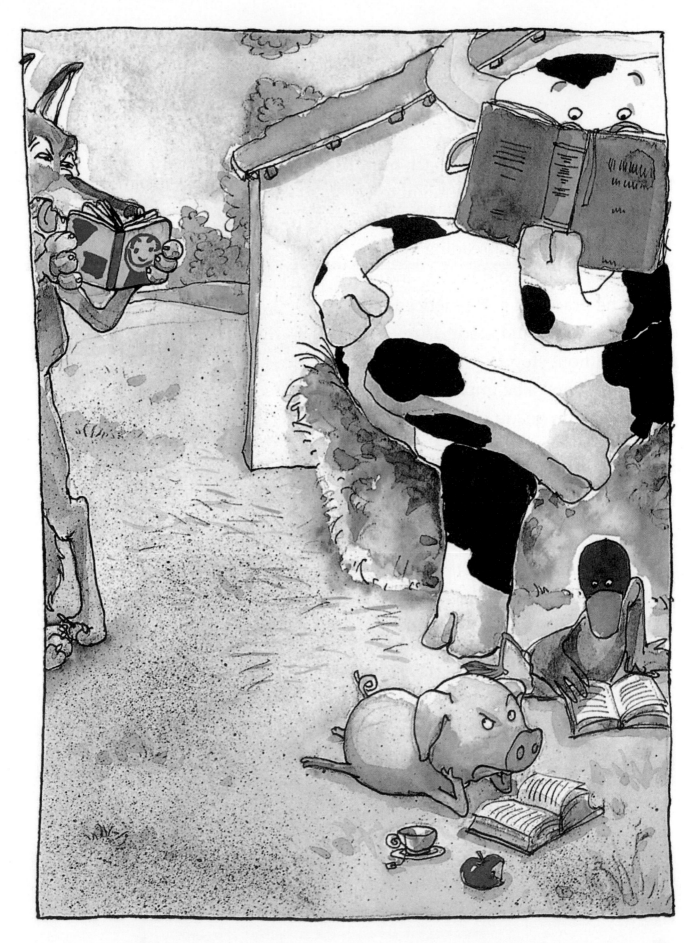

The wolf jumped back over the fence and ran straight to the public library. He studied long and hard, reading lots of dusty old books, and he practiced and practiced until he could read without stopping.

"They'll be impressed with my reading now," he said to himself.

The wolf walked up to the farm gate and knocked. He opened *The Three Little Pigs* and began to read:

"Onceuponatimethrewerethreelittlepigsonedaytheir mothercalledthemandtoldthem—"

"Stop that racket," interrupted the duck.

"You have **improved**," remarked the pig, "but you still need to work on your style."

The wolf tucked his tail between his legs and slunk away.

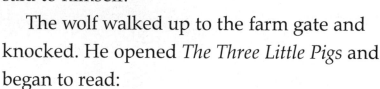

STOP AND CHECK

Visualize How did the wolf feel after he read the story aloud? Which words help you visualize what happens?

But the wolf wasn't about to give up. He counted the little money he had left, went to the bookshop, and bought a splendid new storybook. His first very own book!

He was going to read it day and night, every letter and every line. He would read so well that the farm animals would admire him.

Ding-dong, rang the wolf at the farm gate.

He lay down on the grass, made himself comfortable, took out his new book, and began to read.

He read with confidence and passion, and the pig, the cow, and the duck all listened and said not one word.

Each time he finished a story, the pig, the duck, and the cow asked if he would please read them another.

So the wolf read on, story after story.

One minute he was Little Red Riding Hood,

the next a genie emerging from a lamp,

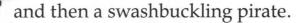

and then a swashbuckling pirate.

"This is so much fun!" said the duck.
"He's a master," said the pig.
"Why don't you join us on our picnic
today?" offered the cow.

And so they all had a picnic—the pig, the duck, the cow, and the wolf. They lay in the tall grass and told stories all the afternoon long.

"We should all become storytellers," said the cow suddenly.

"We could travel around the world," added the duck.

"We can start tomorrow morning," said the pig.

The wolf stretched in the grass. He was happy to have such wonderful friends.

STOP AND CHECK

Visualize How do the animals and the wolf feel about each other? Which words help you visualize their actions?

95

ABOUT THE AUTHOR AND ILLUSTRATOR

BECKY BLOOM was born in Greece but has traveled to many countries to work and go to school. She has many different animals around her, but no wolf. Her other books include *Leo and Lester, Mice Make Trouble,* and *Crackers.*

PASCAL BIET has lived in France his whole life. He was born in the north of France, in Saint-Laurent. He studied visual communication and design. He now lives and works in Paris.

AUTHOR'S PURPOSE
Why do you think Becky Bloom wrote about a wolf learning to read in *Wolf!?*

Respond to the Text

Summarize

Think about the important details in *WOLF!* Summarize what you learned about what stories can teach you. Use your Character Chart to help.

Character	
Wants or Needs	Feelings
Actions	Traits

Write

How has learning to read changed the wolf's life? Use these sentence frames to focus your discussion:

> At the beginning, the wolf . . .
> I noticed that Becky Bloom . . .
> That helps me see that the wolf . . .

Make Connections

What does this story teach you about making friends? **ESSENTIAL QUESTION**

Why is it good for people to read stories?
TEXT TO WORLD

JENNIE AND THE WOLF

Jennie lived in a little cottage in the woods with her mother. They were very poor.

"Oh, dear, we have no more eggs! And it's almost time for dinner!" said Jennie's mother.

"I'll run to the market, mother!" said Jennie. "I'll take the shortcut!" She rushed out with her basket into the forest.

Deep in the forest, Jennie heard a loud moan. Walking on, she made a shocking **discovery**. A huge, gray wolf stood under a tree, crying!

"Please don't run away," the wolf said. "Could you help me? No one else will." The wolf held out his paw. A large, sharp thorn was stuck deep in his paw.

"Is this a trick?" Jennie asked. "I've heard stories about wolves eating people."

"Your knowledge of wolves is out of date," sighed the wolf. "Wolves don't eat people anymore. My brothers and I like to eat eggs. With ketchup!" The wolf cried again and looked at his paw.

Illustration: Anne Wilson

98

Jennie was **inspired** to help. She knelt down and carefully removed the thorn. The wolf gently licked his paw. "Thank you. I will not forget your kindness!" the wolf promised. He bowed and disappeared into the forest.

Later, Jennie hurried home through the forest with her basket of eggs. "*GRRRROOOOWLLLL!*" A pack of hungry wolves appeared out of nowhere and blocked her path.

"What's in the basket?" snarled one wolf. "It looks like eggs!" cried another. "Where's the ketchup?" asked a third.

Then a voice roared, "Let her go!" The wolf whom Jennie had met earlier bounded down the path. "This girl helped me when no one else would." He told the pack how Jennie had helped him.

The other wolves moved aside. Jennie thanked her new friend, the wolf. Then she rushed down the path.

When Jennie got home, she helped her mother finish cooking. At dinner, she told the amazing tale of the gray wolf. Jennie also shared the moral she had learned:
Help others and they will help you.

Make Connections

What did you learn from this fable about helping others? **ESSENTIAL QUESTION**

How are the wolves in this story like other wolves you have read about? How are they different? **TEXT TO TEXT**

Essential Question

How do people make government work?

Read about how a town chooses a new mayor.

Go Digital!

Suppose your town is about to choose a new mayor. How will you do it?

You'll vote!

Voting is a way to choose.

You can vote for favorite books, movie stars, candy bars . . . or even puppies!

If someone wants to be elected mayor, she needs to **convince** as many people as possible to vote for her!

So if Chris gets the most votes, she'll be mayor. What does the mayor do?

The mayor is the leader of the city. Let's go help Chris find some votes.

You have my vote!

I'M going to vote for Brown.

That means people have a right to vote for whoever they want.

GRRR-R! GROWL-L! You can't vote for Brown!

Sparky! Stop that! This country is a democracy!

STOP AND CHECK

Reread What is Chris Smith going to do? Reread to find the answer.

Many people just don't vote. Why not?

Maybe they think their vote is like a little drop of water in an enormous ocean. Their vote is only one out of many, many votes. But sometimes the winner of an election is decided by just a few votes.

Who decided who could vote?

When this country began, the Founding Fathers wrote a constitution. It said how we would govern ourselves. It said people should vote; but it didn't say who could vote. That was left to each state to decide. And that was a problem!

Angry people protested. They wrote letters. They held rallies and made speeches. They marched, were arrested, and went on hunger strikes. Some were killed trying to claim their right to vote. But it took many years, four amendments to the Constitution, and several new laws before all citizens, 18 years or older, were allowed to vote.

If you want to vote, you need to register. Where? At your town office. Or you can download a registration form from the Internet, or you might even find a booth set up at a shopping mall or at a political rally.

Do you want to join a political party? You've probably heard of the Democrats and the Republicans. But you could join the Green Party, the Libertarians, the America First Party, or the Progressives, to name just a few. Or you could be **independent** and not join any party at all.

Before you vote, you'll need to find out about the different candidates. How? Read newspapers, watch TV news, listen to the radio, or surf the Internet. Do you agree with their ideas?

You might have a chance to hear the candidates debate. You might even be able to ask questions!

Before an election, everyone tries to guess who will win. Pollsters ask some of the voters whom they're planning to vote for. Then they **estimate** who will be the winner. But voters can change their minds.

How can you help your **candidate** win? You can volunteer to answer phones, call voters, address envelopes, or hand out flyers. Campaigns need lots of help.

And they need lots of money to help pay for phones, computers, stamps, flyers and bumper stickers, and, most of all, ads and more ads! Where will they find the money?

You might want to donate a few dollars to your favorite candidate's campaign. Or maybe you'll be invited to a fundraising dinner. Would you like to pay $250 for a fancy hamburger and a chance to meet the candidate?

If you donate lots of money, maybe the candidate will listen to you more than to other voters. Is that fair? Does that mean your vote will count more than other voters' votes? There's a lot of disagreement about this.

By the last week of the campaign, everyone is tired. But the candidates make more speeches. They shake more hands, and they run more and more ads. Maybe, just maybe, they will convince another few voters to vote for them.

Some of these ads can be very misleading.

Finally, it's Election Day.

STOP AND CHECK

Reread Why do candidates run more ads during the last week of the campaign? Reread to find out.

Most voters are assigned a particular place to vote—a school, a library, a church basement—wherever there is space for voting booths. What if you're away on voting day? You can get an absentee ballot in advance. Some places let people vote by mail or on the Internet. A few places set up voting machines early. But however you vote, you get just one vote. You can't go back and vote again!

In most places, people use voting machines. Many cities and towns are replacing old machines with new electronic ones. But in very small towns, voters still mark paper ballots with a pencil. However you do it, you'll vote in a private booth. No one can see how you vote.

When the voting ends, the counting begins! Who will win? Stay close to your TV or radio to find out.

Usually a few hours after the polls close, the winner is **announced**.

BUT WAIT!

What if the election is won by only a few votes? The candidate who lost can ask that the votes be counted again. Then it could take a few days—or longer—to carefully recount the ballots and find out who really won.

At last, the election is decided. In the end
someone does win . . . and someone does lose.

You aren't happy? You wish the other candidate had won? Well, remember, the mayor works for everyone—even the people who didn't vote for her. She'll need to listen to *all* the voters.

STOP AND CHECK

Ask and Answer Questions What happens when votes are recounted? Reread pages 115 and 116 to find the answer.

After she is sworn in, the new mayor will have a few years to do her new job.

She won't please all the people all the time, but if she does a good job, maybe the voters will **elect** her again!

★ About the AUTHOR and ILLUSTRATOR

Eileen Christelow had a strange dream when she was just three years old. She dreamed she could read! In first grade, she really did learn to read. From then on, Eileen's nose was almost always in a book.

As Eileen grew up, she discovered art and photography. She also liked children's books and thought about writing and illustrating one of her own. After a lot of work, Eileen's first book was published. She went on to publish many more! Eileen gets her story ideas from newspapers, the radio, and even conversations.

Author's Purpose

Why do you think the author uses two dogs as characters in *Vote!?*

Jeff Baird

120

Respond to the Text

Summarize

Think about what you learned about voting. Summarize what you learned about choosing a new mayor. The details from your Author's Point of View chart may help you.

Details

↓

Point of View

Write

How does the author help you understand how American citizens are responsible for the way our government works? Use these sentence frames to help organize your text evidence.

> Eileen Christelow organizes the text by . . .
> She includes many examples of . . .
> That helps me understand . . .

Make Connections

Why is it important for people to vote in elections? **ESSENTIAL QUESTION**

How can people take part in community government? **TEXT TO WORLD**

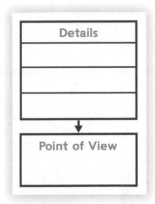

121

Compare Texts

Read how United States leaders wrote the Constitution and set the rules for our government.

The Constitution is the highest law in our country.

A Plan for the
People

The United States **government** started with a plan. Our country's leaders wrote the plan more than 200 years ago. The plan is called the Constitution. All of our laws come from the Constitution.

Saul Loeb/AFP/Getty Images

A New Government

In 1787, the United States was a new nation of thirteen states. The nation's first plan for government had problems. Its leaders decided to meet to talk about a new plan. Fifty-five **delegates** came to the meetings. A delegate is a person who speaks for the **citizens** in each state. George Washington led the meetings. He was the country's first president.

A Summer of Arguments

The meetings began on a hot day in May 1787. The delegates gathered together in the Philadelphia State House. They closed the windows because the meetings were secret. It was hot in the State House. When they opened the windows to cool off, bugs flew in. The delegates argued all summer in the hot, buggy rooms. Making a new plan for government was not easy or fun.

Ben Franklin worried that the delegates would never agree.

Some delegates wanted one person to run the new government. Others thought a group should be in charge. They all agreed on one thing. A group should make laws for the country. But they disagreed on how to pick these leaders. The famous inventor and statesman Benjamin Franklin attended the meetings. He wondered how the group could ever make any **decisions**.

After many months, leaders agreed on a U.S. Constitution.

Making a Plan

The delegates wrote their plan and called it the United States Constitution. The Constitution was only a few pages long, but it was full of big ideas. The Constitution shows how our government works. It says that people are in charge of the government. People vote to pick their leaders. These leaders run the government for the people.

A Government That's Fair to All

The delegates planning the Constitution met for four months. They thought the Constitution was a good plan. But not all delegates signed it on September 15, 1787. Some of them wanted to make sure the government protected people's rights, too. A **right** is something you are allowed to have or do. In 1791, Congress changed the Constitution to protect the rights of American citizens. One right allows people to speak freely. These changes were called the Bill of Rights.

Bettmann/Getty Images

A lot has changed since 1787. Our country is a lot bigger. There are fifty states now. The Constitution has been changed many times, too. But one thing has not changed. The Constitution is still the plan for our government.

Rights for Children

In 1959, many countries signed a Declaration of the Rights of the Child. Here are some of those rights:

- Children should grow up free.
- Children should get an education.
- Children should have the chance to play.

What other rights should children have? This chart shows one class's ideas. Each student voted.

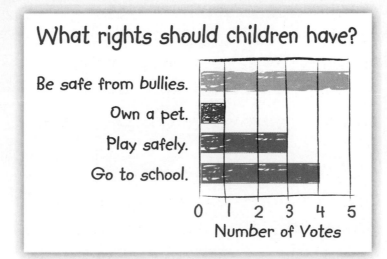

What rights should children have?

Be safe from bullies.
Own a pet.
Play safely.
Go to school.

0 1 2 3 4 5
Number of Votes

Make Connections

Why was the United States Constitution written? **ESSENTIAL QUESTION**

What are ways that people can make government work? Talk about articles and stories you have read. **TEXT TO TEXT**

Genre • Historical Fiction

Essential Question

Why do people immigrate to new places?

Read about how Julie's grandparents came to the United States.

Go Digital!

THE CASTLE ON HESTER STREET

by
Linda Heller

Illustrated by
Boris Kulikov

One day while Julie was visiting her grandparents, her grandfather said, "Did I ever tell you about my good friend Moishe?"

"You told me about Hershel, the famous astronomer," Julie said with a giggle, "the one who discovered that the moon is a matzoh.

"And you told me about Bessie, your little cousin whose braids were so long she used them for jump ropes. But you never told me about Moishe."

"Moishe the goat was from my village in Russia,"
Julie's grandfather said. "He pulled the wagon I rode in
when I came to America. Not only could Moishe leap
across oceans the way others jump over puddles, but he
also could sing. We started singing the moment we left
Russia. '9,092 miles to go, 9,092 miles, after we pass that
small patch of snow we'll have 9,091 miles to go.'"

Julie was about to join in, when her grandmother said, "Sol, what are you telling that child?"

"A true story, just the way I remember it, Rose, dear," Julie's grandfather said. "Moishe's wagon was solid gold. It shone like a shooting star when we flew over the ocean."

"That's a story, all right, but it's not true!" Julie's grandmother said. "Grandpa came on a boat, like I did. It was terrible. Hundreds of families were crowded together. Babies were crying. Bundles were piled over. The boat rocked so much, I thought we would drown. But in Russia, life for Jews was very hard.

"We couldn't live or work where we wanted. Sometimes we were attacked just because we were Jews. We had to leave Russia any way we could."

S.S. BLUCHER

STOP AND CHECK

Make Predictions What will Julie's grandmother say about Grandpa's story? Make a prediction.

As her grandmother spoke, pictures grew in Julie's mind of her grandparents leaving their country and crossing a rough winter ocean on a boat so crowded they could hardly move.

"Grandpa, is that how you really came?" Julie asked, looking sad.

"Yes, it was," Julie's grandfather said. He, too, looked sad, until he added, "But what a welcome I got when I **arrived**. President Theodore Roosevelt rode his horse through a blizzard of ticker tape to greet me. 'Hello, Sol,' he said. 'Mighty glad you could come.'"

"Don't listen to another word," Julie's grandmother said. "Grandpa's brother Morris met him. The boat docked first at Ellis Island. We sat for hours and waited to be **inspected**. Not everyone who came could stay. If you were sick, you had to go back. I was so afraid they would find something wrong with me, but, thank God, I passed every test."

STOP AND CHECK

Confirm Predictions What did Julie's grandmother say about Grandpa's story? Was your prediction correct?

"Hooray!" Julie shouted.

"Thank you, dear," Julie's grandmother said. She
gave her a kiss and said, "I have something to show you."
Then she went to the closet.

Julie's grandfather leaned closer and whispered to
Julie, "Everyone who came here was given a castle. Mine
was on Hester Street. It was so tall the pigeons couldn't
fly all the way up to the roof. I had to carry them there."

Julie's grandmother came back to the sofa carrying a box. "Did Grandpa tell you about the horrible little room he shared with Louie, the cigar maker, and Herman, the tailor?" she asked as she sat down. "In those days people had to take in boarders to help pay the rent. Life was hard. Grandpa had a pushcart. He sold buttons fourteen hours a day, six days a week. The only rest he got was on Sabbath."

"Poor Grandpa," Julie said, and she patted his hand.

Julie's grandfather was quiet for a **moment**, then he said, "But what buttons I had! Buttons carved from diamonds, emeralds, and rubies. Buttons as big as saucers. Buttons as big as plates. Buttons you could use as sleds in the snow."

Julie's grandmother sighed loudly. "Grandpa sold small buttons, small enough to fit through buttonholes. I'll show you," she said as she opened the box. The box was filled with **photographs**. Julie's grandmother took out an old photograph in a cardboard frame. In it Julie's grandfather stood next to his pushcart, which was full of little buttons.

"Grandpa looks so strong," Julie said, feeling proud.

Julie's grandfather found a photograph of a young girl and showed it to Julie.

"This is a picture of your grandmother," he said. "She was very famous in those days.

"Everyone spoke of Mr. Witkin's beautiful daughter Rose, who stayed home all day, nibbling chocolates.

"Her five big brothers had to watch so that nobody stole her away."

"I worked six days a week in a factory then, sewing dresses. But I was very pretty," Julie's grandmother said, smoothing her hair.

"You are still very pretty," Julie's grandfather said, and he kissed her cheek.

"In Russia your grandmother sewed for royalty. She made stitches so small, they couldn't be seen. People wondered how the dresses stayed together."

"That part is true," Julie's grandmother said proudly.

"As soon as I met your grandmother, I wanted to marry her," Julie's grandfather said. "Every night I hired fireflies to fly over her house and spell out 'Rose, my precious flower, I love you every hour.' And Moishe and I sang love songs under her window.

"Finally her father let me marry her. A year later your mother was born. No one had ever seen such a beautiful child. Then Esther, Ruthie, and Bennie were born and they were just as beautiful. I made them tiny jeweled crowns and they rode through the streets in hand-carved golden baby carriages."

139

"Enough is enough," Julie's grandmother said. "From now on I insist that Julie hear only the truth. Grandpa and I had to work even harder to feed all those babies, but we didn't mind. We had something more **valuable** than jeweled crowns and golden baby carriages. We had each other and we were free to live as we wanted."

"That's the truth, Rose, dear," Julie's grandfather said. "And from now on that's all that will pass through my lips."

They sat quietly for a few minutes. Then Julie's grandfather smiled and **whispered** to Julie, "Did I ever tell you about the time Moishe the goat and I sang for President Wilson?"

STOP AND CHECK

Reread How does Grandpa feel about telling tall tales? Reread to find out.

About the Author and Illustrator

Linda Heller

never knew her grandparents, but she heard the story of how they sailed across the Atlantic Ocean from her parents. This inspired Linda to read about and visit Ellis Island and write her own story. Linda's other books include *Today Is the Birthday of the World*.

Boris Kulikov

was born in Saint Petersburg, a big city in Russia. Like the characters in *A Castle on Hester Street*, Boris is also an immigrant. He came to America in 1997 and became an illustrator. Boris now lives in New York City.

Author's Purpose

Why do you think the author includes both Julie's grandmother's story and her grandfather's story?

Respond to the Text

Summarize

Think about the details in *The Castle on Hester Street*. Summarize the grandparents' stories about moving to America. The details from your Theme chart may help you.

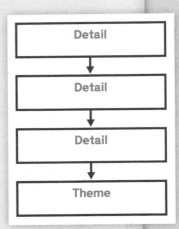

Detail
↓
Detail
↓
Detail
↓
Theme

Write

How does Linda Heller use the stories Julie's grandparents tell to help you compare how they felt about coming to America? Use these sentence frames to organize your text evidence.

> Julie's grandfather's stories are . . .
> Linda Heller tells her grandmother's point of view to show . . .
> This helps me see that they . . .

Make Connections

Why did Julie's grandparents immigrate from Russia? **ESSENTIAL QUESTION**

Why do you think immigrants come to the United States today? **TEXT TO WORLD**

Compare Texts

Read about the first place where many immigrants to the United States stopped.

Next Stop, America!

If you sail to New York, you pass the Statue of Liberty. What you see next is Ellis Island.

The Statue of Liberty stands on Liberty Island in New York Harbor.

(bkgd) Danny Lehman/Corbis Documentary/Getty Images

Today, Ellis Island is part of the Statue of Liberty National Monument. The main building is a museum. Once it was a gateway to America. It was open from 1892 to 1954. More than 12 million people first entered the United States here.

How many people is 12 million? If they all stood in a line, it could stretch like a bridge across the Atlantic Ocean!

Immigrants Arrive

Most of the immigrants to Ellis Island came from Europe. The largest groups came from Italy and Ireland. Others came from Russia, Germany, Sweden, and other countries.

Why did they come? Some were trying to escape war. Millions came seeking jobs. They wanted an **opportunity**, or chance, to make a better life. Many people came seeking freedom. They came to America because they wanted the right to live and speak as they wished.

Families came to America from all over the world. Ellis Island was their first stop in the United States.

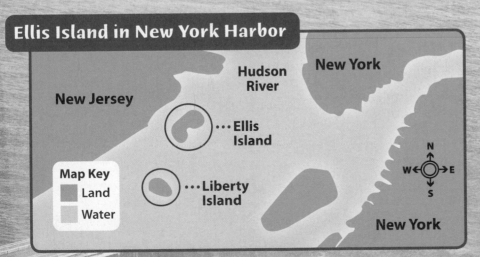

Ellis Island in New York Harbor

New York

Hudson River

New Jersey

···Ellis Island

Map Key
Land
Water

···Liberty Island

N
W←◇→E
S

New York

The immigrants spoke many languages. They had different customs. However, everyone shared one thing. They had all chosen to **immigrate**. They wanted to move to a new country because they wanted to be Americans.

What Happened at Ellis Island

Immigrants crossed the ocean on crowded ships. When the ships arrived in New York harbor, smaller boats took them to Ellis Island. There the travelers hoped to become American citizens. Thousands of people came every day.

First, everyone had to have a check-up. The government didn't want sick people coming into the country. As a result, some sick people stayed in the Ellis Island hospital until they were well. Someone with an eye infection was sent back across the ocean!

People also had to take a written test. They had to answer questions, give their names, and tell what country they were from. They had to tell where they planned to go. They had to promise to obey the laws of the United States.

After hours of waiting, most people got good news. The United States welcomed them to their new home.

Doctors gave everyone who came through Ellis Island a check-up. They checked children, too.

Where They Went

From Ellis Island, some immigrants got on ferries to New York City. Many people's journeys ended there. Thousands settled near friends and family. They stayed in neighborhoods, such as Little Italy and the Lower East Side. Others had more traveling to do. They headed west or south, to other cities and states. Some went to places where they could get a job in a factory or a mine. Others found good farmland. No matter where the immigrants settled, they never forgot Ellis Island.

Make Connections

What did many of the immigrants want? ESSENTIAL QUESTION

What stories have you read about immigrants to America? How are those stories like this article? TEXT TO TEXT

Essential Question

How do people figure things out?

Read about different ways of flying.

Go Digital!

The Inventor Thinks Up
Helicopters

"Why not
a
vertical
whirling
winding
bug,
that hops like a cricket
crossing a rug,
that swerves like a dragonfly
testing his steering,
twisting and veering?
Fleet as a beetle.
Up
down
left
right,
jounce, bounce, day and night.
It could land in a pasture the size of a dot...
Why not?"

—*Patricia Hubbell*

149

Ornithopter

Circa 1903, Great Britain

While observers were whooping and clapping,
The pilot was happily snapping
   Bird wings into place
   For a wild goose chase,
And the plane was repeatedly flapping!

But no matter the wind or the weather,
A pilot whose wings swing together
   On a plane so absurd
   As to think it's a bird
Needs an engine as light as a feather.

—J. Patrick Lewis

Respond to the Text

Summarize

Use details from "Ornithopter" to summarize the poem. Details from your Point of View chart may help you.

Details

↓

Point of View

Write

Think about the two poems you just read. How do the poets help you understand how people invent things? Use these sentence frames to organize your text evidence.

The inventors' machines . . .
The poet of "The Inventor Thinks Up Helicopters" . . .
The poet of "Ornithopter" . . .

Make Connections

What do these poems tell you about inventors and how they figure things out? **ESSENTIAL QUESTION**

How many different ways of flying are described in the poems? Describe the inventions in these poems. **TEXT TO WORLD**

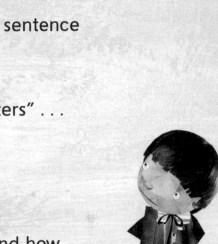

Genre · Poetry

Compare Texts
Read how a poet describes
the first balloon flight.

Montgolfier Brothers' Hot Air Balloon

1783, France

We stuffed the straw in the burner,
We stoked it furiously,
And ours was the first balloon to rise
Merrily aerially!

We might have gone much farther,
We flew superhumanly
Till our smart little cart started falling apart,
Sagging diagonally.

Our adventure over Paris
Was a twenty-five-minute flight.
And who was there but Benjamin Franklin,
Waving (without his kite)!

—J. Patrick Lewis

Make Connections

How did the brothers figure out how to fly?
Use details from the poem. **ESSENTIAL QUESTION**

Compare this poem to "The Ornithopter."
How are the poems similar? How are they
different? **TEXT TO TEXT**

Whooping Cranes
in Danger

by Susan E. Goodman

Essential Question

How can people help animals survive?

Read about whooping cranes. Find out how a group of scientists are helping these birds survive.

Go Digital!

There are many types of heroes. Superheroes in comics catch bad guys. Astronauts risk their lives to explore space. Doctors devote their careers to finding cures for dreadful diseases. Our story has heroes, too. Scientists and their helpers are saving the whooping cranes.

Whoopers Need Help

Long ago, whooping cranes lived all over North America. Then people started hunting them. Farmers and builders took over the marshes these birds called home. Whoopers were losing the resources they needed.

By 1941, only fifteen whooping cranes were left in the wild. It looked as if they could die out forever. Some people refused to let this happen. The government reserved land for these cranes to live on. Hunters could not enter this wildlife refuge.

Scientists guarded this tiny flock in Texas. Seventy years later, its **population** has grown to two hundred birds. But one flock is not enough. A disease or storm could wipe it out completely. Scientists decided to create a new flock in Wisconsin. Two groups of birds are safer than one.

Without places to get food and raise families, the whooping crane could not **survive**.

A Tough Problem

Building a new flock of whoopers is harder than it seems. These cranes are born up north. Then they migrate south in fall to avoid the cold winter. In spring, they fly back north for the summer. (Who says birds aren't smart?)

Scientists had a big problem to solve. They couldn't just grab some whoopers from the first flock to start a new one. When returning north, adult birds will only go back to the place they were born. So all members of the second flock had to be born in the new spot. How could that happen? Who would their parents be?

A Clever Solution

Eleven eggs were about to hatch in spring of 2001. Their parents were ready to welcome these chicks to the world. Their puppet parents, that is!

This puppet takes the place of this whooping crane chick's mother.

Scientists had to raise the chicks, but the whoopers weren't supposed to get used to people. The birds needed to be wild to stay safe. So humans pretended to be whooping cranes. They wore white costumes to hide their faces and bodies. They wore puppets on their arms to deal with the chicks.

The **caretakers** never spoke near the birds. They "talked" to the chicks by playing tapes of real whooping cranes. They also had real whoopers in the refuge. The chicks needed to know what actual grown-up whooping cranes looked like.

Caretakers used the puppets to teach the chicks the same skills that real parents would. The puppets showed them where to swim and where to sleep. They even taught the chicks how to get along with other cranes!

The puppets could teach most things. But they couldn't teach the chicks how to fly!

Scientists used puppets to train the babies how to eat and drink, and where to find the right kind of food.

STOP AND CHECK

Reread Why did the scientists wear white costumes and use puppets? Reread to find the answer.

The Biggest Parent of Them All

Pilots of ultralight planes could do the job. They put on their costumes and got to work.

At first, the plane just rolled across the ground. A pilot played a special crane call, which meant, "Come on, follow me!" That's exactly what the chicks did. Of course, the treats given out by the pilot's puppet helped a lot!

As days passed, the plane sped up. The chicks did, too. Flapping their wings helped them go faster. It also made their wings stronger. At last, they ran fast enough and flapped hard enough. And . . . UP they went!

Soon the cranes were flying almost every day. They had to. Fall was coming. They had to be strong enough to migrate more than 1,200 miles to Florida.

The whoopers learned to follow the ultralight on the ground and in the air. They had to learn to recognize their Wisconsin home from the air, because the plane would not lead them back the next spring.

Paul K. Cascio/USGS

159

Operation Migration

Finally, the Big Day came. This experiment started with eleven eggs. Two chicks had gotten sick and died. One couldn't fly well and moved to a zoo. The other eight whoopers were ready to go!

Two ultralights revved their engines. One would lead the birds. The other would track down cranes that strayed from the flock. The planes took off. The birds did, too. They were on their way!

Planes and birds were only part of the migration. A crew drove south, too. The birds had to eat and rest each night. Scientists had chosen safe places along the way. The crew rushed ahead to set up pens for them to stay in.

This ultralight plane led the whooping cranes to their winter home in Florida.

The trip was hard. The cranes flew up to ninety-five miles on good days, only twenty on bad ones. Often rain or wind kept them from flying at all.

One sad night, a giant storm ripped their pen apart. Caretakers spent hours searching and calling for their whoopers. All were fine, except one. He had flown into a power line and died.

After forty-eight days, the plane flew over the birds' winter home in Florida. A caretaker on the ground played the whooping crane call. The whoopers swooped in for a landing. The first part of the journey was a **success**!

Whooping Crane Migration

Wisconsin

Map Key

Land

Water

N
W — E
S

Florida

This map shows where the whooping cranes flew when they migrated.

A Warm Winter

What was one of the first things the whoopers learned about Florida? Crabs are delicious! The shells were hard, but the meat was soft. Puppet parents helped the whoopers learn to peck them apart.

At first, the cranes stayed in a pen as big as a football field. It even had a pond with a fake whooper parent in it to make them feel safe. Actually, they *were* safer in the pond. Cranes usually sleep in the water at night. Splashing sounds warn them if a predator is nearby.

In time, caretakers took the top off the pen. The cranes flew out to explore more of their new home. Caretakers hid, watching them enjoy yummy shrimp and snails.

Generally the whoopers returned to the pen at night. Sometimes they didn't. Two cranes were killed by bobcats; now there were five.

The whoopers learned to eat new foods, such as crabs, in their winter home in Florida.

Klaus Nigge/National Geographic/Getty Images

162

In spring, the birds started eating more. That was a good sign. They were storing energy for a trip north. Still, the scientists wondered, would the cranes know when to leave?

Scientists wondered if the whoopers would know when to fly north to Wisconsin.

Homeward Bound?

One day, caretakers heard radio signals. The cranes had leg bands that sent out these sounds. The whoopers were on the move!

Caretakers jumped in two trucks to follow the signals. They had to hurry. The trip home would be much faster. Air has currents just like water does. Birds ride these currents the same way that surfers ride waves.

The cranes traveled more than two hundred miles the very first day. They were headed north. But would they remember their route?

Soon scientists had another thing to worry about. One crane left the group. A truck turned to track her. Where was she going, and why?

STOP AND CHECK

Reread What were the scientists worried about? Reread to find the answer.

PhotoStockFile/Alamy

Day by day, the cranes kept flying. Then the group of four reached Lake Michigan. They began to circle. Oh no, thought the trackers. They do not know which way to go! The whoopers kept circling around and around. After two hours, they finally turned west. They were on course!

Eleven days after leaving Florida, these four cranes came in for a landing. They were very close to the pen they grew up in.

What about that last crane? She ended up visiting a flock of sandhill cranes for a while. Sandhill cranes are **relatives** of whooping cranes. Two weeks later, she came back home to the refuge.

The number of whooping cranes is beginning to grow again.

Klaus Nigge/National Geographic/Getty Images

A New Beginning

This first migration was finished, but the whooping crane's recovery had just begun. The next year, these five cranes flew south by themselves. The ultralights were busy leading sixteen new chicks.

The planes still lead migrations each fall. But now, whooping crane parents are leading their own chicks down South. Some of these chicks have grown up enough to have babies of their own.

The whooping crane is still threatened. It remains one of America's most endangered birds, but scientists are hopeful. Luckily, the flock keeps getting bigger.

STOP AND CHECK

Summarize How are the whooping cranes doing now? Summarize what you learned from "A New Beginning."

About the Author

Susan E. Goodman likes to write about topics that excite her. The whooping crane is one of those topics. "When I first heard this story, I knew I had to write about it," she says. "It's so sad, and happy, funny and amazing. It gives me hope."

Susan has written more than thirty nonfiction books for children. Her writing has taken her all over the world. She has flown in a helicopter. She has taken a plane to the Arctic. She has even ridden in a machine that trains astronauts to fly the Space Shuttle. However, she has never flown in an ultralight plane on its way to Florida. Not yet, anyway!

Author's Purpose

Why do you think the author wanted to tell this story?

Respond to the Text

Summarize

Summarize how scientists helped save the whooping cranes. The details from your Author's Point of View chart may help you.

Details
↓
Point of View

Write

How does the author show that saving the whooping cranes is important? Use these sentence frames to organize your text evidence.

> The author thinks the scientists are . . .
> She shows that the survival of the whooping crane is important by . . .
> I know that she thinks that . . .

Make Connections

How are scientists helping the whooping cranes survive? **ESSENTIAL QUESTION**

Why are people all over the world helping endangered animals? **TEXT TO WORLD**

Compare Texts

Read about a group of people that helps manatees.

Help the Manatees!

Places to See Manatees in Florida

Tallahassee ★ FLORIDA

Key
■ Places to see manatees
★ State Capital
● City

Miami

People in Florida are worried. The manatees are in trouble. Hundreds of these super-sized marine mammals are dying every year. The population dropped from 3,000 to 2,500 in just twelve months. What caused the problem? People.

Manatees can be seen throughout Florida. They live along the coast, and in rivers, springs, and bays.

Why Are Manatees in Trouble?

Manatees make their home in warm, shallow water. They live in Florida rivers and bays and in the ocean. They eat weeds and grasses that grow in water.

Manatees don't have many enemies because they are so large. After all, they're related to elephants! However, people have **threatened** their habitat. Many people live in Florida now. Lots of people take vacations there, too. More people than ever are using the manatees' habitat.

Manatees can be ten feet long and weigh up to 1,200 pounds.

What Hurts the Manatees?

People race power boats in shallow waters where manatees live. Some boaters crash into manatees and hurt them. Fishing hooks and nets hurt manatees, too. Swimmers also like to use the warm waters where manatees live. That can drive the creatures away.

Taking Action

The Save the Manatee Club has taken action to help manatees. The group educates people about these gentle giants. They teach kids and grown-ups how to keep the manatees safe and healthy. They rescue injured manatees. They work to change laws to help manatees.

The club gives away banners and signs. These remind boaters to go slow around manatees. The group also teaches people to use less water. Manatees need **resources** such as clean water.

Now people in Florida are more careful when they use the manatees' habitat. Manatees have a better chance to survive. They can thank their friends in the Save the Manatee Club!

Signs like this teach people how to protect manatees.

Make Connections

How does the Save the Manatee Club help manatees survive? ESSENTIAL QUESTION

How is the Save the Manatee Club like other groups that help animals? TEXT TO TEXT

Essential Question

Why is working together a good way to solve a problem?

Read about how a group of animals work with Desert Woman to stop a bully.

 Go Digital!

ROADRUNNER'S DANCE

by Rudolfo Anaya • pictures by David Diaz

"*Ssss*," hissed Snake as he slithered out of his hole by the side of the road. He bared his fangs and frightened a family walking home from the cornfield.

The mother threw her basketful of corn in the air. The children froze with fright.

"Father!" the children called, and the father came running.

"*Ssss*," Snake threatened.

"Come away," the father said, and the family took another path home.

"I am king of the road," Snake boasted. "No one may use the road without my permission."

That evening the people of the village gathered together and spoke to the elders.

"We are afraid of being bitten by Snake," they protested. "He acts as if the road belongs only to him."

The elders agreed that something should be done, and so the following morning they went to Sacred Mountain, where Desert Woman lived. She had **created** the desert animals, so surely she could help.

"Please do something about Snake," the elders said. "He makes visiting our neighbors and going to our fields impossible. He frightens the children."

Desert Woman thought for a long time. She did not like to **interfere** in the lives of the people and animals, but she knew that something must be done.

"I have a solution," she finally said.

Dressed in a flowing gown, she traveled on a summer cloud across the desert to where Snake slept under the shade of a rocky ledge.

"You will let people know when you are about to strike," Desert Woman said sternly. And so she placed a rattle on the tip of Snake's tail.

"Now you are Rattlesnake. When anyone approaches, you will rattle a warning. This way they will know you are nearby."

Convinced she had done the right thing, Desert Woman walked on the Rainbow back to her home in Sacred Mountain.

However, instead of inhibiting Rattlesnake, the rattle only made him more threatening. He coiled around, shaking his tail and baring his fangs.

"Look at me," Rattlesnake said to the animals. "I rattle and hiss, and my bite is deadly. I am king of the road, and no one may use it without my permission!"

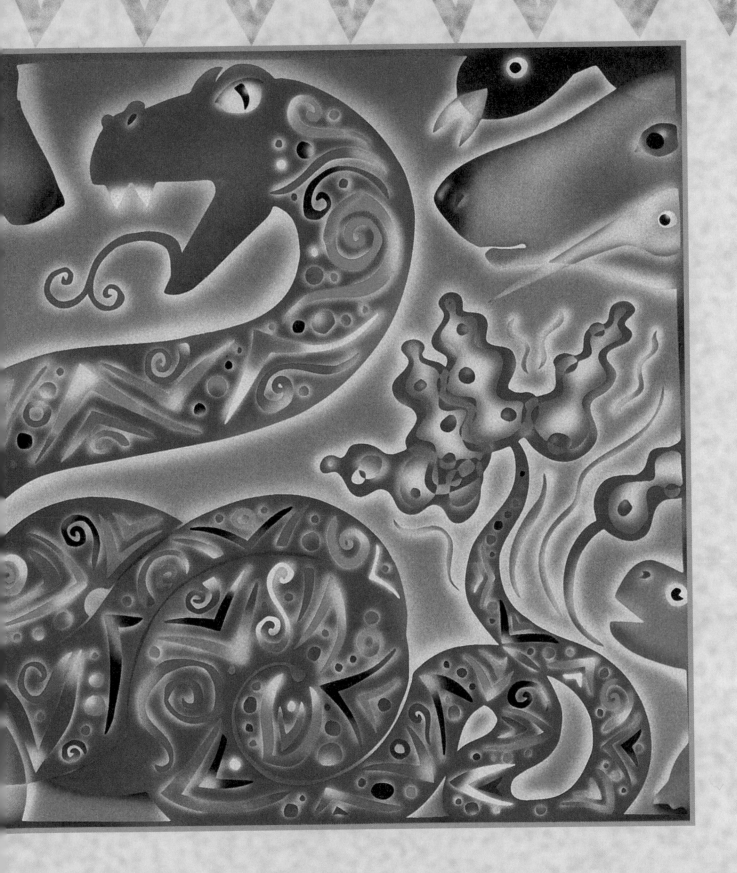

Now the animals went to Desert Woman to complain.

"Who, who," Owl said, greeting Desert Woman with respect. "Since you gave Rattlesnake his rattle, he is even more of a bully. He will not let anyone use the road. Please take away his fangs and rattle!"

"What I give I cannot take away," Desert Woman said. "When Rattlesnake comes hissing and threatening, one of you must make him behave."

She looked at all the animals assembled. The animals looked at one another. They looked up, they looked down, but not one looked at Desert Woman.

"I am too **timid** to stand up to Rattlesnake," Quail whispered.

"He would gobble me up," Lizard cried and darted away.

"We are all afraid of him," Owl admitted.

Desert Woman smiled. "Perhaps we need a new animal to make Rattlesnake behave," she suggested.

"Yip, yip," Coyote barked. "Yes, yes."

"If you help me, together we can make a guardian of the road," Desert Woman said. "I will form the body, and each of you will bring a gift for our new friend."

She gathered clay from the Sacred Mountain and wet it with water from a desert spring. Working quickly but with great care, she molded the body.

"He needs slender legs to run fast," said Deer. He took two slender branches from a mesquite bush and handed them to Desert Woman.

She pushed the sticks into the clay.

"And a long tail to balance himself," said Blue Jay.

"Caw, Caw! Like mine," croaked Raven, and he took long, black feathers from his tail.

"He must be strong," cried the mighty Eagle, and he plucked dark feathers from his wings.

"And have a long beak to peck at Rattlesnake," said Heron, offering a long, thin reed from the marsh.

"He needs sharp eyes," said Coyote, offering two shiny stones from the riverbed.

As Desert Woman added each new gift to the clay body, a strange new bird took shape.

"What is your gift?" Owl asked Desert Woman.

"I will give him the gift of dance. He will be agile and fast," she answered. "I will call him Roadrunner."

Then she breathed life into the clay.

Roadrunner opened his eyes. He blinked and looked around.

"What a strange bird," the animals said.

Roadrunner took his first steps. He tottered forward, then backward, then forward, and fell flat on his face.

The animals sighed and shook their heads. This bird was not agile, and he was not fast. He could never stand up to Rattlesnake. He was too **awkward**. Disappointed, the animals made their way home.

Desert Woman helped Roadrunner stand, and she told him what he must do. "You will dance around Rattlesnake and peck at his tail. He must learn he is not the king of the road."

"Me? Can I really do it?" Roadrunner asked, balancing himself with his long tail.

"You need only to practice," Desert Woman said.

Roadrunner again tried his legs. He took a few steps forward and bumped into a tall cactus.

"Practice," he said. He tried again and leaped over a sleeping horned toad.

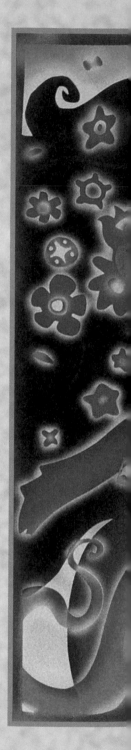

STOP AND CHECK

Make Predictions Will Roadrunner be able to beat Rattlesnake? Use clues in the story to make a prediction.

He tried jumping over a desert tortoise, but landed
right on her back. The surprised turtle lumbered away,
and Roadrunner crashed to the ground.

"I'll never get it right," he moaned.

"Yes, you will," Desert Woman said, again helping him
to his feet. "You need only to practice."

So Roadrunner practiced. He ran back and forth,
learning to use his skinny legs, learning to balance with
his tail feathers.

"Practice," he said again. "Practice."

With time, he was swirling and twirling like a twister.
The once awkward bird was now a graceful dancer.

"I've got it!" he cried, zipping down the road, his
legs carrying him swiftly across the sand. "Thank you,
Desert Woman."

"Use your gift to help others," Desert Woman said, and she returned to her abode on Sacred Mountain.

"I will," Roadrunner called.

He went racing down the road until his sharp eyes spied Rattlesnake hiding under a tall yucca plant.

"*Sssss,* I am king of the road," Rattlesnake hissed and shook his tail **furiously**. "No one may use *my* road without *my* permission."

"The road is for everyone to use," Roadrunner said sternly.

"Who are you?"

"I am Roadrunner."

"Get off my road before I bite you!" Rattlesnake glared.

"I'm not afraid of you," Roadrunner replied.

The people and the animals heard the ruckus and drew close to watch. Had they heard correctly? Roadrunner was challenging Rattlesnake!

"I'll show you I *am* king of the road!" Rattlesnake shouted, hissing so loud the desert mice trembled with fear. He shook his rattle until it sounded like a thunderstorm.

He struck at Roadrunner, but Roadrunner hopped out of the way.

"Stand still!" Rattlesnake cried and lunged again.

But Roadrunner danced gracefully out of reach.

Rattlesnake coiled for one more **attempt**. He struck like lightning, but fell flat on his face. Roadrunner had jumped to safety.

Now it was Roadrunner's turn. He ruffled his feathers and danced in circles around Rattlesnake. Again and again he pecked at the bully's tail. Like a whirlwind, he spun around Rattlesnake until the serpent grew dizzy. His eyes grew crossed and his tongue hung limply out of his mouth.

"You win! You win!" Rattlesnake cried.

"You are not king of the road, and you must not frighten those who use it," Roadrunner said sternly.

Confirm Predictions What happens when Roadrunner and Rattlesnake meet? Was your prediction correct?

"I promise, I promise," the beaten Rattlesnake said and quietly slunk down his hole.

The people cheered and praised the bird.

"Now we can visit our neighbors in peace and go to our cornfields without fear!" the elders proclaimed. "And the children will no longer be frightened."

"Thank you, Roadrunner!" the children called, waving as they followed their parents to the fields.

Then the animals gathered around Roadrunner.

"Yes, thank you for teaching Rattlesnake a lesson," Owl said. "Now you are king of the road."

"No, now there is no king of the road," replied Roadrunner. "Everyone is free to come and go as they please. And the likes of Rattlesnake had better watch out, because I'll make sure the roads stay safe."

STOP AND CHECK

Ask and Answer Questions Why does Roadrunner say there is no king of the road? Reread to find the answer.

ABOUT THE AUTHOR AND ILLUSTRATOR

As a child, **Rudolfo Anaya** played in the fields near Santa Rosa, New Mexico, and swam in the Pecos River. He also listened to the *cuentistas*, storytellers who told Mexican folktales. Today, Rudolfo is also a storyteller. He writes his own tales to share his Mexican and Native American heritage.

David Diaz remembers when he first knew he wanted to be an artist. He was in first grade, and he had just finished drawing a face. David has been drawing faces ever since then. He likes to try new styles and new ideas.

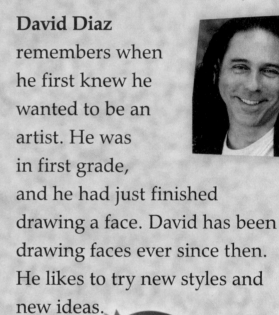

AUTHOR'S PURPOSE
Why do you think Rudolfo Anaya wrote this story?

Respond to the Text

Summarize

Think about the details from *Roadrunner's Dance.* Summarize the main events in the story. The details from your Theme chart may help you.

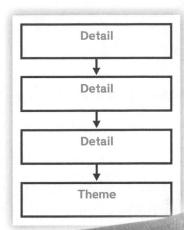

Detail
↓
Detail
↓
Detail
↓
Theme

Write

How does the author's use of dialogue help you understand how Desert Woman solves the problem the animals have? Use these sentence frames to organize your text evidence.

> The author uses dialogue to . . .
> He describes the problem using . . .
> This helps me understand how the animals . . .

Make Connections

How did the animals and Desert Woman work together to solve their problem? ESSENTIAL QUESTION

Why is it important to work together to solve problems? TEXT TO WORLD

Compare Texts

Read about how people in one Florida town worked together to solve a problem.

Deltona Is Going Batty

Buzz! Buzz! Slap! Buzz! Buzz! Slap!

In Deltona, Florida, those are the sounds of summer. When summer comes, so do bugs.

The mayor of Deltona worked with a group of people to solve the bug problem. A man **involved** with the group came up with a fantastic answer. Bats! Bats like to eat bugs. Why not bring bats to Deltona? Let bats get rid of Deltona's bugs!

The mayor and the city government liked this idea. But people in Deltona had questions. Where would the bats live? Who would pay for the bats?

The people who ran the city had to find answers. Then they had to decide what to do.

People in Deltona enjoy spending time outside in nice weather. But in summer, bugs take over!

Local Government Decides

The mayor and other city officials met. They came up with a plan for the bats. It would not cost the town any money.

Bats can live in bat houses. Local business people will pay for them. Volunteers will put the bat houses in parks and public places.

The city officials talked to the people of Deltona about the plan. Their **cooperation** was important for the plan to work. Most people agreed. They wanted to try the plan.

The officials met again to vote on the plan. They decided to bring bats to Deltona!

The Bats Get a Home

Soon the first bat house was placed at City Hall. People celebrated. It was Bat House Day!

Will bats solve Deltona's bug problem? It is too soon to tell. It takes time for a group of bats to find a bat house and move in. The people of Deltona are willing to wait and see. If bats don't help, their local government will try something else. That's why Deltona is a good place to live.

Deltona is north of Orlando.

ALABAMA GEORGIA

FLORIDA

Deltona

Orlando

N W E S

Miami

This is the bat house at Deltona City Hall. It is 20 feet above the ground.

(c) SuperStock/age footstock @ Robert L. Sjoberg, Nature's Friend

How Local Government Works

Deltona has a local government. Like many other towns, it has a mayor and a city commission.

The mayor of Deltona works closely with the city commission. It has seven members. Each one comes from a different part of the city. Each is elected by the voters who live in that part of town.

LOCAL GOVERNMENT

CITY COMMISSION

MAYOR

CITY MANAGER

Many towns, including Deltona, have a local government like this.

SPENDING   PARKS   UTILITIES   FIRE   LIBRARIES   POLICE

The mayor and city commission members meet with the people in their communities. They talk with the people to find out what they need.

Because it takes many people to keep things running smoothly, Deltona hires a city manager. The city manager works with the mayor, the commission, and town departments, such as the fire and police departments, to provide services.

The people of Deltona know the secret of a successful community. People and government must work together. When people have a problem, such as too many bugs, they can ask their local government for help.

People in a town meet with the mayor to tell him their ideas.

Make Connections

How did working together help the people of Deltona solve the bug problem? ESSENTIAL QUESTION
They f:

Compare this story about people working together to other stories you have read. TEXT TO TEXT

CDC/Cade Martin

Essential Question

What do we know about Earth and its neighbors?

Read about how Earth is different from the other planets and the Moon.

Go Digital!

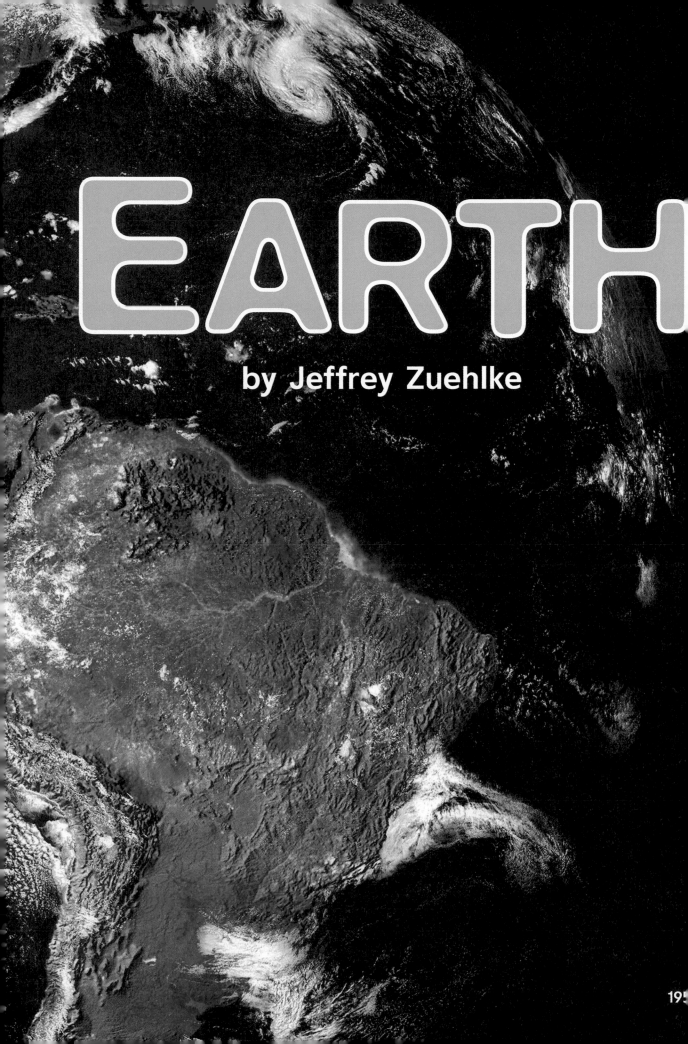

EARTH

by Jeffrey Zuehlke

Our Home Planet

Have you ever seen this planet before? This is Earth. It is home to you and everyone you know. Billions of people live on this planet. Billions more plants and animals live here too. That makes Earth a special planet. As far as we know, no other planet has living beings on it.

How does Earth support life when other planets do not? Our planet has everything creatures need to live. It has water. It has air we can breathe.

From space, you can see Earth's blue oceans and brown land. How is our planet different from other planets?

People enjoy the bright sunshine and warm temperatures on a beach. Earth's water and air make it an ideal place for living things.

Earth has **warmth** too. Gases covering the planet hold in heat from the Sun. That keeps our planet warm. But not too warm. Some planets are much too cold to **support** life. Others are much too hot. Earth is just the right **temperature** to support life.

We can study Earth in our own backyard. But scientists have also learned about Earth by studying space. They have learned how other planets are different from ours. Learning more about space helps us understand why our planet is one of a kind.

Studying space has allowed us to learn a lot about Earth.

STOP AND CHECK

Summarize What did you learn about Earth in this section? Summarize the first section in your own words.

NASA

Earth and Its Neighbors

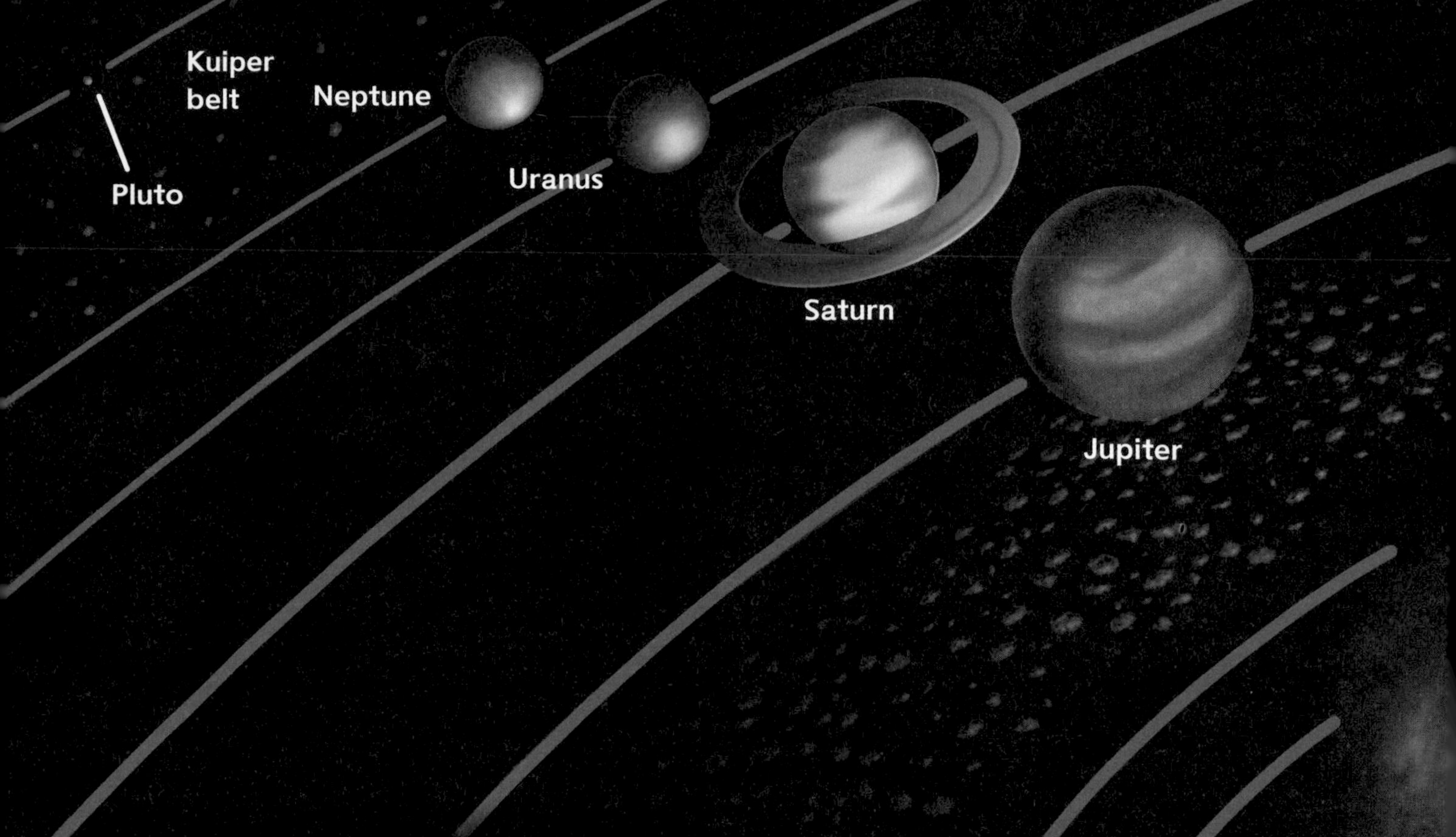

Kuiper belt
Neptune
Pluto
Uranus
Saturn
Jupiter

Earth shares its neighborhood in space with many other planets. Earth is part of the solar system. The solar system includes the Sun and eight planets. It also includes rocks called asteroids. Dwarf planets are part of the solar system too. Dwarf planets are smaller than the eight main planets.

The Sun lies at the center of the solar system. The planets closest to the Sun are Mercury, Venus, Earth, and Mars. These planets are made mostly of solid rock. Scientists call them the rocky planets.

Illustration: George Hamblin

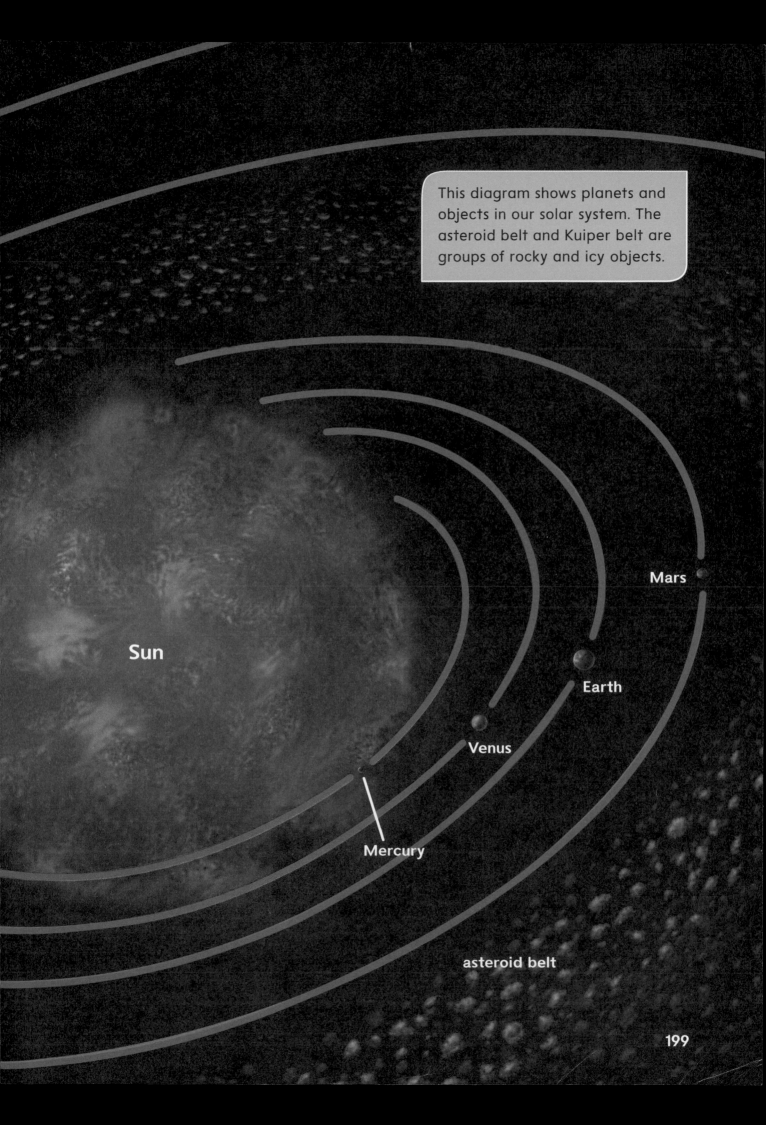

This diagram shows planets and objects in our solar system. The asteroid belt and Kuiper belt are groups of rocky and icy objects.

Mars

Sun

Earth

Venus

Mercury

asteroid belt

Jupiter, Saturn, Uranus, and Neptune are called gas giants. They are mostly made of gas. They are the largest planets in the solar system. They are also farthest from the Sun.

Earth is the largest of the rocky planets. It is the fifth-largest planet in the solar system. Earth is nearly 8,000 miles (12,800 kilometers) wide. But our planet is much smaller than the gas giants. More than 1,000 Earths could fit inside Jupiter, the biggest planet.

Neptune, Uranus, Saturn, and Jupiter (LEFT TO RIGHT) are gas planets. They are much larger than the rocky planets.

Mercury Venus Earth Mars Jupiter Saturn Uranus Neptune Pluto

This picture shows the eight planets in our solar system. The Sun appears on the left, and the dwarf planet Pluto is on the right. This picture shows the size of each planet compared to others.

Earth is the third planet from the Sun. The Sun is about 93 million miles (150 million km) away from Earth. To travel that far on Earth, you would have to circle the **globe** 3,733 times!

The Sun may be very far from Earth, but its rays warm the planet. Deserts like the Sahara get very hot.

(t) The International Astronomical Union (b) Jean-Claude Winkler/Photographer's Choice RR/Getty Images

STOP AND CHECK

Summarize What have you learned about Earth and its neighbors in this section? Summarize this part of the article in your own words.

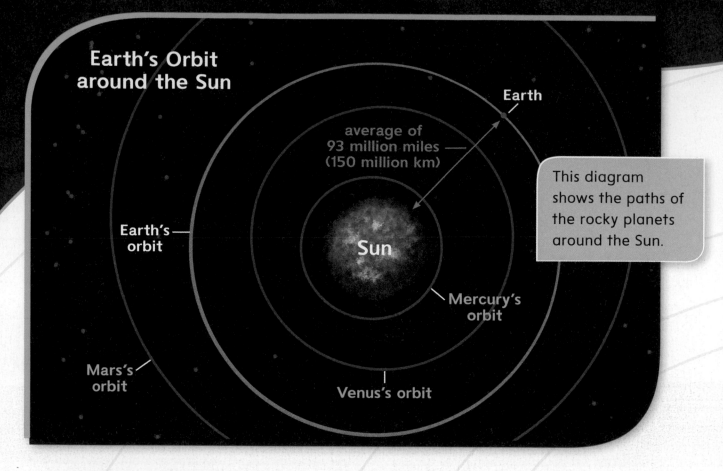

Earth's Orbit around the Sun

Earth

average of 93 million miles (150 million km)

Earth's orbit

Sun

Mercury's orbit

This diagram shows the paths of the rocky planets around the Sun.

Mars's orbit

Venus's orbit

Each planet follows its own path around the Sun. The path is called an orbit. The orbits are a little bit elliptical (ee-LIHP-tih-kuhl). That means they are oval-shaped paths. Earth takes a little more than 365 days to orbit the Sun. One trip around the Sun equals one year.

Planets also rotate (ROH-tayt) as they travel. They spin around like a top. Each planet rotates around its axis (AK-sihs). An axis is an imaginary line that runs through the center of the planet from top to bottom. Earth's axis is tilted. So Earth leans to one side as it spins. It rotates all the way around in 24 hours. That's exactly one day.

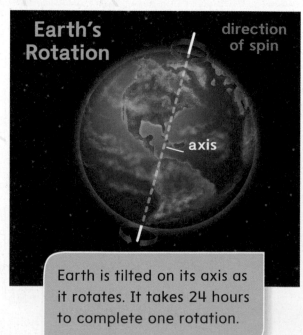

Earth's Rotation

direction of spin

axis

Earth is tilted on its axis as it rotates. It takes 24 hours to complete one rotation.

Earth's Closest Neighbor

Everyone knows about Earth's closest neighbor. We see it in the sky almost every night. It is the Moon.

The Moon is much smaller than Earth. It is about 2,160 miles (3,475 km) wide. About 50 moons would fit inside Earth.

Our Moon orbits Earth, just as Earth orbits the Sun. The Moon takes about 27 days to travel around Earth.

Like our planet, the Moon also rotates. But it rotates much more slowly than Earth. The Moon takes a little more than 27 days to turn all the way around. Since it travels around Earth in the same amount of time, the same side of the Moon always faces us.

The Moon looks small when shown side by side with Earth. (It is actually much farther from Earth than shown here.)

NASA/JPL/USGS

From night to night, the Moon seems to change shape. Sometimes we can see the full moon. Other times, it looks as if it has been cut in half. The Moon's shape seems to change just a little each night. Over about one month, it grows into a full moon and then gets smaller and disappears again.

Phases of the Moon over 28 Days

The Moon seems to grow bigger until half of its round shape shows (TOP ROW, LEFT TO RIGHT). This is called the moon's first quarter. It grows larger until we see the full moon. The full moon shines for a night or two. Then it looks smaller bit by bit, until we see the last quarter (THIRD ROW FROM TOP). Finally, the crescent disappears into a new moon.

The Moon is closer to
Earth than any planets are.
But it is still very far away.

We see only the parts of the Moon that are lit
by the Sun. As the Moon travels around Earth,
sunlight hits the Moon from different directions.
When it hits the side of the Moon facing Earth,
we see a full moon. If it mostly lights the side
facing away from Earth, we see only a sliver.

The Moon may not seem far away. But it is
very far. Our Moon is 238,855 miles (384,400 km)
from Earth. Imagine you could drive from Earth
to the Moon in a car going 50 miles (80 km) per
hour. It would take nearly 200 days of nonstop
driving to get there.

STOP AND CHECK

Reread Why does the Moon seem to
change shape? Reread to find the answer.

The Moon's surface has craters of many different sizes. These craters are on the side of the Moon that faces away from Earth.

Once you reached the Moon, what would you see? The Moon's **surface** is mostly gray rocks and dirt. You would see some mountains and many deep valleys. You would also see many craters (KRAY-turs). Craters are bowl-shaped pits in the surface. Some craters are just a few miles wide. The largest ones are more than 1,000 miles wide (1,610 km).

Craters are formed when rocks or ice from space slam into the Moon's surface. These objects are called meteorites (MEE-tee-uh-ryets) and comets (KAH-mehts).

This image shows the gray surface of the Moon. The dark patches are areas filled with lava rock. This is the side of the Moon we see from Earth.

What else would you notice? There is no life on the Moon. The Moon has almost no atmosphere. So there is no air to breathe.

Without an atmosphere, nothing protects the Moon from the Sun's heat. Nothing holds in any of the Sun's warmth either. So the Moon gets very hot and very cold. Sunny parts of the Moon get as hot as 253°F (123°C). Other places get as cold as -387°F (-233°C).

• • • • • •

Look up at the night sky. Can you see the Moon, our nearest neighbor in space? The Sun and the planets are out there, too, even if you can't see them now. Look down at the ground. That's Earth, our home planet. We are all part of the solar system.

The Moon is seen through a thin layer of Earth's atmosphere. The Moon has no atmosphere of its own.

National Aeronautics and Space Administration (NASA)

About the Author

Jeffrey Zuehlke is the author of more than forty-five nonfiction books for children about amazing people, places, and objects. Jeffrey has told stories about sports stars and leaders from history. And if you are curious about vehicles—from snowplows to space shuttles—he has probably written a book for you. Some of his books take readers to faraway countries. Others explore exciting places in the United States, such as the Grand Canyon.

Author's Purpose
Why do you think the author included photographs and diagrams in *Earth?*

Respond to the Text

Summarize

Tell the main ideas that you learned about Earth and its neighbors. The information from your Main Idea and Details chart may help you.

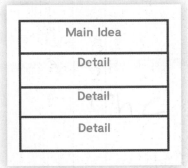

Main Idea
Detail
Detail
Detail

Write

How does Jeffrey Zuehlke use text features to help you learn about Earth? Use these sentence frames to organize your text evidence.

> Jeffrey Zuehlke uses diagrams and labels to . . .
> He uses illustrations to . . .
> This helps me understand . . .

Make Connections

How can we learn more about Earth and its neighbors? ESSENTIAL QUESTION

Why do people study the solar system? TEXT TO WORLD

Compare Texts

Read this Lithuanian legend about why the Sun is red.

Why the Sun Is Red
A Lithuanian Legend

"I'm wondering," said the King to his horseman while pointing to the rosy sunset. "Why is the Sun red while setting and rising, but yellow the rest of the day?"

"Perhaps it is not for us to know," said the horseman.

"The Sun's mother must know," said the King. "You're just the one to find her, in her amber house. Its **surface** glows bright orange. If you find the answer to my question, I'll fill your hat with gold!" said the King. "But if you don't, you must leave my kingdom forever."

For seven days the horseman searched. Then, one rainy evening, he saw a glow. It was the amber house! An old woman opened the door. It was the Sun's mother.

"What brings you here?" she asked.

"It's about your daughter," said the horseman. "Can you tell me why she is red when she rises and sets, but yellow the rest of the day?"

"You've traveled all this way to ask that?" said the Sun's mother.

"My King ordered me," explained the horseman. "If I don't get an answer, I must leave his kingdom."

"I'll ask my daughter when she returns tonight," said the woman. "Hide quietly in the kitchen."

The Sun returned, and the mother said, "A man was here. He wished to know why you are red when you rise and set, but yellow the rest of the day."

"How dare he ask!" shouted the Sun.

"He left," said her mother. "But why are you angry? It's a simple question."

"I'm angry because every morning and evening I draw near the sea and see her," said the Sun.

"Her?"

"She is the most beautiful princess in the world. She makes me red with envy."

The horseman had his answer. He sped away on his horse.

The pleased King had his answer. He filled the horseman's hat with gold. The horseman bowed and left quickly, eager for the **warmth** of his own bed.

Make Connections

How does this legend explain about one of Earth's neighbors? ESSENTIAL QUESTION

Compare this story to nonfiction articles you have read about space. TEXT TO TEXT

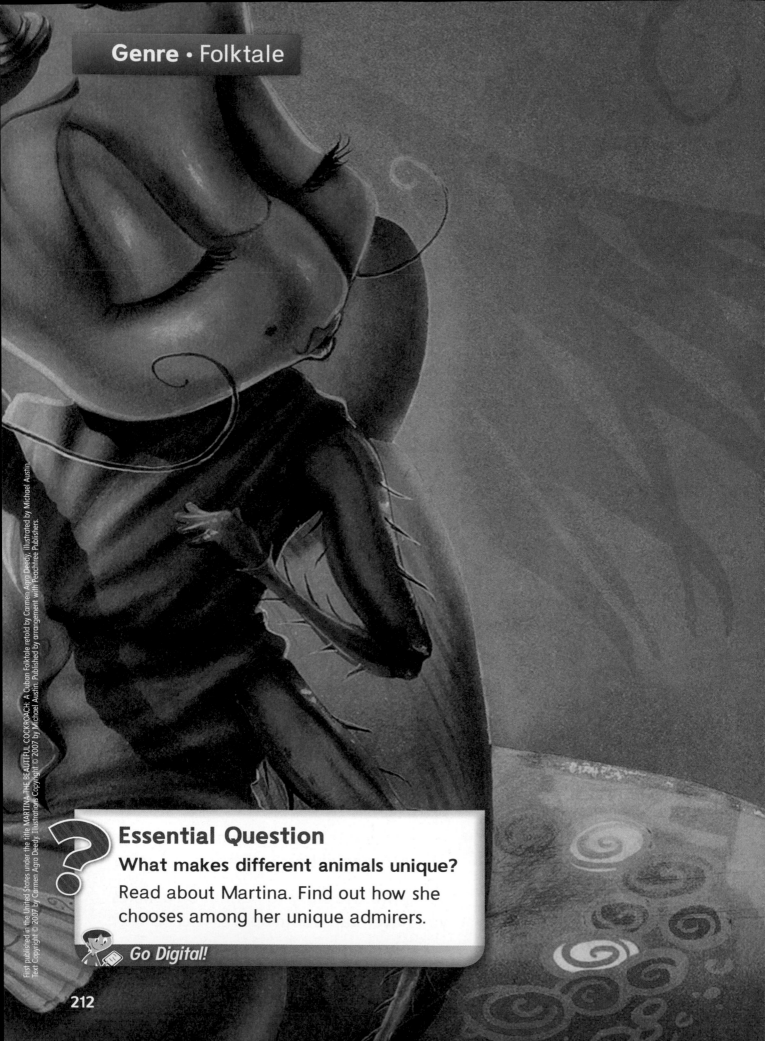

First published in the United States under the title MARTINA THE BEAUTIFUL COCKROACH: A Cuban Folktale retold by Carmen Agra Deedy; illustrated by Michael Austin. Text Copyright © 2007 by Carmen Agra Deedy. Illustrations Copyright © 2007 by Michael Austin. Published by arrangement with Peachtree Publishers.

Essential Question

What makes different animals unique?

Read about Martina. Find out how she chooses among her unique admirers.

Go Digital!

Martina

the Beautiful Cockroach

A Cuban Folktale

retold by
Carmen Agra Deedy

illustrated by
Michael Austin

Martina Josefina Catalina Cucaracha was a beautiful cockroach.

She lived in a cozy street lamp in Old Havana with her big, lovable family.

Now that Martina was 21 days old, she was ready to give her leg in marriage. The Cucaracha household was crawling with excitement! Every *señora* in the family had something to **offer**.

Tía Cuca gave her *una peineta,*
a seashell comb.

Mamá gave her *una mantilla,*
a lace shawl.

But *Abuela,* her Cuban
grandmother, gave her *un consejo
increíble,* some shocking advice.

215

"You want me to do WHAT?" Martina was aghast.

"You are a beautiful cockroach," said *Abuela*. "Finding husbands to choose from will be easy— picking the right one could be tricky."

"B-b-but," stammered Martina, "how will spilling COFFEE on a suitor's shoes help me find a good husband?"

Her grandmother smiled. "It will make him angry! Then you'll know how he will speak to you when he loses his temper. Trust me, Martina. The Coffee Test never fails."

Martina wasn't so sure.

Meanwhile, *Papá* sent *el perico*, the parrot,
to spread the word.

Soon all Havana—from the busy sidewalks
of El Prado to El Morro castle—was abuzz
with the news.

Martina the beautiful cockroach was ready
to choose a husband.

As was the custom, Martina would greet her suitors from the balcony, under her family's many **watchful** eyes.

Daintily, she sat down
and crossed her legs,
and crossed her legs,
and crossed her legs.

She didn't have long to wait.

Don Gallo, the rooster, strutted up first. Martina tried not to stare at his **splendid** shoes.

Keeping one eye on his reflection, Don Gallo greeted her with a sweeping bow. "¡*Caramba!* You really are a beautiful cockroach. I will look even more **fabulous** with you on my wing!"

With that, he leaned forward and crooned,

"Martina
Josefina
Catalina
Cucaracha,
Beautiful *muchacha,*
Won't you be my wife?"

Martina hesitated only for an instant. "Coffee, *señor?*"

Right on cue, *Abuela* appeared.

With a quick glance at her grandmother, Martina nervously splattered coffee onto the rooster's spotless shoes.

"Oh my!" she said with mock **dismay**. "I'm all feelers today!"

"*¡Ki-ki-ri-kiiii!*" The rooster was furious. "Clumsy cockroach! I will teach you better manners when you are my wife."

Martina was stunned. The Coffee Test had worked!

"A most humble offer, *señor*," she said coolly, "but I cannot accept. You are much too cocky for me."

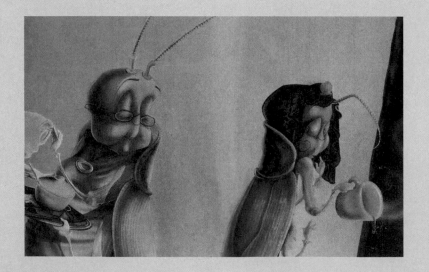

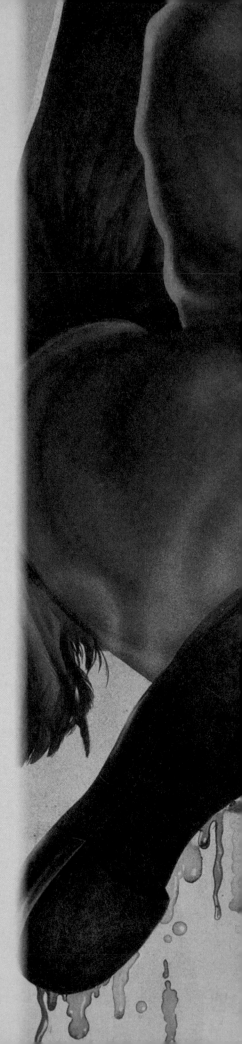

STOP AND CHECK

Visualize What is the Coffee Test? Use the descriptions to visualize the events in the story.

Don Cerdo, the pig, hoofed up next. His smell curled the little hairs on Martina's legs.

"What an unimaginable scent," Martina wheezed. "Is it some new pig cologne?"

"Oh no, *señorita*. It's the sweet aroma of my pig sty. Rotten eggs! Turnip peels! Stinky cheese!" Don Cerdo licked his chops and sang,

"Martina
Josefina
Catalina
Cucaracha,
Beautiful *muchacha*,
Won't you be my wife?"

Martina had already left in search of coffee.

She wasted no time with the pig.

"*¡Gronc! ¡Gronc!*" squealed Don Cerdo as he dabbed at the coffee on his shoes. "What a tragedy for my poor loafers!"

He really is quite a ham, thought Martina.

"Calm yourself, *señor*. I'll clean them for you!"

"I'll say you will!" he snorted. "When you are my wife, there'll be no end to cleaning up after me!"

Martina rolled her eyes in **disbelief**.

"A most charming offer, *señor*," she said drily, "but I must decline. You are much too boorish for me."

The Coffee Test had saved her from yet another unsuitable suitor.

STOP AND CHECK

Visualize What happens when Martina pours coffee on the pig? Use the descriptions to visualize the events in the story.

The pig was scarcely out of sight when Don Lagarto, the lizard, crept over the railing. His oily fingers brushed the little cockroach's lovely *mantilla*.

"You shouldn't sneak up on a lady like that!"

"I don't sneak. I creep," he said, circling Martina.

For some reason this fellow really bugged her. "I've had enough of creeps for one day," said Martina. *"Adíos."*

"But I need you! Wait!" The lizard fell on one scaly knee and warbled,
"Martina
Josefina
Catalina
Cucaracha,
Beautiful *muchacha,*
Won't you be my wife?"

Martina sighed. "Let me see if there's any coffee left."

This time she wasn't taking any chances. Martina returned with TWO cups for the lizard.

"*¡Psssst! ¡Psssst!*" he spat. Don Lagarto was livid. He changed colors three times before he finally found his true one. "And to think," he hissed. "I was going to eat—er—MARRY you!"

Martina stared at the lizard. You could have heard a breadcrumb drop.

"Food for thought, *señor,*" Martina said icily, "but I must refuse. You are much too cold-blooded for me."

When her grandmother returned to collect the day's coffee cups, Martina was still fuming.

"I'm going inside, *Abuela*."

"So soon?"

"*¡Sí!* I'm afraid of whom I might meet next!"

Abuela drew Martina to the railing and pointed to the garden below. "What about him?"

Martina looked down at the tiny brown mouse, and her cockroach heart began to beat faster.

Ti-ki-tin, ti-ki-tan.

"Oh, *Abuela*, he's adorable. Where has he been?"

"Right here all along."

"What do I do?"

"Go talk to him . . . and just be yourself."

Martina handed *Abuela* her *peineta* and *mantilla,* then scurried down to the garden. The mouse was waiting.

Ti-ki-tin, ti-ki-tan.

"*Hola*, hello." His voice was like warm honey. "My name is Pérez."

"*Hola*," she whispered shyly, "I'm Martina—"

"—the beautiful cockroach," he finished for her.

"You think I'm beautiful?"

The little mouse turned pink under his fur. "Well, my eyes are rather weak, but I have excellent EARS. I know you are strong and good, Martina Josefina Catalina Cucaracha." Then he squinted sweetly. *"Who cares if you are beautiful?"*

TI-KI-TIN, TI-KI-TAN.

"Martina-a-a-a-a! Don't forget the coffee!" It was *Abuela*.

No, thought Martina. No coffee for Pérez!

"Martina Josefina Catalina Cucaracha!"

"Sí, Abuela." Martina knew better than to argue with her Cuban grandmother.

With a heavy heart, she reached for the cup.

But Pérez got there first. Quick as a mouse, he splashed *café cubano* onto Martina's shoes.

Now the coffee was on the other foot.

Martina was too delighted to be angry. At last, she'd found her perfect match. But she had to ask, "How did you know about the Coffee Test?"

Pérez grinned. "Well, *mi amor*, my love . . .

. . . I too have a Cuban grandmother."

STOP AND CHECK

Reread Why doesn't Martina want to pour coffee on the mouse? Reread to find the answer.

About the Author and Illustrator

Carmen Agra Deedy loves spinning stories. She travels around the world entertaining people with her tales. Carmen came to the United States from Cuba in 1960. She and her family settled in Georgia. Carmen has not forgotten her Cuban culture. She shares it with the world through her stories.

Michael Austin grew up in a small town in Florida, where he combined his imagination and love of drawing. He drew on rocks, paper plates, boxes, and even the walls. He grew up to be an illustrator of many award-winning books.

Author's Purpose
What message did the author want to tell readers?

Respond to the Text

Summarize

Think about how Martina finds a husband. Summarize the events in the story. The information from your Problem and Solution chart may help you summarize.

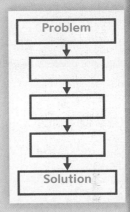

Write

How does Carmen Agra Deedy help you predict how the coffee test will turn out for each character? Use these sentence frames to organize your text evidence.

> Carmen Agra Deedy describes each animal by . . .
> Then she . . .
> This helps me understand why Martina . . .

Make Connections

What makes Pérez unique among Martina's suitors? **ESSENTIAL QUESTION**

Why do people like to watch animals? What is interesting about animals? **TEXT TO WORLD**

Get a Backbone!

Most animals in the world fit in one of two groups. Some have backbones. The others do not. People, lizards, owls, frogs, and sharks all have backbones. Touch the back of your neck. That's where your backbone starts. It's a string of bones that goes all the way down your back to your tailbone.

What would you be like without a backbone? You couldn't walk or sit up. You'd have to slither around like a worm or swim like an octopus. Those animals have no backbones.

backbone

A rooster is a vertebrate. Its backbone helps hold up its body.

234

Types of Vertebrates

Animals with backbones are called **vertebrates**. All vertebrates have backbones. However, not all vertebrates are alike. They have different **features**. Some are tiny. Others are huge. Some swim, while others fly.

Vertebrates can be birds, amphibians, fish, reptiles, or mammals. Animals in each group share a **unique** quality that makes them special.

Birds

Most birds can fly, but bees and bats can, too! Some birds, like ostriches and penguins, can't fly at all. Ostriches run. Penguins walk and swim. So what makes birds special?

Feathers, of course! Feathers keep birds warm. They can help birds to fly and steer through the air. The color of a bird's feathers can help it hide from predators or attract other birds.

A parrot is a bird. It has feathers and a backbone.

Reptiles

Lizards and snakes are reptiles. All reptiles have scales covering their bodies.

Because reptiles are cold-blooded, they must live in warm places. Some snakes, turtles, and crocodiles live mostly in warm water. Some reptiles live in dry deserts. Most reptiles have low bodies, four short legs, and a tail. Only snakes have no legs at all.

A chameleon is a reptile. It is a cold-blooded vertebrate with scaly skin.

(t) Salvador Manaois III/Flickr/Getty Images (b) Corey Hochachka/Design Pics/Corbis

235

Amphibians

Amphibians spend part of their lives in water and part on land. Frogs, toads, and salamanders are amphibians.

Most amphibians start out as an egg floating in water. When they hatch, they look like fish. They breathe through gills. As they grow older, they grow legs and lungs and begin to live on land.

A frog is an amphibian. These vertebrates live in water and on land.

Fish

Fish are vertebrates with a special ability. They can live in water. Fish don't have lungs to breathe air. They breathe oxygen using body parts called gills.

Fish have more species than any other type of vertebrate. There are about 32,000 kinds of fish! These cold-blooded animals live all over the world in rivers, streams, oceans, lakes, and ponds.

Clownfish are vertebrates that spend their whole lives in water.

Vertebrates

This chart compares animals with backbones.

Animal	Mouse	Clownfish	Frog
Group	mammal	fish	amphibian
Body Covering	fur	wet, scaly skin	smooth, moist skin
Where They Live	woodlands	oceans	lakes, ponds
How They Breathe	breathe through lungs	breathe through gills	breathe though gills, skin, or lungs

Mammals

A mouse and an elephant are related! How? They are vertebrates, and they are mammals. Mammals are warm-blooded animals. Most have hair or fur that covers their bodies. Their unique feature is milk! Mammal mothers feed their babies milk.

All mammals have lungs to breathe air. Most live on land. Some, like whales and dolphins, live in water. Bats are the only mammals that have wings and can fly. They also sleep while hanging upside down!

Look around you. The next time you see animals, think about them. Are they vertebrates? What are their special features?

A mouse and an elephant look different, but they are both mammals. Both have backbones.

Make Connections

What one thing makes vertebrates different from other animals? ESSENTIAL QUESTION

How are these animals like other animals you have read about? TEXT TO TEXT

(l) Image Source/Getty Images (r) Digital Zoo/Digital Vision/Getty Images

237

Birth of an Anthem

Francis Scott Key was filled with a love of his country when he saw the American flag still waving over Fort McHenry.

Essential Question

How is each event in history unique?

Read to see how America found its national anthem.

It Began in Baltimore

"The Star-Spangled Banner" officially became the U.S. national anthem less than 100 years ago. But the song itself is much older. Francis Scott Key wrote the words as he watched the British Navy attack Fort McHenry during the War of 1812 in the Battle of Baltimore. But why was Key in Baltimore?

This is a copy of Francis Scott Key's handwritten lyrics. The phrase "star-spangled banner" describes the enormous American flag he wrote the poem about.

The answer comes down to a Maryland doctor. In August 1814, British soldiers marched into Upper Marlboro, Maryland. Dr. William Beanes was an **agreeable** man. He greeted the soldiers as friends. He let the British officers use his home.

Then a few days after they left, word reached Beanes that the soldiers were stealing from his neighbors. He had the soldiers held in a jail. The British officers did not **appreciate** this. When they found out, they arrested Beanes and brought him aboard a British ship.

> **STOP AND CHECK**
>
> **Summarize** Why did the British officers arrest Dr. William Beanes?

239

Watching and Waiting

Key was sent to Baltimore to help Beanes. He was one of the **descendants** of Englishmen who came to America to live in the early 1700s. He was also a respected lawyer. His business **boomed**. When Key boarded the British ship, he persuaded the British to free the doctor. After Beanes was released, the two men got on an American ship. Then the British Navy arrived in ships and barges, or large sea **vehicles** used for the **transportation** of cannons and other **resources**. They attacked the Americans at Fort McHenry. Beanes and Key were forced to stay on the ship. There, they watched the battle.

More Songs to Sing

"The Star-Spangled Banner" is our official national anthem. But some patriotic songs have been considered unofficial anthems. In 1789, a composer named Philip Phile wrote "The President's March." This music was written to honor George Washington at the beginning of his first term as president. Lyrics were later added and the song was retitled "Hail, Columbia." The song is still played today to honor the vice president of the United States.

Some other patriotic songs considered unofficial anthems are "My Country 'Tis of Thee" and "America the Beautiful."

Making It Official

This timeline shows important dates in the creation of our country's anthem.

July 1889	April 1918	Jan 1930	Mar 1931
"The Star-Spangled Banner" becomes the official song to be played when raising the flag.	A bill is introduced to make "The Star-Spangled Banner" the national anthem, but it does not pass.	Five million people sign a petition to make the song the U.S. national anthem.	Herbert Hoover signs a bill to make the song the official national anthem.

Dawn's Early Light

The battle continued through the night. When morning arrived, Key saw that the American flag still flew above the fort. The Americans had won this battle! The sight inspired him to write a poem. Key's words later became "The Star-Spangled Banner."

Sheet music shows the music notes and lyrics to a song. This sheet music was published in Philadelphia, Pennsylvania, at around 1815.

First, Key showed the poem to friends. Then, they showed it to others. By the time of the Civil War, most of America's **population** was singing "The Star-Spangled Banner." It had become the country's most beloved song. Then, in 1931, Congress passed a resolution to make "The Star-Spangled Banner" the U.S. anthem. Finally, President Herbert Hoover signed the law. Americans have been singing it ever since.

Respond to the Text

Use important details from the selection to summarize.
SUMMARIZE

How does the author help you understand how Francis Scott Key wrote "The Star-Spangled Banner"?
WRITE

When do people sing the national anthem today?
TEXT TO WORLD

241

Compare Texts
Read about a special way of finding out about important events in the past.

Discovering Life Long Ago

In the past, people wrote in diaries and journals. They wrote letters to friends and families. They also wrote autobiographies to tell their life stories. Diaries, journals, and autobiographies tell us what people thought and felt. They also give details about daily life in the past. They describe the food people ate. They tell what kind of **transportation** they used.

Posters, newspapers, and old photographs also give details about events in the past. So do speeches and songs. Photographs show people's clothes and how they had fun.

Both words and pictures from the past help us see how people lived long ago. They tell a history of people, places, and things. They take us back in time.

This poster was an ad for the transcontinental railroad in 1869.

A Pioneer's Diary

Sallie Hester was fourteen years old when she traveled west in a wagon train in 1849. She kept a diary. You can read a part of it below. What details about **emigration** can you learn from Sallie's diary?

In the 1840s, thousands of families moved west to Oregon and California in covered wagons.

Spring, 1849

When we camp at night, we form a corral with our wagons and pitch our tents on the outside. Inside of this corral we drive our cattle, with guards stationed on the outside of the tents. . . .

We have a portable table, tin plates and cups, cheap knives and forks, camp stools, etc. . . . We live on bacon, ham, rice, dried fruits, molasses, packed butter, bread, coffee, tea and milk, as we have our own cows.

Make Connections

What can we learn about history from diaries, newspapers, and photographs? ESSENTIAL QUESTION

What have you learned about transportation west from old photos and diaries? TEXT TO TEXT

Big Ideas *from* Nature

by Adrienne Mason

Essential Question

What ideas can we get from nature?

Read how ideas from nature inspired new inventions.

Go Digital!

Inspiration

Sometimes a sticky situation can lead to a great invention. In the 1940s, George de Mestral went for a walk with his dog. Along the way, George's pants and his dog's fur caught tiny seeds called burrs. George was curious. Why did the burrs stick so well? He looked closer. The burrs were covered in tiny hooks. George used this idea to invent a two-sided fastener. It had hooks on one side and loops on the other. Today these hook and loop fasteners are used on everything from shoes to spacesuits!

Idea

hooks
fasteners

Observing how burrs stick to cloth and fur inspired one inventor to create a new fastener.

Those sticky burrs gave de Mestral a great idea. Nature provided a **model** that George could imitate. Copying, or imitating, designs from nature is called biomimicry [bigh-o-MIM-i-kree]. (*Bio* means life and *mimicry* means to copy.) From owls' sharp claws to elephants' bendy noses, nature is full of models. We can learn from each one.

Thomas Northcut/Photodisc/Getty Images

245

Observing nature gives us ideas for new things. George de Mestral didn't set out on his walk thinking he would create a new fastener. But by being curious and observant, he did just that.

Nature Did It First

Designers often start with a problem. They may look for solutions in the natural world. Nature has been making and testing designs for a long time! Nature often has the answers to questions people ask.

More than a hundred years ago, the Wright brothers, Orville and Wilbur, wondered how to fly. For an answer, they watched birds, the flying experts. Watching bird wings gave them ideas on how to design airplane wings. While bird wings are not **identical** to plane wings, they both can fly. The Wright Brothers built an airplane in 1903. It was the first to lift up, up, and away!

Leonardo da Vinci was an artist and inventor. He lived more than 400 years ago. He looked at birds' wings and then drew plans for many flying machines.

Idea

Inspiration

Inspiration

Idea

Smart Shapes

Fish and cars share a problem. It takes energy to move a fish through water and a car through air. Fish get energy from food. Cars get it from fuel.

To create a new fuel-saving car, designers studied the shape of fish. They found that the boxfish's square shape was streamlined. This means that the fish slips through the water without wasting energy. By making the new car's shape **similar** to that of the boxfish, they created a car that saves gas.

The car's frame is also similar to the fish's skeleton. The metal frame is thick in some places and thinner in others, just like the fish's bones. This saves on materials and puts strength where it is needed most.

Watching fish gave car designers a new idea for a car's shape.

Energy Savers

Air conditioners keep buildings cool. The shape of a building can also help. In Africa, termites gave builders an **example** of a self-cooling structure. Holes at the bottom of termite mounds catch the wind. The air rises through tunnels and flows out the top. The termites designed an **effective** way to cool a structure. The builders borrowed their ideas. During the day, fans on the first floor blow cool air into the building. The air rises and flows through chimneys on the roof. This design saves money and energy.

How is a termite mound like this building in Africa? They both need a way to stay cool.

STOP AND CHECK

Summarize What did you learn from reading the section called "Energy Savers"? Tell what the section is about.

Idea

Inspiration

(bkgd) John Beatty/Stone/Getty Images (inset) Ken Wilson-Max/Alamy

248

Inspiration

Idea

Grasshoppers and the robot, Jollbot, can both jump.

Master Movers

You can't travel to Mars, but a robot can. Robots can explore places that are not safe for people. Robots can't walk, but they still have to travel over dips and bumps. Sometimes they get stuck. Designers are working on a robot called Jollbot to fix the problem. The name Jollbot comes from the words *jump* and *roll*. The Jollbot can do both. The super spring of grasshopper legs gave designers their idea.

Tunnel Makers

More than 200 years ago, an engineer was trying to drill a tunnel under a river. But each attempt failed. The walls kept falling in. Then he saw how shipworms bored through wood. The animal uses a tough shield to drill. Then it builds a hard tube along the tunnel walls. What a great idea! The engineer copied the shipworm to build the Thames Tunnel. As he drilled, workers lined the tunnel walls with bricks.

Shipworms and tunnel-builders need a way to drill through wood or rock safely.

Idea

Inspiration

shipworm

shipworm's tunnel

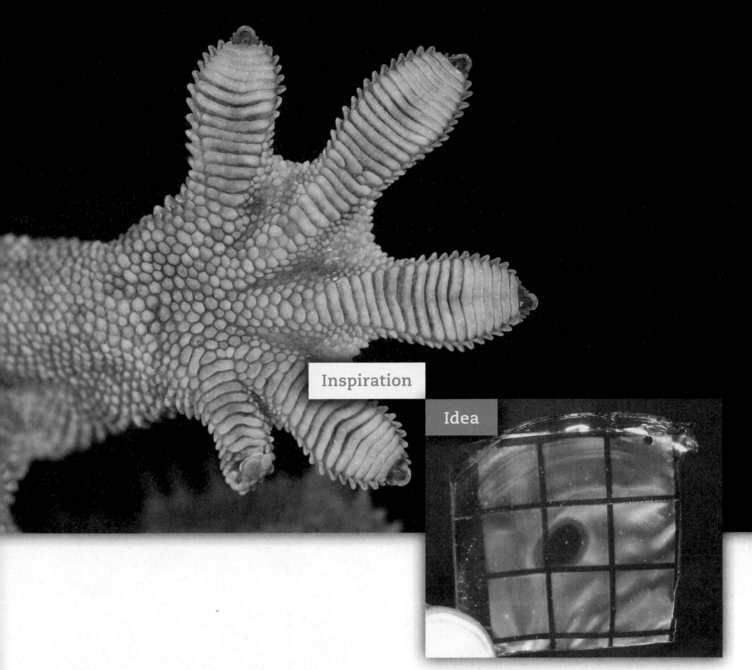

Inspiration

Idea

Mixing New Materials

Tiny hairs on a gecko's foot help it climb walls. It can cling to ceilings, too. Scientists studied gecko feet to create a bandage with bumps. The bandage is so sticky it can even attach wet surfaces (like a human heart!).

Sticky gecko feet gave doctors an idea for a super sticky bandage.

(bkgd) Volker Steger/Photo Researchers, Inc. (inset) Robert Langer and Jeff Karp

STOP AND CHECK

Summarize What did you learn from reading the section called "Mixing New Materials"? Tell what the section is about.

Inspiration

Idea

Working Together

Birds fly in flocks. Fish swim in schools. They do this without hitting one another. Cars move in large groups, too. But they often crash. Today, car designers are learning from locusts. They study how the insects travel together safely. One day you might drive a car that "sees" the cars around it.

Ideas from locusts are helping to design safer cars.

STOP AND CHECK

Ask and Answer Questions Why are car designers studying locusts? Reread page 252 to find the answer.

Learning from the Experts

Biomimicry shows that ideas that work for nature can work for people, too. It makes sense. Need a **material** that is strong and stretchy? Learning about spider silk would be a good place to begin. Spider silk is one of the strongest fibers in nature. It is as flexible as an elastic band and strong like steel. Need a type of glue that will harden in salt water? What do the sea creatures barnacles and mussels use to stick to rocks? Maybe nature already has a plan or a recipe people can use!

Observing how nature works also shows us ways to help the planet. Nature does not waste materials or energy. And natural designs do not pollute the air or water. Learning new things while protecting Earth's resources—that's an idea worth copying!

This cloth was woven from the silk that spiders use to spin webs.

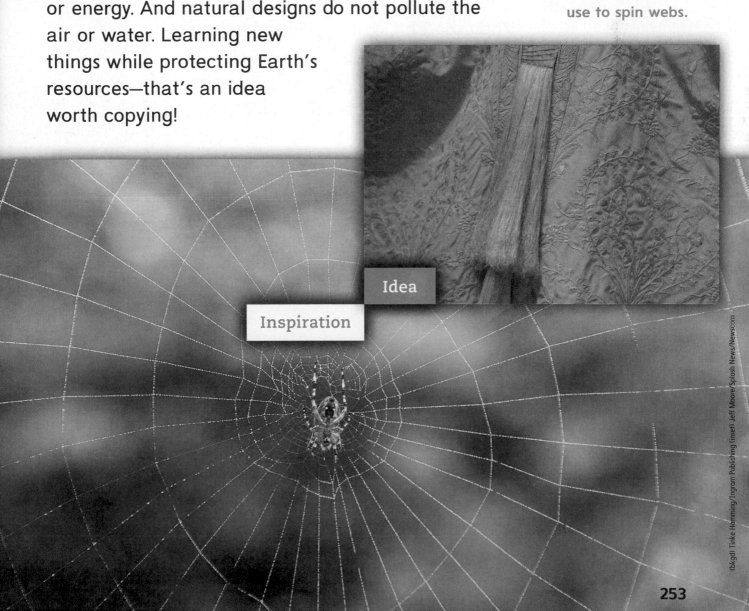

Idea

Inspiration

About the Author

Adrienne Mason studied to be a scientist. Later on she decided that a life in a lab was not for her. Because she loved talking and writing about science, she began to write books instead. She has written more than twenty books for children. Most are about science, nature, and history. When she isn't writing, Adrienne likes to spend time outdoors. She hikes, camps, bikes, and walks on the beach near her home in western Canada.

Author's Purpose

Why do you think the author included pairs of photographs? What do the two photographs show?

Respond to the Text

Summarize

What ideas from nature led inventors to create new products? Information from your Main Idea and Details chart may help you summarize.

Main Idea
Detail
Detail
Detail

Write

How does the author organize the text to help you understand that each new idea starts with a problem? Use these sentence frames to cite your text evidence.

> The author describes problems to . . .
> Then she compares to help me . . .
> This helps me understand how . . .

Make Connections

Describe how something in nature led someone to a new idea. ESSENTIAL QUESTION

Think about one of the inventions in this article. How has it made our world better? TEXT TO WORLD

Genre · Myth

Compare Texts
Read about how fish bones inspired a young inventor long ago in Athens.

PERDIX Invents the SAW

In the days of gods and goddesses, there lived an inventor named Daedalus (DED-uh-lis). He was famous throughout Greece for his good ideas and his bad temper.

One day Daedalus heard a knock on his workshop door. "Who's interrupting my work?" he growled.

"It's me, Uncle," said his twelve-year-old nephew Perdix (PER-dix). "I want to be a great inventor, too. Will you teach me?"

Daedalus's back hurt from chopping firewood. His shoulder ached from sweeping. He didn't really want to teach Perdix. Then he got an idea. "If you do all the chores, I'll let you watch me invent things," he said.

Perdix did the chores, cooked meals, and **observed** how Daedalus worked. The boy had some clever ideas. He wanted to make a smaller ax for cutting branches for firewood. Daedalus disagreed. "Just leave the inventing to me," he always hissed.

One afternoon Perdix roasted a large fish for lunch. After eating, Daedalus licked his fingers and smacked his lips. "That was pretty good, Perdix, but I've eaten better," he said.

Perdix sighed and started washing the dishes. In the process he cut his finger on the jagged backbone of the fish. He held the backbone up and studied its sharp edges. "I can **imitate** this design and make a fine tool for cutting wood," he thought.

The next day, Perdix sawed all the firewood before Daedalus awoke. "How did you finish your work so early?" Daedalus snarled.

"It was easy with my new invention," said Perdix. He showed his uncle the saw.

Daedalus was reluctant to praise his clever nephew.

"It should be *my* invention because you cooked that fish for me," he sniffed.

Perdix just smiled. He now realized that he was a great inventor, too.

Make Connections

How did nature inspire Perdix? ESSENTIAL QUESTION

What other inventions have you read about that were inspired by nature? TEXT TO TEXT

WHITES ONLY

Essential Question

How can one person change the way you think?

Read how a librarian opens doors for Louis in Alabama in 1951.

Go Digital!

258

Finding Lincoln

by **Ann Malaspina**
paintings by **Colin Bootman**

PUBLIC LIBRARY
SINCE 1929

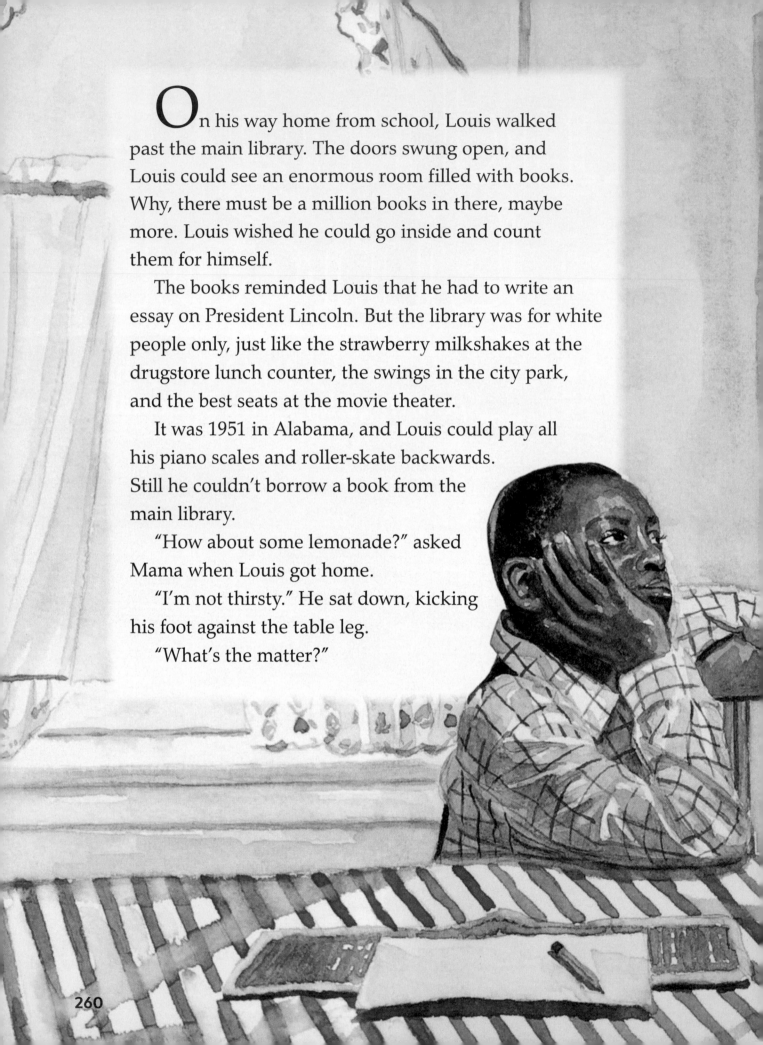

On his way home from school, Louis walked past the main library. The doors swung open, and Louis could see an enormous room filled with books. Why, there must be a million books in there, maybe more. Louis wished he could go inside and count them for himself.

The books reminded Louis that he had to write an essay on President Lincoln. But the library was for white people only, just like the strawberry milkshakes at the drugstore lunch counter, the swings in the city park, and the best seats at the movie theater.

It was 1951 in Alabama, and Louis could play all his piano scales and roller-skate backwards. Still he couldn't borrow a book from the main library.

"How about some lemonade?" asked Mama when Louis got home.

"I'm not thirsty." He sat down, kicking his foot against the table leg.

"What's the matter?"

Louis didn't feel like talking. He was thinking that Daddy always had books piled high by his bed. But he had read those books again and again. Now Daddy wanted a book on honeybees so he could learn how to keep beehives. If Mama was ever going to have fresh honey, Daddy needed to get inside that library, too.

"Maybe a little homework will cheer you up," teased Mama, as she let the biscuit dough rise for supper.

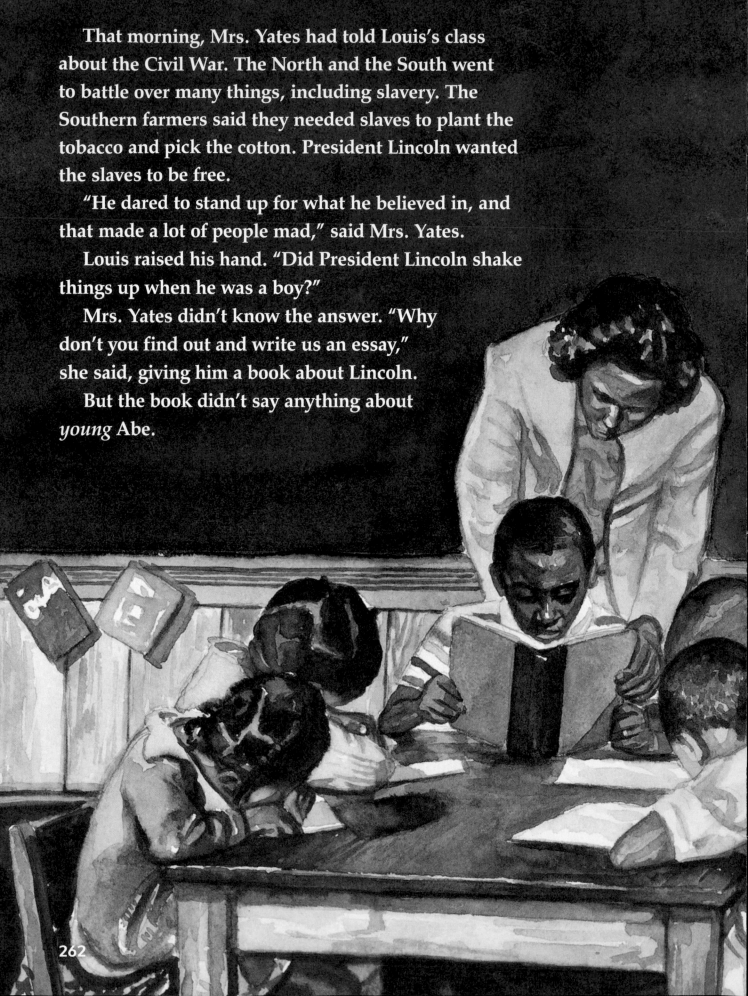

That morning, Mrs. Yates had told Louis's class about the Civil War. The North and the South went to battle over many things, including slavery. The Southern farmers said they needed slaves to plant the tobacco and pick the cotton. President Lincoln wanted the slaves to be free.

"He dared to stand up for what he believed in, and that made a lot of people mad," said Mrs. Yates.

Louis raised his hand. "Did President Lincoln shake things up when he was a boy?"

Mrs. Yates didn't know the answer. "Why don't you find out and write us an essay," she said, giving him a book about Lincoln.

But the book didn't say anything about *young* Abe.

Now Louis stared at his blank paper. "I need to find a book about President Lincoln when he was a boy," he told Mama.

"I have an idea," Mama said.

After the biscuits were baked, she took Louis to the basement of their church. She and her friends had started a small library where people **donated** books they didn't want anymore. Louis saw cookbooks, mysteries, and a book of maps, but no books about President Lincoln or honeybees.

"One day soon we'll be checking books out of the main library. Just you wait," Mama said on the way back home.

Louis didn't want to wait anymore. And he wasn't going to!

The next day after school, Louis stopped in front of the main library. Holding his breath, he climbed the wide steps and pushed open the door. Everywhere he looked, books were shelved high. Louis didn't have time to count, but a million seemed about right.

The library was also full of people. Every one of them turned to stare at Louis.

In the quiet room, Louis's heart was beating as loud as a tin drum. He began walking to the front desk. He was so **nervous** that he bumped into a man's chair.

STOP AND CHECK

Visualize How does Louis feel in the public library? Use the descriptions to visualize the events in the story.

"Watch where you're going, boy," said the man.

"Excuse me," mumbled Louis. On the polished floor, his sneakers squeaked like an old rusty hinge.

Two librarians sat at the desk, looking at him. "Can't you read?" said one, pointing at the "Whites Only" sign next to the door.

Louis's face burned like it did when he ran fast on a hot day in August.

The second librarian put down the book she was holding. "You'd better go home," she said, leading Louis back to the door. As she gently pushed him outside, she whispered, "Come back tomorrow after five."

Louis didn't see how tomorrow would be any different. Still, Mrs. Yates was waiting for that essay. He had to go back.

The next afternoon, Louis told Mama he needed to run an errand. Before she could ask a question, he was off.

He ran all the way to the library and up the front steps. It was after five o'clock. The door wouldn't budge when he pushed it. Just as Louis turned to go, he heard a voice.

"Shh, come in quickly." The door cracked open, and the librarian from yesterday peeked out.

Inside, the library was dark and quiet. "Now, what book did you want?" she asked.

"I need a book about President Lincoln when he was a boy."

"Follow me."

Louis followed her down one stack of books, then another. She stopped, moving her finger along a high shelf.

"Here it is."

She pulled down a book. Her hand was shaking, like Louis's insides. She could get in big trouble for helping him. She might have to pay a fine or even lose her job.

Louis read the cover, *Abe Lincoln Grows Up,* by Carl Sandburg. She had found just the right book!

Then Louis thought of something. "Don't I need a library card?"

Even Daddy and Mama couldn't get a library card. Staring down at his sneakers, Louis wished he could **disappear**.

The librarian was quiet for a moment. Then she tapped him on the shoulder.

"Come on. I'll give you a **temporary** one. You do live in town, don't you?"

Louis raised his head. "Yes, ma'am." This librarian didn't seem to mind shaking things up at all!

Walking slowly down the street, Louis looked at the book and his library card all the way home.

Louis burst in the kitchen door. He couldn't wait to tell everybody.

When she heard what had happened, Mama threw up her hands in **amazement**. Daddy shook his head like he had when Louis caught the catfish up at the lake last summer. "Isn't that something!" he kept saying.

Mama put her arm around Louis. "I hope no one got in trouble."

Daddy cleared his throat. "Mama and I just want you to be careful."

STOP AND CHECK

Visualize How do Louis's parents feel when Louis comes home with the library book? Use the descriptions to visualize how they act.

That night, Louis and Daddy read about young Abe and his kindness to animals. Though he grew up in the wilderness, Abe didn't like to shoot game. When he saw his friends hurting a turtle, Abe **refused** to join in. He didn't care if he wasn't like the other boys.

Abe also liked to have fun. Once he lifted a boy upside down so he could walk across the ceiling. Abe had to clean up the muddy footprints.

Abe could swing an ax, drive a plow, and win a wrestling match with anyone he met. What he liked best was to read a book. Some people said he was lazy and thought too much. Abe was just in a hurry to learn everything he could.

When Louis sat down to write his essay,
he filled up three whole pages.

"President Lincoln did what he thought was right, even when it shook people up," Louis said at bedtime.

Mama leaned to give him a hug. "Just like you, Louis."

Before Louis fell asleep, he remembered something. The next time he went to the main library, he needed to find a book about honeybees for Daddy. Out of a million books, Louis was sure he could find the perfect one.

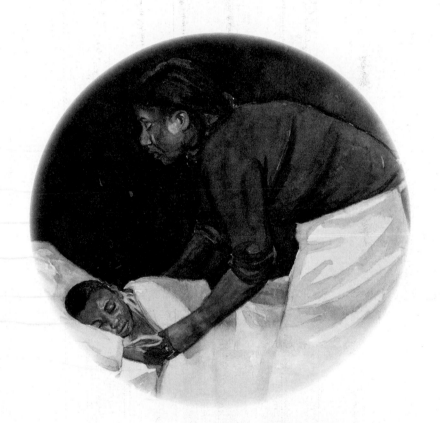

STOP AND CHECK

Reread Why does Louis's mother say "Just like you, Louis" and give Louis a hug? Reread to find the answer.

About the
Author and Illustrator

Ann Malaspina

was inspired to write by her fourth-grade teacher. The teacher told students to write for five minutes without stopping. "We could write anything at all, as long as we kept our pencils moving for five minutes," says Ann. Ann's pencil has been moving ever since. She has written seventeen nonfiction books for children. Several of them are about people who fought for their civil rights.

Colin Bootman

was born in Trinidad. The beauty and the culture of the island still inspire him. After moving to New York as a child, he discovered comic books. He loved the art in them. Colin is now the award-winning illustrator of twenty books for children. He wants young people to follow their own passions, too.

Author's Purpose
Why does the author tell a story about Louis's problem?

(t) Ann Malaspina, Author of Finding Lincoln, Published by Albert Whitman & Company 2009
(b) Colin Bootman, Illustrator of Finding Lincoln, Published by Albert Whitman & Company 2009

Respond to the Text

Summarize

What are the important events in *Finding Lincoln?* Tell them in order. Use your Cause and Effect chart to help you summarize.

Character		
Setting		
Cause	→	Effect
Cause	→	Effect
Cause	→	Effect

Write

How do you know that both the librarian and Louis are brave? Use these sentence frames to organize your text evidence.

The author describes Louis by . . .
Then she says that the librarian is . . .
This helps me understand how brave they are because . . .

Make Connections

How did the helpful librarian change the way Louis thought? ESSENTIAL QUESTION

Who is a person who inspires people in our country today? TEXT TO WORLD

Genre · Biography

Compare Texts
Read about how one woman helped many African Americans to get an education.

Mary McLeod Bethune

A Great American Teacher

In the past, some children in the United States could not get an **education**. Mary McLeod Bethune helped change that.

Mary was born in 1875 in South Carolina. Her family lived in a tiny cabin on their cotton farm. Mary and her sixteen brothers and sisters worked on the farm. Back then, few schools in South Carolina taught African American children.

Mary's Early Life

One day, Emma Wilson came to the farm. She wanted to teach African American children. Mary was eager to learn. Although her parents needed her help on the farm, they let her go to school. Miss Wilson inspired Mary to learn, and soon she finished school. Mary wanted to continue going to school, but her family had no money.

Then Mary Crissman helped. She paid for Mary to go to college. It was not easy for Mary. Some people wanted to **deny** African Americans the chance to learn. Mary showed her **bravery** by standing up for her right to an education.

After Mary finished college, she became a teacher. She dreamed of opening a school for African American girls.

Everyone Gets a Chance

In 1904, many African Americans moved to Daytona Beach, Florida to build a railroad. Mary decided to open a school for the railroad workers' children.

Building a school was hard work. Mary rented an old cottage for the school. Her neighbors helped her fix it up. The first students were five girls and Mary's own son. The students used burnt wood for pencils and crushed berries for ink. Mary biked around town asking people to **contribute** to the school. More students came. They sold vegetables and gave concerts to raise money for the school.

Changing Lives

By the 1920s, Mary needed a bigger building for her school. She opened a larger school that joined with another school nearby. The school became Bethune-Cookman College.

Mary grew up poor, but she helped many African Americans have more opportunities. Because of her, many African Americans received an education. She was a **leader** who was inspired to teach. Mary's story still inspires us.

Mary with her students in 1905

Mary's childhood home

Make Connections

How did Mary McLeod Bethune change the way people thought? ESSENTIAL QUESTION

Who else has changed people's lives? TEXT TO TEXT

(l) Courtesy of The State Archives of Florida (r) Courtesy of The State Archives of Florida

Excerpt from

The Talented Clementine

by Sara Pennypacker
pictures by Marla Frazee

Clementine has a big problem. She has no **talents**, and tonight is the big Talent-Palooza. Every third and fourth grader will be dancing, singing, or turning cartwheels—except Clementine. Even Margaret, her best friend, has an act. Now Clementine has to tell Mrs. Rice, the principal, and Margaret's teacher why she won't be performing. What can Clementine say? For once, she is completely out of ideas.

Essential Question

How can you use what you know to help others?

Read about how Clementine finds her special talent.

 Go Digital!

When I walked into the auditorium, I saw Margaret's teacher and Mrs. Rice sitting at the side of the stage on tall director's chairs. I tried to hide, but Margaret's teacher saw me. She looked down at her clipboard and frowned. Then she yelled so loud all the kids in the auditorium stopped what they were doing to listen.

"Clementine, I don't seem to have you listed here. No matter, we'll fit you in. What's your act?"

I went over there and whispered in her ear that I didn't have one. I hoped the kids watching thought I was saying I couldn't choose one because I had too many talents.

"What do you mean, you don't have one?" Margaret's teacher yelled, even though I was right there.

Okay, fine. Maybe she didn't yell it. But all the kids were listening so hard, they heard anyway.

"Hey, Clementine," one of the fourth graders called out. "Your face looks like it's burning up! Maybe that could be your act!"

STOP AND CHECK

Ask and Answer Questions Why does Clementine whisper in the teacher's ear? Reread page 280 to find the answer.

About a million kids laughed, even though
he was N-O-T, *not* funny. But he was right—when
I get **embarrassed** my face gets red and hot. So
I didn't yell anything back to him. I just stood
there with my red, hot face hanging down.

Mrs. Rice called me over. "Come sit beside
me, Clementine," she said. "You can keep me
company during the rehearsal."

So I had to sit in between Mrs. Rice and Margaret's teacher, right there at the side of the stage where all the kids could see me and know that I had no talents.

The first act was called A Dozen Doozie Cartwheelers. Twelve kids lined up, six on each side of the stage.

"Wait!" I yelled. I ran into the gym and dragged a tumbling mat back into the auditorium. I placed it on the floor in front of the stage. Then I got some of the Dozen Doozies to help me. Pretty soon we had all the mats piled up.

Margaret's teacher was glaring at me. She tapped her watch.

"They're going over," I explained. "No matter how they start off aiming, some of them are going over."

And they did. At least half a dozen of the Doozies went flying off the stage and right onto the mats. As soon as we got those kids back up and checked them for broken bones, I saw something else with my amazing corner-eyes.

"Stop!" I yelled. Then I ran over and grabbed a handful of crackers from one of the third graders just before they went into his mouth.

"You're up next," I reminded him. "And you're whistling 'Yankee Doodle Dandy.' No crackers!"

When I got back, Margaret's teacher gave me a look that said she was going to remember all this nonsense when I got into her grade.

But Mrs. Rice gave me a thumbs-up. "Thank you, Clementine," she said. "Those crackers could have been a problem."

And you will not believe what happened next: Margaret's teacher **apologized**!

"I'm sorry," she said. "I'm a little antsy tonight."

I wanted to stick around to hear about why she was antsy, but just then I noticed that the Super-Duper Hula-Hoopers had been Hula-Hooping for a while. I went over and asked them how long they were planning to go on.

284

The girl on the right said, "I once went for five hours and thirteen minutes."

The girl on the left made a face that said, "That's nothing!"

"Well, you need to have an ending tonight," I said. "There are a lot of acts after yours." I borrowed the jump-ropers' CD player and explained about how they could Hula-Hoop to the music and then S-T-O-P, *stop* when it was over.

And I didn't even get to sit down again for the rest of the afternoon because everybody needed my help for something. Finally, after everyone had a chance to practice their acts, I went over to Mrs. Rice.

"May I go into your office and use the phone? I need to call my parents and tell them not to come."

"I think it's a little late for that." Mrs. Rice showed me her watch and then called out, "Take your places, people. Five minutes to showtime!"

Everybody ran to their places. I ran to the curtains and peeked out: every seat in the **audience** was filled.

Margaret's teacher clapped her hands for attention.

"Before we get started," she said, "I just want to thank you all for being part of the show. Each and every one of you is helping to raise money for the big school trip next spring. Except Clementine."

Okay, fine, she didn't actually say, "Except Clementine," but you could see everyone was thinking it.

Just then, the secretary came over and handed her a note.

"Oh! Oh, my goodness!" she cried. She jumped up out of her seat faster than I thought a grown-up should. "Oh, my goodness gracious, it's now! My daughter's having her baby! My first grandchild!"

"Go," said Mrs. Rice. "It's all right. We can handle the show. Just go be with your daughter."

"Oh, thank you!" Margaret's teacher said. And then she left so fast she really did lose one of her bobby pins. It didn't look like lightning, though. It just looked like a bobby pin falling to the floor.

"Wow," I said to Mrs. Rice. "So now you have to run the whole show by yourself."

"No, not by myself," Mrs. Rice said. "I have an assistant. And that's you."

"Me? Oh, no. I can't!"

"You can. And I'm certainly not doing this alone."

"I really can't. I don't pay **attention**, remember?"

"You do pay attention, Clementine. Not always to the lesson in the classroom. But you notice more about what's going on than anyone I know. And that's exactly what I need tonight."

"I don't think this is a very good idea at all."

"Well, I do think it's a good idea. I'll prove it to you." Principal Rice called over one of the Hula-Hoopers. "Hillary, what's the second act after intermission?"

Hillary looked around. "I don't have a program," she said. "Do you want me to get you one?"

Mrs. Rice told her No thanks, then she turned to me. "Clementine, what's the second act after intermission?"

"Caleb from the fourth grade is going to burp 'The Star-Spangled Banner'," I told her.

"Does he need any props?"

"A two-liter bottle of root beer."

"How long will it take?"

"Forty-one seconds. Forty-eight if he has to stop to drink extra soda at the 'rockets' red glare' part."

"I rest my case," Principal Rice said. She pointed a "no buts" finger at the empty director's chair.

When a principal orders you to do something, it is impossible to refuse. Some part of you always gives in. So I climbed into the chair.

"Open the curtains!" Principal Rice said. And the worried scribbling feeling exploded all through my body.

STOP AND CHECK

Ask and Answer Questions How does Clementine feel about being the principal's assistant? Reread page 288 to find the answer.

289

Well, you would think those kids had never had a rehearsal.

First thing: all Dozen Doozies cartwheeled off the edge of the stage. Well, except for one girl, who forgot to move at all. Maria and Morris-Boris-Norris, from my class, went on next, and they cartwheeled right off the stage, too.

Nobody had to go to the emergency room, though, and the audience thought the whole thing was supposed to happen that way, so it was okay.

The next act was the O'Malley twins. Lilly had convinced Willy not to do the thing with his lunch, and to play a duet on the piano with her instead. But when Lilly got up to the mike to announce the act, she got so nervous she threw up.

I looked at Willy, sitting on the piano bench. Willy does everything Lilly does. And sure enough, he was getting ready.

"Not on the piano!" I yelled. Just in time.

Then I ran over and closed the curtains quick, so the whole audience wouldn't get started, too.

When the janitor came running out to clean everything up, I had a good idea.

"Send Sidney out now, in front of the curtains," I told Mrs. Rice.

"Why?" she asked. "There's no microphone out there."

"That's okay. Sidney's really loud. And she's going to recite a poem so there's no cartwheeling, just standing still. Besides, she's got really skinny feet, so she can fit out there if she stands sideways."

So Sidney went onstage and stood sideways and yelled her poem. By the time she was done, the stage was all mopped clean.

Next came the Hula-Hoopers, and they completely forgot what I'd told them about stopping. The music ended, but they just kept on going. Finally, I had to close the curtains to pull them off the stage so the jump-ropers could go on.

The jump-ropers must have figured that if the Hula-Hoopers didn't have to stop at the end of the music, neither did they. So I had to close the curtains on them, too.

Then came Margaret.

She did fine at the walking-on-stage-on-time thing, which not everybody did. But just as she got to the microphone, Alan took a picture of her from the audience. Which was a bad mistake.

Whenever anyone takes a picture of Margaret that she isn't expecting, she freezes. She says it's the horror of not knowing if she looks perfect or not. Which I don't understand, because Margaret always looks perfect.

No matter, there she was, frozen on the stage with her mouth hanging open. For one tiny second, a little part of me thought, *Good! No showing off for you tonight!*

But then my empathetic part took over.

I ran over to where Margaret could see me and waved until I got her eyes to unfreeze. I pointed to my hair and pretended to brush it.

Margaret nodded like a robot. She turned to
the audience. "First, always brush your hair.
Even if it's cut off like mine."

She looked back at me. I pretended to do up
some buttons, then I pointed to my right.

"Always make sure you're buttoned up right,"
Margaret told the audience.

Then I lifted my foot and crossed my fingers over my sneaker.

"Never wear green sneakers!" Margaret said. "Green sneakers are the worst!" Then she shook herself, as if she'd been asleep. She went up closer to the mike.

"Wait a minute," she said. "I was just kidding about that one. You can wear any color sneakers you want. And green is the most fashionable of all."

She zoomed me a smile so huge all her teeth-bracelets sparkled like diamonds in the spotlight. I zoomed her one back—except with no teeth-bracelets because I don't have them yet. After that, Margaret was okay.

I went back and climbed up onto the director's chair, and Principal Rice gave me a huge smile, too. She leaned over and said, "I have the answer for you now, Clementine. About why you can't have a substitute. It's because there is no substitute for you. You are one of a kind!"

And that's when I **realized** I didn't have the worried feeling anymore. Instead, I had the proud feeling: like the sun was rising inside my chest.

The proud, sun-rising feeling stayed with me all through the rest of the show. And no matter what went wrong, which was plenty, Mrs. Rice and I just fixed it.

STOP AND CHECK

Visualize Use the descriptions to visualize Clementine's actions at the end of the story. How does she feel?

About the Author and Illustrator

Sara Pennypacker was shy as a girl. She loved books, art, and baseball. In fact, her dream was to play major league baseball. Sara has not yet lived her baseball dream. But she has been able to combine her other two loves. She works with books and art! First she was a watercolor painter with her own studio. After that, she started writing children's books.

Marla Frazee has written and illustrated five books. She has also illustrated many other books, including the Clementine series. Marla studied art at a college in California. Now, in addition to writing and illustrating, she shares her talents by teaching other people how to create illustrations for children's books.

Author's Purpose

Why do you think the author chose Clementine as the story's narrator?

Respond to the Text

Summarize

What are the most important events in this story? The details from your Point of View chart may help you summarize.

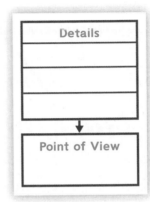

Details

↓

Point of View

Write

How does the author use what the characters do and say to help you understand how Clementine has changed? Use these sentence frames to focus your discussion.

> The author describes Clementine . . .
> She uses dialogue to tell me that her teachers . . .
> I can see how Clementine has changed because the author . . .

Make Connections

How does Clementine use what she knows to help others? **ESSENTIAL QUESTION**

Why do people perform in talent shows? **TEXT TO WORLD**

From

Clementine
and the Family Meeting

by Sara Pennypacker
pictures by Marla Frazee

It's almost time for the family meeting at Clementine's house, and Clementine is really nervous. What did she and her little brother do this time? Did she eat too much junk food? Maybe she misplaced one of Dad's tools? Both Mom and Dad have assured her that this meeting is only about good news. But Clementine is not so sure . . .

My dad called the meeting to order.

"We are a very lucky family," he said. "Very lucky."

"What's on the agenda?" I asked.

"I'm getting to that," my dad said. "Now, families change. They grow. It's hard to believe, but you're eight and a half now, and your brother's almost four."

I clapped my hands over my brother's ears. "Should we have a surprise party for him? You know what would make a great present? A gorilla!"

"His birthday's not for a few months," my mom said. "I vote we table that discussion for another time."

"Well, so what's the good thing we have to talk about tonight?" I asked.

My dad looked at my mom and raised his eyebrows. My mom looked back at him and smiled. She waved her palm to him like a game show host, as if to say "Show us these great prizes, Bill!"

My dad looked at my mom again, and this time he looked like he was going to cry! Not in a sad way, but in an "I can't believe how lucky I am that you're here" way. Which was nuts because my mom is *always* here.

"Families grow," he said again. "And tonight . . ." He stopped and smiled at my mom again. "Tonight, your mother and I want to talk to you about . . . an addition to our family. Our family is about to grow again."

And then finally, I figured out what he was saying! I slid Pea Pod off my lap and jumped up to give my dad and mom a hug.

"Yes! Thank you! Yes! You won't be sorry, I promise I'll take good care of it, you'll barely even notice it's here . . . Thank you!"

Cauliflower was sitting on the floor, looking between me and our parents, completely clueless, I leaned over and squeezed him hard. "We're getting a gorilla, after all!"

My mom fell back against her chair, laughing. "Oh, Clementine," she said. "It's definitely not a gorilla!"

I was a little tiny bit relieved. The truth is, since I got my kitten, I'm not sure I really want a gorilla anymore. That would be a really big litter box.

I studied my parents. "What is it then? A pony? We're getting a *pony?*"

My dad pulled me over to him and held my hands. "We're talking about a new baby. A brother or a sister for you two. What do you think about that?"

What I thought about that was N-O, *no thanks!*

I yelled it.

"No thanks!" Parsnip echoed. Then he looked up at me. "No thanks what?"

"No thanks to more people! Our family is four. There are four sides to a puzzle so we can all work on it at once. Hot dogs come in packages of eight, so we can each have two. At the playground, four is an even number for the seesaws. Four can all be together in the car. Four can be two and two sometimes, and nobody is lonely. Two kids and two grown-ups. Two boys and two girls. There are four sides to the kitchen table, so we each get one. Four is a perfect number for a family!"

While I'd been explaining all this, my brother had snuck over to his favorite cupboard and thrown all the pots and pans out, like a personal-size tornado. He was sitting inside now, crashing lids together.

I pointed to the mess in the kitchen. "Look at us! Lima Bean puts toy trucks in the ziti and we used a drill gun to stir the muffins this morning because we couldn't find the mixer and my rat is missing, which isn't my fault, and so is my hat, and maybe that *is* my fault, but how is a baby going to help with anything, that's what I want to know! It's all moving too fast and we're not ready."

"Oh, honey," my mom said. "Life is *always* moving too fast and we're *never* ready. That's how life *is.* But somehow that's just perfect." She dragged Zucchini out of the cupboard and hauled him off to get his pajamas on.

"Your mother," my dad said, "is exactly right. Things are always changing—that's life. And this?" He spread his hands to the tornadoed kitchen. "Us? Toy-truck ziti, missing hats, drill-gun mixers? Well, this is how we roll, Clementine. This is how we roll."

Make Connections

How do Clementine's parents help her understand the changes in her family? **ESSENTIAL QUESTION**

How are the plot and setting and theme in the two stories about Clementine alike? How are they different? **TEXT TO TEXT**

Amazing Wildlife of the

Mojave

By Laurence Pringle

? Essential Question

How do animals adapt to challenges in their habitat?

Read about how different animals in the Mojave Desert survive in a dry, hot place.

Go Digital!

Deserts are challenging places to live. They are dry and often very hot. Each year only a few inches of rain fall in the Mojave (Mo-HA-vee). It is North America's smallest desert. It lies mostly in parts of southern California and southern Nevada. The Mojave has both mountains and valleys. It includes Death Valley, the lowest and hottest place in North America.

On a car ride through the Mojave desert, you may pass by many miles of bare, dusty earth and scattered bushes. However, on a morning hike you can discover that a desert is a lively place. Birds sing. Lizards scurry after insects. Jackrabbits and roadrunners dash among the bushes and cactus plants.

A Living Place

Although it is very dry, the Mojave is a living place or environment for many fascinating animals and plants. Over many years they have changed, or adapted, so they live very well in a dry, hot environment. They do this in different ways. In the Mojave you might see several kinds of lizards. They are all **related**. All lizards are reptiles. Reptiles all have scaly skin. However, they are different in many ways. The desert spiny lizard, for example, is only a few inches long. Most of its food is insects.

This hawk looks out for food from the top of a yucca palm.

The name Mojave means "alongside water." It comes from the Mojave people. They were Native Americans who once lived along the Lower Colorado River. The river flows through part of the Mojave desert.

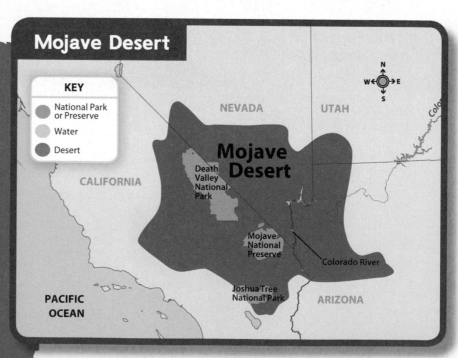

Mojave Desert

KEY

National Park or Preserve

Water

Desert

NEVADA   UTAH

CALIFORNIA

Mojave Desert

Death Valley National Park

Mojave National Preserve

Colorado River

Joshua Tree National Park

PACIFIC OCEAN

ARIZONA

The chuckwalla is very different. It can grow to almost three feet long. This big lizard eats leaves, flowers, and fruit of plants. It also has a special way of protecting itself. If a chuckwalla senses danger, it quickly hides in a crack between rocks. Then it gulps in air, making its body fatter. It becomes tightly wedged in so that a predator cannot pull it out.

This chuckwalla will quickly squeeze itself between rocks if a predator comes near.

Marka/SuperStock

Getting Water in the Desert

Animals get water in different ways in the Mojave. Coyotes, bobcats, and other large mammals can travel a long distance for a drink. So can some birds. Small lizards, snakes, and mice are different. They cannot travel far. They might **prefer** to drink from a stream or even a puddle, but these are rare treats in a desert. They find water in different ways. They get some from tiny drops of dew that form overnight on plants or stones. Their main source of water is the food they eat. Flowers, seeds, and leaves contain water. The bodies of insects, scorpions, and other animals are all at least half water. Some desert animals get most or all of the water they need simply by eating food.

STOP AND CHECK

Reread What are some different ways that animals in the Mojave get water? Reread to find the answer.

This coyote can travel far to find water.

NPS Photo by Robb Hannawacker

Light-colored fur helps this kangaroo rat hide from predators.

Light Colors Help

People who live in or visit deserts often wear light-colored clothes. This is smart because dark colors take in, or absorb, Sun energy, while light colors reflect it. You can avoid overheating by wearing light colors. Desert animals do the same by being light-colored.

Being light-colored can help animals in another way. In the Mojave, the land is often colored tan, gray, and light brown. Pale mice, insects, or lizards are hard to see against this background. This gives the animals some **protection** from predators that try to catch and eat them.

Not all desert animals are light-colored. In some parts of the Mojave, mice and lizards are much darker. They are different because they live among rocks and soil that are black or dark brown. In those places, darker colors help them hide and survive.

Escaping the Heat

Desert animals are all alike in one way. They find ways to avoid midday heat. Different animals do this in different ways. Most of them rest during the hottest time of day. They are active in cooler times, such as mornings, evenings, or at night.

Different animals avoid heat in different ways. Scorpions usually hide in shady places. However, if a scorpion must be out in daytime, it can stand tall on its legs. This is called "stilting." It keeps the scorpion's body from touching the hot surface. A snake, of course, cannot "stilt" because it has no legs! On a hot day some snakes and lizards crawl up into bushes. There, the air is cooler than on the hot soil surface.

STOP AND CHECK

Reread How do scorpions avoid the heat? Reread to find the answer.

A scorpion uses its legs to raise its body above the hot ground.

Nico Smit/iStock/360/Getty Images

A jackrabbit's long ears help it stay cool.

Most desert animals also escape the heat by seeking shelter under bushes, rocks, and other shady places. Black-tailed jackrabbits sprawl in the shade. They lose body heat by panting or breathing rapidly. Heat is also given off from many tiny blood vessels in their large ears.

Cool and Safe Underground

Many desert animals seek the coolness of underground burrows. The afternoon soil temperature may be as hot as 140 degrees F! Just a foot or two underground, the temperature might be 85 degrees. Burrows protect animals from heat and also from cold. Desert nights are often chilly. Winter snow sometimes falls in the Mojave.

Desert tortoises spend most of their lives in burrows they dig. They come out in the spring to eat plant leaves, flowers, and fruit. Because their burrows are big and often several feet long, there is room for other animals too. A tortoise burrow is an **excellent** hiding and resting place for kangaroo rats, rabbits, snakes, lizards, owls, and other small desert creatures. Some join a sleeping tortoise. Others use an abandoned burrow.

These owl chicks make a comfortable home in this abandoned burrow.

The hard shell of a desert tortoise protects it from predators.

Some desert animals also use their hideouts in a different way. In the evening, scorpions wait just inside their shelters for their next meal. A lizard, beetle, or even another scorpion might pass by. These moving animals make ground vibrations that scorpions can feel. The vibrations **alert** scorpions that an animal is nearby. Some scorpions can sense vibrations in the air caused by a flying insect. They can reach out and grab a low-flying moth!

NPS Photo by Stacy Manson

The desert iguana's skin turns pale in the afternoon to help it stay cool.

Morning Warmth

Desert animals have many different ways to avoid overheating. Sometimes, however, they need to get warm! At night, the desert air is quite cool. By dawn, some animals need to warm up. Lizards and snakes crawl to a sunny place. They turn their bodies toward the Sun to raise their body temperature.

Desert iguanas have an amazing ability for warming and also for cooling. They change color! In the morning, their skin is dark. This helps them absorb heat from the Sun. Then the day gets hotter and hotter. By early afternoon the iguanas' skin has turned white, reflecting sunlight. Then, as the air becomes cooler in the evening, their skin darkens again.

The desert iguana's skin is dark in the morning. This helps the animal warm up.

STOP AND CHECK

Ask and Answer Questions Why do desert iguanas change color? Reread the page to find the answer.

Like iguanas, some birds need to warm their bodies after a chilly night. Roadrunners turn their backs toward the Sun and raise their body feathers. Their skin is black. It absorbs Sun energy. When warm enough, roadrunners join in the **competition** for food. They dash to hunt for lizards and small snakes.

This roadrunner cools off in the shade of a tree.

Roadrunners live very well in deserts. Like all the other Mojave animals, they are wonderfully adapted to thrive in a dry, hot environment. So are scorpions, jackrabbits, chuckwallas, and tortoises. They all make the Mojave a lively, fascinating place.

After warming up, this roadrunner is ready to run fast to catch its prey.

About the Author

Growing up, **Laurence Pringle** loved to explore the outdoors—tramping through the woods, splashing through ponds and streams, and fishing in the ocean. His other strong interest was reading, so writing about nature made perfect sense. Among his other books are *Snakes! Strange and Wonderful, Come to the Ocean's Edge,* and *A Dragon in the Sky: The Story of a Green Darner Dragonfly.* When he's not writing, he still enjoys hiking and fishing.

Author's Purpose

Why do you think the author calls the animals of the Mojave "amazing"?

Respond to the Text

Summarize

How have different animals in the Mojave adapted to the challenges in their habitat? Information from your Venn Diagram may help you summarize.

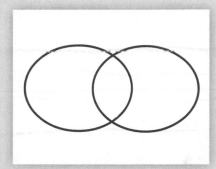

Write

How do you know how the author feels about the wildlife in the Mojave desert? Use these sentence frames to organize your text evidence.

> The author says that living in the desert is . . .
> He tells about how the animals . . .
> This helps me know that he feels . . .

Make Connections

Describe how one of the animals in the selection has adapted to its environment. **ESSENTIAL QUESTION**

How do animals in cities or towns adapt to their habitat? **TEXT TO WORLD**

Compare Texts

Read about Little Half Chick. Find out what he learns about helping.

Little Half Chick

Once in Mexico, an unusual chick hatched. He had only one eye, one wing, and one leg. He was named Little Half Chick. He quickly learned to hop faster on one leg than most chickens could walk on two. He was a curious and adventurous chick and soon grew tired of his barnyard **environment**. One day he decided to hop to Mexico City to meet the mayor.

Along the way, he hopped by a stream blocked with weeds. "Could you clear these weeds away so my water can run freely?" the stream gurgled. Little Half Chick helped the stream. Then he hopped on.

It started to rain. A small fire on the side of the road crackled, "Please give me **shelter** from this rain, or I will go out!" Little Half Chick stretched out his wing to protect the fire until the rain stopped.

Further down the road Little Half Chick met a wind that was tangled in a prickly bush. "Please untangle me," it whispered. Little Half Chick untangled the wind. Then he hopped on to Mexico City.

Little Half Chick did not meet the mayor. He met the mayor's cook. She grabbed him, plunged him into a pot of water, and lit a fire. However, the fire and the water remembered Little Half Chick's kindness. The fire refused to burn, and the water refused to boil. Then, the grateful wind picked him up and carried him safely to the top of the highest tower in Mexico City.

Little Half Chick became a weather vane. His flat body told everyone below the direction the wind blew. And he learned this lesson: Always help someone in need because you don't know when you'll need help.

Make Connections

Explain how Little Half Chick adapted to his new habitat. **ESSENTIAL QUESTION**

Compare Little Half Chick to other animals you have read about. **TEXT TO TEXT**

The Winningest Woman
of the
Iditarod Dog Sled Race

Susan Butcher (1956–2006) Four-Time Winner

? Essential Question

How can others inspire us?

Read about people who are courageous.

Go Digital!

320

I rode the whole Iditarod
From Anchorage to Nome!
The husky sleigh, eleven day
Iditarod to Nome.

Two moose can cause a traffic jam.
(There is no word in Moose for *"Scram!"*)
And over trails of ice and snow,
No musher knows which way to go.
The weather? Forty-two below
Could freeze the whiskers in a beard!
The huskies up front disappeared
And though it sounds a little weird—
Okay, you're right, extremely odd—
I did I *did* Iditarod—
A bitter cold Iditarod—
My sled slid the Iditarod
From Anchorage to Nome.

—*J. Patrick Lewis*

The Brave Ones

We hear the bell clanging
we come in a hurry
we come with our ladders and hoses
our hoses
we come in a hurry
to fight the fire
the furious fire
to smother the smoke
the smoke
we don't have much time
we climb, we spray
we are the brave ones who save
who save
we are the brave ones who save

—*Eloise Greenfield*

Respond to the Text

Summarize

Use key details from "The Winningest Woman of the Iditarod Dog Sled Race" to summarize the poem. Use your Theme chart to help you.

Detail

↓

Detail

↓

Detail

↓

Theme

Write

How do the poets use repetition to help you understand the message in their poems? Use these sentence frames to organize your text evidence.

> In "The Winningest Woman of the Iditarod Dog Sled Race" the poet repeats words to . . .
>
> The poet of "The Brave Ones" uses repetition to . . .
>
> These words help me understand the theme of each poem by . . .

Make Connections

What words did the poets use to show that Susan Butcher and the firefighters are inspiring? **ESSENTIAL QUESTION**

Why do people like to read poems about courage and bravery? **TEXT TO WORLD**

Compare Texts

Read how nature inspires a young girl to dream of great things.

Narcissa

Some of the girls are playing jacks.
Some are playing ball.
But small Narcissa is not playing
Anything at all.

Small Narcissa sits upon
A brick in her back yard
And looks at tiger-lilies,
And shakes her pigtails hard.

First she is an ancient queen
In pomp and purple veil.
Soon she is a singing wind.
And, next, a nightingale.

How fine to be Narcissa,
A-changing like all that!
While sitting still, as still, as still
As anyone ever sat!

–Gwendolyn Brooks

Make Connections

Why do you think Narcissa inspires the poet? **ESSENTIAL QUESTION**

Compare Narcissa to Susan Butcher in "The Winningest Woman of the Iditarod Dog Sled Race." How are they alike? How are they different? **TEXT TO TEXT**

The REAL STORY OF STONE SOUP

by Ying Chang Compestine
illustrated by Stéphane Jorisch

Essential Question

What choices are good for us?

Read how three brothers choose healthful foods to make a surprising soup.

 Go Digital!

By now, you have probably heard the old folktale about stone soup. A hungry soldier tricks some stingy villagers into making him a big pot of soup. The truth is that stone soup was invented here in China, and without any sly tricks.

Here is the real story.

It all began when I hired those troublesome Chang brothers to help me on my fishing boat. Nice boys, but lazy and, I'm sorry to say, somewhat stupid. The only good thing is I could get away with not paying them very much.

Even with three of them, I did most of the work, and I kept the hardest job for myself. I steered the boat.

STOP AND CHECK

Ask and Answer Questions What kind of person is the narrator? Use the illustrations and what you have read to find the answer.

One summer day, after a full morning of fishing, I decided to stop early for lunch.

"Time to eat, boys!" I yelled. "Dock the boat."

After the Chang brothers got the boat tied up, my work really began. Those boys were too dull to know what to do. "Ting! Gather firewood. Pong! Prepare the cooking pot and clean the fish. Kuai! Get some fresh water."

"The cooking pot isn't here," **interrupted** Ting, the oldest, a troublemaker. He always talked back to his elders.

"What do you mean the pot isn't here? Where is it?"

They looked at one another and shrugged.

"You boys forgot the cooking pot? How could you?" I asked.

"It's your pot," said Ting. "You should have remembered to bring it."

Those stupid potato heads! What were we to do now? Pong, the middle one and the most well-mannered of the three, tried to apologize. "Sorry, Uncle. We left in a hurry this morning, and we—"

Kuai, the youngest, interrupted. "We don't really need a pot to cook lunch." He whispered something to his brothers. Kuai is always full of silly ideas.

"How are we supposed to cook lunch?" I asked. "With a hole in the ground?"

Those crazy boys must have thought I meant it. No sooner had those words left my mouth than they started digging a hole in the sandy beach.

"What are you doing?" I asked.

"Cooking lunch, of course," said Kuai. He began to line the hole with banana leaves. Meanwhile, Ting and Pong started a huge fire next to the hole.

"Now we need some stones," said Kuai.

"For what?" I asked

Kuai didn't answer. He picked up a nearby rock and held it to his ear. "This is a fish stone," he announced. Then he threw the rock in the fire.

"Come now," I said. "Even you can't be foolish enough to believe—"

"Shh!" Ting interrupted, holding a stone to his ear. "I need to hear what it is telling me. Aha! This is a fine vegetable stone." He tossed his rock into the fire, too.

I tried listening to a couple of stones. I didn't hear a thing. The hunger must have gone to their heads. "If you're so clever, what kind is this?" I handed a stone to Pong. He listened for a moment.

"Aha! Uncle, you are brilliant. You picked out a yummy egg stone." He pitched my stone into the fire.

I had no idea what he was blabbering about. But by this time I was hungry enough to eat anything, even stones.

"We need something to carry water from the river and to eat the soup with," said Kuai.

"Oh, Uncle," said Pong. "Could you use your mighty ax to make some bowls from bamboo stalks?"

"*Ai yo!*" I grumbled. "I have to do all the work, as always!" But it was true that none of them could be trusted with my sharp ax.

With a few quick chops, I made four bowls from a thick stalk. The boys used them to fill the hole with water.

I shook my head at them. "Now we have a puddle and a fire. How do you **expect** to get the water over the fire?" I asked.

"Leave that to us," said Ting.

"Uncle, you made the best bowls in the village with nothing more than an ax," said Pong. "Could you use your **graceful** knife to make some chopsticks to go with them?"

"*Ai yo!*" I cried. "You lazy boys want me to do all the work." Nevertheless, I carved out some chopsticks. Unlike the Chang brothers, I wasn't stupid enough to eat hot stones with my fingers.

When I finished, I gave each boy a pair of my skillfully carved chopsticks. "How long does it take the stones to cook?" I worried that the stones might burn like potatoes. Then I couldn't believe what those crazy boys did next. With long sticks, Ting picked a stone out of the hot fire, and instead of offering it to his elder first, he held it before Kuai and Pong!

They didn't eat it, though. They whispered to it, "*Yú, yú, yú*" ("Fish, fish, fish"), and blew on it.

Then Ting dropped the stone into the hole. *Sploosh!*

"*Ai yo!*" I yelled.

Bubbles of steam shot off the stone as it sank to the bottom. The steam carried a wonderful fish smell. I saw pieces of fish floating in the soup. Those boys had told the truth—it really was a fish stone! My stomach purred like a kitten.

STOP AND CHECK

Ask and Answer Questions
Look at the illustration on page 334. Why are there pieces of fish floating in the soup?

335

Kuai gently stirred the soup. "Hmm, this is turning into a tasty soup. If only we had a little salt, it would be a soup fit for a schoolmaster."

"Ting!" I said. "Get the salt off the boat."

"It's your salt. You get it," Ting said rudely. I was too hungry to teach him good manners. So I went to get the salt.

As I returned with the salt, Ting picked up the second stone and held it before his brothers. *"Cài, cài, cài."* They whispered the word for vegetables three times and blew on the stone. Ting dropped it into the soup.

Shoosh! More steam leapt into the air. Surprisingly, I smelled vegetables! The **aroma** was so yummy, my stomach growled like an angry tiger.

Kuai stirred the soup again and sprinkled in a little salt. "This is a wonderful vegetable stone. If only we had a little sesame oil, this would be a soup fit for an emperor," said Kuai.

"Just a moment!" I cried. "I'll be right back with the sesame oil."

When I returned with the sesame oil, Ting was holding up the last stone. All three boys yelled, *"Dàn, dàn, dàn!"* ("Egg, egg, egg!") Then they each blew hard on the stone, one at a time.

"Why are you shouting at that stone, you potato heads?" I asked.

"Egg stones don't hear very well," said Ting. He dropped the stone into the soup.

Shoom! The hot stone brought the soup to a wild boil. I couldn't believe it when I saw threads of egg float to the top. A **luscious** fragrance filled the air. Even the monkeys came closer to get a whiff.

Kuai drizzled in the sesame oil. More delectable smells! By now I was sure the sounds from my hungry stomach could be heard back in the village.

Finally, Ting did something right. He filled
one of the bamboo bowls with soup and served
me, his elder, first.

I could hardly wait to taste it. I lifted the steaming bowl to my lips and took a sip. "Mmmmm . . . *Hăo chí! Hăo chí!*" ("Tastes good! Tastes good!") I must tell you that I have never tasted such a wonderful soup! The fish from the fish stone was tender and fresh. The wild mushrooms and onions from the vegetable stone were **flavorful**. The threads of egg from the egg stone were cooked just right.

Thanks to the bowls and chopsticks I had made, now the boys could enjoy the soup, too. The rest of the afternoon, they were happy and even worked a little harder. Not harder than me, of course.

From that day on, I always carried rocks in my pockets and told everyone the secret of making stone soup. I even demonstrated how to whisper to fish and vegetable stones, and how to yell at egg stones. But the truth is, I still haven't had time to make it. You know, I work too hard already.

And that, my friends, is how I invented the *real* stone soup. I don't know how people ended up with that silly old folktale.

STOP AND CHECK

Summarize How did the brothers make stone soup? Tell the events from the story in order.

About the
Author and Illustrator

Ying Chang Compestine says that writing keeps her close to China, where she grew up. Ying writes cookbooks as well as children's books. She travels around the world talking about her life and her writing. Ying says that traveling to new places lets her find the best food and the best stories.

Stéphane Jorisch lived near a big river in Canada as a teenager. He loved floating in boats of all kinds. Stéphane's father illustrated comic strips. That inspired Stéphane to become an artist. Stéphane also illustrated *Emily's Piano* and *Anancy and the Haunted House*. He now lives in Montreal, Canada.

Author's Purpose
Why are the illustrations an important part of this story?

Respond to the Text

Summarize

Summarize the main events in the story. Use the details from your Point of View chart to help you.

Details

↓

Point of View

Write

How does the author use dialogue to help you understand how the Chang brothers solved their problem? Use these sentence frames to focus your discussion.

> The author uses what the narrator says to . . .
> What the Chang brothers say is important because . . .
> The author helps me see how they . . .

Make Connections

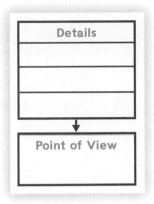

Which healthful foods do the Chang boys choose to put in the soup?
ESSENTIAL QUESTION

What are some healthful choices that people make every day?
TEXT TO WORLD

Compare Texts

Read about how people can choose healthful food to get energy.

Healthful Food Choices

Food Is Energy

What's for dinner? There are so many choices. Every time you go to the market you find a **variety** of foods to eat. Which ones do you choose? Why does it matter what you eat?

It matters because you move around and think all day long. You go to school. You play with friends. You do chores and homework. All that activity takes energy. You get energy from the food you eat. You need to eat energy-producing food because, unlike a plant, your body can't make its own food.

Energy from the Sun

Think about the tomato you ate for lunch. It began as a tiny seed. A seed contains just enough food to begin growing. The plant uses energy from the Sun. It changes water and air into food. It uses the food to produce tomatoes. A farmer picks the tomato and sends it to a supermarket.

Plants can make their own food from sunlight.

346

The next time you go to the market, what will you buy? You might choose a juicy red tomato for two reasons. It's **healthful** and delicious, and it's good for you, too. It gives you energy!

You can get many healthful vegetables at a grocery store.

Recipe for Easy Salsa

Use a tomato to make a healthful snack. Try this recipe! Ask an adult to help.

What You Need
1 large tomato
¼ red onion
½ cup cilantro
½ lime
salt
hot sauce

1. Chop tomato, onion, and cilantro.
2. Place the chopped vegetables in a small bowl.
3. Squeeze the lime juice into the bowl.
4. Add a little bit of salt and hot sauce.
5. Mix everything together with a spoon.

Enjoy your salsa with baked corn chips!

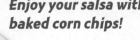

Make Connections

Why is it important to choose healthful foods? ESSENTIAL QUESTION

Compare the food choices in this article to food choices in other stories you have read. TEXT TO TEXT

Genre • Expository Text

Essential Question
How are people able to fly?
Read to find out what it's like
to fly in a hot air balloon.

Go Digital!

Hot Air Balloons

By Dana Meachen Rau

Ready for Take Off

It is early morning. People unload a huge colorful bag in an open field. They turn on a strong fan. They aim it into the opening of the bag. The bag starts to grow. It's a balloon! But it isn't the kind of balloon you get at a birthday party. This balloon is taller than sixteen men!

Suddenly, fire roars into the balloon. It starts to rise. People climb into the basket under the balloon while others hold it steady. Then the balloon takes off, carrying its **passengers** into the sky. They float higher than the houses, higher than the trees, up to where the birds fly.

Can you imagine what it would be like to float so high? Cars would look like tiny dots. You'd be able to see for miles. The wind would be your guide. What would it feel like to ride with the wind?

Hot air is lighter than cool air. A burner heats the air in a balloon so it will rise from the ground.

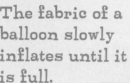

The fabric of a balloon slowly inflates until it is full.

Balloon riders get a bird's-eye view.

Jean-Pierre Blanchard crossed the English Channel from England to France in a balloon.

Ballooning History

Throughout history, people have wondered what it would be like to fly. The Chinese watched their kites move with the wind. The Greeks told stories of men who made wings to help them fly. People drew pictures of flying machines. But flying seemed **impossible**.

In the late 1700s in France, the Montgolfier [mont-GOL-fee-ay] brothers noticed something about paper and fire. If paper got too close to the flames, it burned. But they saw that if the paper was above the fire, the hot smoke seemed to make it float and rise. So in 1783 they made a balloon out of paper and silk. They lit a fire under it. People were amazed when the Montgolfier brothers sent a sheep, a duck, and a rooster as passengers in this first hot air balloon. The animals had a successful flight. Soon after, two men rode in a Montgolfier balloon. They traveled more than 5 miles for 25 minutes.

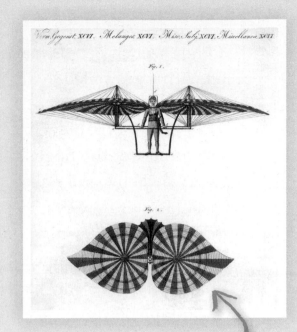

Early inventors drew pictures of unbelievable flying machines.

Greek stories tell of Daedalus and his son Icarus, who made their own flying wings.

Other French people made balloons filled with a **gas** called hydrogen. Hydrogen can rise like hot air does. In 1785 Jean-Pierre Blanchard flew a gas balloon over the English Channel, a waterway between England and France. He also flew the first balloon in America. George Washington watched Blanchard's balloon **launch** in 1793 from Pennsylvania on its way to New Jersey.

Ballooning became very **popular**. Pilots tried flying balloons higher and farther than ever before. People found uses for balloons during war. Balloons could carry messages. They could spy from the sky.

Soldiers used balloons to scout out the battlefield.

The stiff framework of an airship helped the balloon keep its shape.

The Wright brothers' first airplane gave people another way to travel the sky.

By the early 1900s, **airships** flew in the sky. An airship had a gas-filled balloon with a frame to give it a sausage shape. The basket in which people rode, called the gondola, was enclosed and often very large. It also had an **engine** and **propellers**. Pilots could steer these new types of balloons in the direction they wished to go. Some airships were used in war. Others were used for travel and the gondolas looked like fancy hotels inside.

In the early 1900s, the Wright brothers also flew the first airplane. After that, people rode airplanes for travel instead.

But people didn't forget about balloons. They built gas balloons that could study the weather and even travel around the world. In 1960, modern hot air balloons were developed by Ed Yost, and were later used for sport. Today, people join hot air balloon clubs. Teams hold balloon races. Passengers take rides in the sky to see the beautiful land below.

STOP AND CHECK

Reread Why were airships better than hot air balloons? Reread page 355 to find the answer.

The burner heats the air inside the envelope to inflate the balloon.

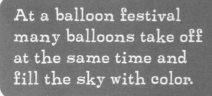

At a balloon festival many balloons take off at the same time and fill the sky with color.

The parachute valve in the top of a balloon lets out hot air.

How Hot Air Balloons Work

The science called **physics** helps us understand how hot air balloons rise in the sky. Physics is the science of how things move.

Air is all around you. You can't see it. But you can feel it when the wind blows. Air also has **weight.** Hot air is light. Cold air is heavy. That means that hot air rises up in the sky. Cold air sits closer to the ground.

A hot air balloon works because the hot air trapped inside the balloon is lighter than the cold air outside the balloon. So the balloon rises up into the sky!

STOP AND CHECK

Reread What causes a balloon to rise in the air? Reread page 357 to find the answer.

(t) Kevin Fleming/Corbis Documentary/Getty Images (b) Jason Todd/Photonica/Getty Images

Crowds wait for the big launch.

The big balloon is called an envelope. Most envelopes are larger on the top and narrower on the bottom. They come in all colors. The envelope is made out of strong, light cloth called nylon.

Just like a paper envelope holds a letter, the balloon envelope holds the hot air. Pilots heat the air in the balloon with a burner. The burner sends out a huge flame into the envelope. When the balloon is full of hot air, it starts lifting off the ground.

A basket hangs below the burner. This basket carries the pilot and the passengers. The basket is light, but strong enough to carry several people. Some baskets can carry up to twenty passengers at a time if the balloon is big enough to lift them.

When the pilot wants the balloon to go up, he fires up the burner. This can be very loud. The flame grows bigger. It heats the air in the envelope so the balloon will rise.

When the pilot wants the balloon to go down, he pulls a cord that lets out some of the hot air. The cord opens the parachute valve. The parachute valve is a cut-out circle of nylon in the top of the balloon. The balloon stops rising. As more hot air escapes, the balloon sinks toward the ground.

A basket hangs below the balloon to hold passengers.

Up to the Wind

You turn your handlebars to steer your bike. But a pilot can't steer a balloon. He can make it fly higher or lower, but he can't make it go from side to side. He needs some help from the wind.

Wind moves in different directions. Wind might be moving one way high in the sky. It might be moving another way lower in the sky. These paths of wind are called **currents.** A pilot uses these currents to move the balloon from place to place. He moves the balloon up and down with the burner and parachute valve. When he finds a current going in the **direction** he wants to go, he lets the balloon ride the wind right or left.

Balloon pilots use wind currents to push them in the direction they want to go.

Pilots can't control how fast or how slow the balloon moves. That's **controlled** by the wind. But too much wind can be dangerous. It can tear the balloon or send it in the wrong direction.

So pilots always check the weather. A day with clear skies and not too much wind is best for ballooning. They often launch right after the sun comes up when the wind is calm and the air is cool. They can also launch in the evening, but must land before the sun sets.

Balloons don't usually land in the same place they started. A pilot talks to his crew on the ground with a radio. They look for a safe place to set the balloon down. The crew meets the balloon when it lands. They will let the air out of the balloon and pack it up again.

Riding a hot air balloon is an adventure. Where will the wind take you?

STOP AND CHECK

Summarize How does the wind cause a hot air balloon to fly? Tell what you learned on pages 360 and 361.

Thitisan/Shutterstock.com

About the Author

As a child, **Dana Meachen Rau** drew pictures everywhere. She illustrated the family's mailbox and the walls of their garage! Then her father brought her big stacks of paper so she could write and draw on them. That was the beginning of Dana's love for writing. Today, she has written more than 200 books for children and young adults. Besides fiction stories, Dana has written nonfiction books on many topics such as nature, cooking, and science. She continues to write every day.

Author's Purpose

The author uses many photographs and captions in *Hot Air Balloons*. How do these text features help you understand what you read?

Respond to the Text

Summarize

Tell the important ideas and details that you learned about hot air balloons. The details from your Cause and Effect chart may help you summarize.

Cause	→	Effect
First	→	
Next	→	
Then	→	
Finally	→	

Write

How does the way the author organizes the text in this selection help you understand how people are able to fly? Use these sentence frames to focus your discussion.

> The author helps me understand how hot air balloons fly by . . .
> She also uses words and phrases to . . .
> The way the text is organized helps me . . .

Make Connections

Why do you think people like to ride in hot air balloons? **ESSENTIAL QUESTION**

In what ways are hot air balloons a good way to fly? In what ways are they not so good? **TEXT TO WORLD**

Genre · Myth

Compare Texts
Read about how a
hero finds a way to fly.

Bellerophon and Pegasus

A Greek Myth

Bellerophon (buh-LAIR-uh-fawn) lived long ago in Greece. He wanted to marry King Iobates's (ee-oh-BAH-tees-ez) daughter. But the king wanted to test Bellerophon first. He commanded him to defeat the Chimera (kigh-MIR-uh), a terrible monster. It had a lion's head, a goat's head, and a giant snake for a tail. It was attacking helpless people across the kingdom.

Bellerophon worried about his task. How could one man stop the Chimera? He asked the goddess Athena for help. In a dream, she showed him where to find the flying horse Pegasus.

Illustration: Anna Vojtech

364

Bellerophon woke up from the dream holding a golden bridle. It shone as brightly as the sun!

Bellerophon caught Pegasus with the golden bridle and leaped onto the creature's back. Pegasus snorted and stamped his hooves. He stretched his mighty wings with a strong **motion**. Then he carried his new master up, up, up, into the sky. They were in **flight**!

Bellerophon and Pegasus soared and circled above the countryside as they hunted the Chimera. At last they found the dreadful beast.

The monster's heads roared and hissed so loudly that the ground shook. Fire shot from the monster's mouths. Pegasus flew swiftly around the Chimera, swooping down and away. Again and again the monster lunged at the flying horse and his rider. Each time it missed them. Bellerophon swung his sword with all his might, three times. The monster fell.

Bellerophon and Pegasus flew back to King Iobates. To prove his victory, Bellerophon brought King Iobates a strand of lion's mane, a snake's scale, and a goat's horn from the Chimera.

At last King Iobates agreed to let Bellerophon marry his daughter. Everyone in the kingdom was invited to the wedding feast. And Pegasus got a golden bucket filled with the finest oats in the land.

Make Connections

Why was Bellerophon able to fly?
ESSENTIAL QUESTION

Compare flying in this myth with other stories you have read. **TEXT TO TEXT**

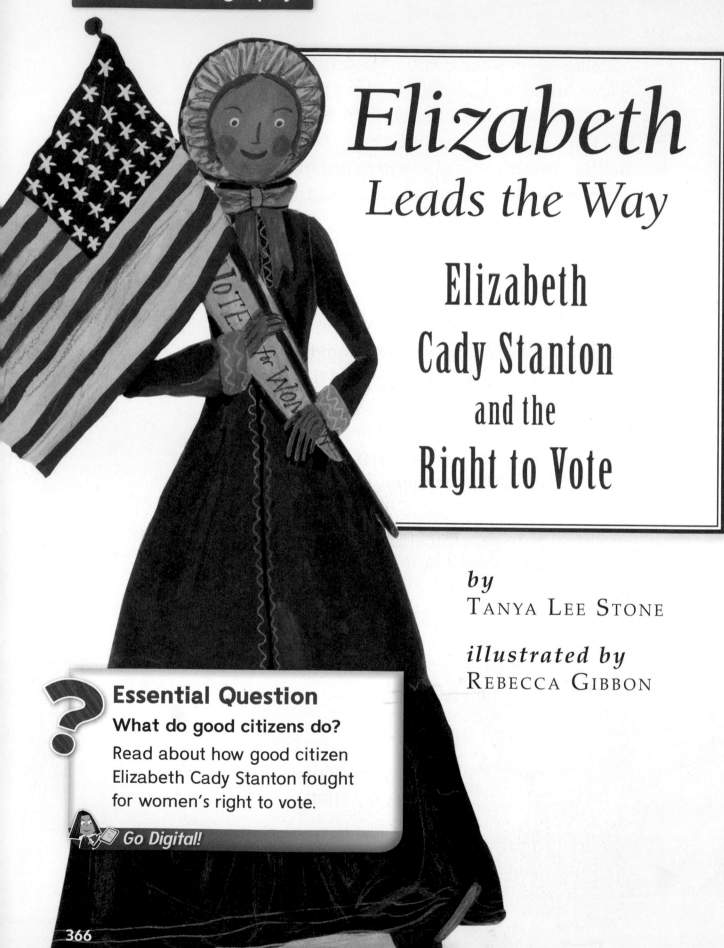

Elizabeth
Leads the Way

Elizabeth
Cady Stanton
and the
Right to Vote

by
TANYA LEE STONE

illustrated by
REBECCA GIBBON

? Essential Question

What do good citizens do?

Read about how good citizen Elizabeth Cady Stanton fought for women's right to vote.

Go Digital!

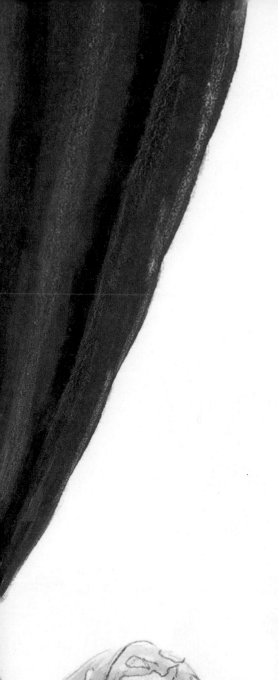

W hat would you do
if someone told you
you can't be what you want to be
because you are a girl?

What would you do
if someone told you
your vote doesn't count,
your voice doesn't matter
because you are a girl?

Would you ask why?
Would you talk back?
Would you fight . . .
for your rights?
Elizabeth did.

All of these things used to be true
back when Elizabeth Cady was a girl.

And all of these things might still be true
today if Elizabeth hadn't led the way.

She was only four years old the first time she heard someone, a *woman*, say life was better for boys.

The woman had come to visit Elizabeth's new baby sister. "What a pity it is she's a girl!"

How could anyone look at a little baby and feel sad? What could be wrong about being a girl?

She was thirteen years old
when her father, Judge Cady,
told a woman whose husband had died
that the farm she had spent her whole life working on
would be taken from her.
Without a husband, the law stated,
nothing belonged to her.

Elizabeth was **horrified** by this **unfairness**.
She said that the law should be cut out of every book!
Judge Cady told her that wouldn't
change anything.

Pre**pos**terous!

The law was still the law.
And only men were allowed to change laws.

STOP AND CHECK

Ask and Answer Questions
What law did Elizabeth feel
was unfair? Reread pages 369
and 370 to find out.

She decided
right then and there
that she could do anything
any boy could do.

She jumped over high hurdles on horseback.

She rafted across a raging river.

She won a prize for being the best in Greek studies.

Her father was proud.
But he worried about his strong-spirited,
rule-breaking daughter.

"Ah, you should have been a boy!"
He knew how much easier
her life would be.
But Elizabeth wasn't interested in easy.

At sixteen, since colleges would not let girls in,
Elizabeth begged her father to send her
to a girls' school to **continue** her learning.

So, while most young ladies were
getting married,
washing dishes,
doing laundry,
and having babies,

Elizabeth was studying religion, math,
science, French, and writing.

Several years later, Elizabeth Cady
met Henry Stanton.

He was an abolitionist,
speaking out against slavery.

He understood how unfair it was for people
not to have rights or power.

He did not laugh
when Elizabeth talked
about freedom.

He did not laugh
when Elizabeth said all people
should be able to live life
the way *they* chose.

And he did not laugh
when she told him
she would add his name to her own
but she would not give up hers
just to marry him.

So Elizabeth Cady
became Elizabeth Cady Stanton and
had babies, cooked meals, washed dishes,
mended clothes, and did laundry.

She loved her babies, but she did *not* love
cooking and dishes and mending and laundry.

One day her friend Lucretia Mott invited her to a lunch.

Lucretia had always shared Elizabeth's ideas
about all the things women could do, and would do,
if only they had the right.
The other women at lunch shared them, too.

Elizabeth got fired up. She **proposed** they hold a meeting.

A meeting that would gather together
lots and lots of women
from all around to talk.

But what would they talk about?

There were so *many* things
that needed to be set straight.

Married women
couldn't own property
or even the money
they worked to earn!

Elizabeth had learned long ago
that only men could change the laws.

Because only men could vote.

That was it!

That was the *one* thing
that could change *every*thing.

If women could vote,
they could help change
all kinds of laws!

This idea was so shocking,
so huge,
so **daring**—
Elizabeth's friends gasped out loud!

If they were flabbergasted,
what would other
people think?

Elizabeth did not **waver**.
She knew voting was the only way
to make a difference.

Her battle cry for the right to vote rang out:
"Have it, we must. Use it, we will."

Even her Henry thought she had gone too far.

STOP AND CHECK

Ask and Answer Questions How did people feel about Elizabeth's ideas? Reread pages 378 and 379 to find out.

But on July 19, 1848,
when Elizabeth arrived at the meeting place,
she saw for herself that she hadn't.

The small church in Seneca Falls, New York,
was filled with hundreds of people.

Elizabeth read aloud
what she and a few of the women
had written together.

Their Declaration of Rights and Sentiments
challenged the idea from the Declaration of
Independence
that "all *men* are created equal."

When she was finished,
she looked into the faces of the crowd and waited.

The room was silent!
Then a rumbling began.
It grew louder and louder and louder
as people argued whether or not
women should be allowed to vote.

STOP AND CHECK

Summarize How did
Elizabeth try to win rights
for women? Summarize the
important events in order.

Word of the meeting
spread like wildfire.

Newspapers across the
country scolded
Elizabeth for her
boldness.

But other women joined
her in battle.

The idea of women having
the right to vote
began to buzz in the ears of people
from Maine to California.

Elizabeth had tossed a stone in the water
and the ripples grew wider and wider and wider.

Many said Elizabeth must be stopped.
But she was unstoppable.
She changed America forever.

About the Author and Illustrator

Tanya Lee Stone
likes to write fiction
and nonfiction for
children. Going to
school and helping
other people write children's
stories helped her grow as
a writer. Tanya has traveled
around the world from Russia
to Australia. She has written
more than ninety books for
young people. She especially
likes to write stories about
strong women and girls.

Rebecca Gibbon
loved picture books
as a young girl.
She dreamed of
illustrating books one
day. Today she is the illustrator
of several picture books. She
illustrated *Players in Pigtails*, a
true story of a baseball league
for girls. She also illustrated
a book of poems and a book
about famous trees. She lives
in London, England.

Author's Purpose

Why do you think the author
wrote a book about Elizabeth
Cady Stanton's life?

Respond to the Text

Summarize

Tell about the important events in Elizabeth Cady Stanton's life. The details from your Author's Point of View chart may help you summarize.

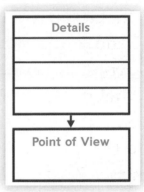

Details

↓

Point of View

Write

How does Tanya Lee Stone use Elizabeth's biography to teach you about what it means to be a good citizen? Use these sentence frames to organize your text evidence.

> Tanya Lee Stone tells that Elizabeth . . .
> She shows how Elizabeth . . .
> This helps me understand that she . . .

Make Connections

In what ways was Elizabeth Cady Stanton a good citizen? **ESSENTIAL QUESTION**

How did Elizabeth Cady Stanton's fight for women's rights change life in the United States? **TEXT TO WORLD**

Compare Texts

Read about how one person's good citizenship made a difference for women in the United States.

Susan B. Anthony
★ Takes Action! ★

Susan Brownell Anthony was born in Massachusetts in 1820. Her family believed that all people are equal. At the time Susan was born, however, this idea of equality was very unusual. Men and women did not have the same rights. Women could not do many of the things men did. Women could not vote and they could not own property. Life was different for Susan. She learned to read and write at the age of three, even though she was a girl.

Early Struggles

When Susan went to school, she saw that boys and girls were not treated the same way. One of her teachers refused to teach Susan long division. She said that girls did not have any reason to know math. As a result, Susan's family took her out of school and taught her at home.

Susan's family felt strongly about equality and good citizenship. They spoke out against slavery. When Susan was twenty-six years old, she became a school teacher and fought for the rights of students. She wanted boys and girls to be able to learn together. She also wanted children of former enslaved people to be able to learn in these same classrooms.

In 1978, the United States mint released a dollar coin to honor Susan B. Anthony.

A Friend in the Fight

When she was twenty-eight, Susan heard about a meeting to discuss how women might get the right to vote. She was very excited about this idea. She went with her family to Seneca Falls, New York, to hear Elizabeth Cady Stanton give a speech about the topic. Susan and her sister and parents signed papers to support the idea. Susan felt so strongly about it that she started working with Elizabeth Cady Stanton. Together they started a weekly newspaper and gave speeches around the country.

In 1848, Elizabeth Cady Stanton spoke about women's right to vote at a meeting in Seneca Falls, New York.

Women Can Vote!

This time line shows important dates in the life of Susan B. Anthony and in the fight for women's right to vote.

1820	1848	1852	1868
Susan Brownell Anthony born in Adams, Massachusetts	Attended Seneca Falls conference	Started working with Elizabeth Cady Stanton	Started a weekly paper

Women Get the Vote!

Susan gave as many as 100 speeches around the country every year for forty-five years. She always stayed excited and hopeful about her work.

Not everyone agreed with her ideas. Susan and her friend Elizabeth Cady Stanton had to fight hard for many years for the rights of all people. They always did their work peacefully. It was not until fourteen years after Susan died that women in the United States were allowed to vote. The long struggle would not have been successful without the work of Susan B. Anthony.

Susan B. Anthony and Elizabeth Cady Stanton worked hard to support the rights of women in the United States.

1869	1872	1906	1920
Founded National Woman Suffrage Association with Elizabeth Cady Stanton	Arrested for trying to cast a vote in an election	Died in Rochester, New York	Women get the right to vote

You Can Be a Good Citizen, Too!

You can **participate** in your community, just like Susan B. Anthony did.

- Volunteer your time.
- Get to know your neighbors.
- Talk to people. Listen to their ideas. Tell them your ideas.
- Work peacefully with others.
- Help others.
- Make your community a great place to live!

Good citizens help people in their community.

Make Connections

In what ways was Susan B. Anthony a good citizen?
ESSENTIAL QUESTION

Tell about some other leaders you have read about. How did they show good **citizenship**? TEXT TO TEXT

Clever Jack
TAKES *the* CAKE

by
Candace Fleming

illustrated by
G. Brian Karas

Essential Question

How do we get what we need?

Read how a poor boy gets what he needs to make a royal gift.

Go Digital!

One summer morning long ago, a poor boy named Jack found an invitation slipped beneath his cottage door. It read:

His Majesty the King

cordially invites all the children of the Realm to the Princess's Tenth Birthday Party tomorrow afternoon in the Castle Courtyard

"A party!" exclaimed Jack. "For the princess!"
His mother sighed. "What a shame you can't go."
"Why not?" asked Jack.

"Because we've nothing fine enough to give her," his
mother replied. "And no money to buy a gift."

Jack had to **admit** his mother was right. His pockets
were empty except for the matchsticks he always carried.
As for their few belongings—a spinning wheel, a
threadbare quilt, a pitted ax—what princess wanted those?

The boy thought a moment. "Then I will make her
something," he declared. "I will make her
a cake."

"From what?" asked his mother.
"From the dust in the cupboard?
From the dirt on the floor?"

"I have a better idea," said Jack.

And that same morning, he traded his ax for two bags of sugar, and his quilt for a sack of flour.

He gave the hen an extra handful of seed in exchange for two fresh eggs, and he kissed the cow on the nose for a pail of her sweetest milk.

He gathered walnuts.

He dipped candles.

And in the strawberry patch, he searched ... and searched ... and searched until he found the reddest, juiciest, most succulent strawberry in the land.

"Delicious!" said Jack as he plucked it from its stem.

STOP AND CHECK

Summarize How did Jack get what he needed to make a cake? Tell the events in order.

Then he set to work, churning, chopping,
blending, baking.

That same night, Jack stood back to admire his **creation**—two layers of golden-sweet cake covered in buttery frosting and ringed with ten tiny candles. Across the cake's top, walnuts spelled out "Happy Birthday, Princess." And in the very center—in the place of honor—sat the succulent strawberry.

"What a fine, fine gift," said Jack's mother.

Jack grinned.

Early the next morning, with combed hair and clean shirt, Jack set off for the castle, holding the cake proudly before him.

Before long, he came to a bloom-speckled meadow.

Perhaps I should pick a bouquet for the princess, thought Jack, just as four-and-twenty blackbirds rose into the air. Like a sudden summer storm cloud, they swirled around the cake, pecking, nipping, flapping, picking.

"Get back!" hollered Jack.

"I'm taking this cake to the princess."

"Aw-caw-caw-caw-caw!" cackled the birds.

And as quickly as they had come, they were gone, taking with them the walnuts that spelled "Happy Birthday, Princess."

Jack looked at his gift. "At least I still have two layers of cake, ten candles, and the succulent strawberry," he said. Holding the cake proudly before him, Jack continued on to the castle.

Before long, he came to a bridge.

"Toll!" a voice demanded.

Out stepped a wild-haired troll.

"No one crosses my bridge without paying."

"But I haven't any money," said Jack.

The troll licked his lips. "But you do have a cake."

"I'm taking this to the princess," said Jack.

"And just how will you get it there?" growled the troll. "You and your cake are on *this* side of the river. The princess is on *that* side, and my bridge is the *only* way across."

Jack **considered** the problem. "I will make you a deal. If you let me cross, I will give you half this cake."

"Agreed," grunted the troll.

So Jack slid out one layer and, as the troll slobbered and gobbled, crossed the bridge.

On the other side, he looked down at his gift. "At least I still have a layer of cake, ten candles, and the succulent strawberry," he said.

Holding the cake proudly before him, Jack continued on to the castle.

Before long he came to the forest. No birds chirped here. No squirrels chittered.

As if under a spell, the entire wood lay silent, sleeping. Only the wind seemed to whisper, "Beware! Beware!"

Pulling the cake closer, Jack pressed on.

The road grew narrower. The trees grew thicker. The light grew dimmer. Soon it was so dark that Jack couldn't see the cake in front of his face.

"Turn back!" the wind whispered. "Turn back!"

"I can't!" cried Jack. "I'm taking this cake to the princess."

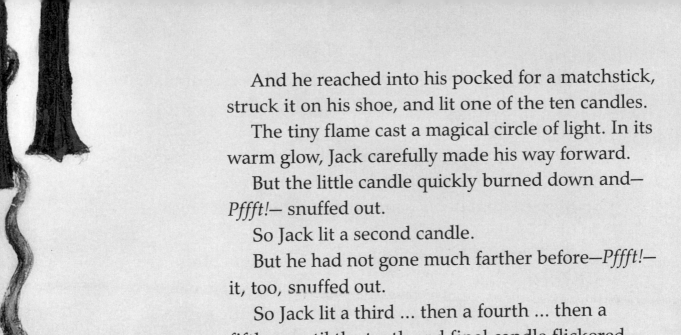

And he reached into his pocked for a matchstick, struck it on his shoe, and lit one of the ten candles.

The tiny flame cast a magical circle of light. In its warm glow, Jack carefully made his way forward.

But the little candle quickly burned down and—*Pffft!*— snuffed out.

So Jack lit a second candle.

But he had not gone much farther before—*Pffft!*— it, too, snuffed out.

So Jack lit a third ... then a fourth ... then a fifth ... until the tenth and final candle flickered, fluttered, sputtered to its end.

And as it did, the road widened, the trees thinned, and the bright sunlight shone once more.

Jack looked down at his gift. "At least I still have a layer of cake and the succulent strawberry," he said.

Holding the cake proudly before him, Jack continued on to the castle.

Before long he came to a clearing.

"Good morning, young sir!" called out an old gypsy woman. "Have you come to see Samson dance?"

At the sound of his name, the bear beside her rose up on his hind legs.

"I don't have time," replied Jack. "I'm taking this cake to the princess."

"Then we shall make it a quick jig," said the gypsy, snatching up her concertina.

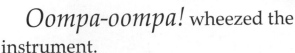

Oompa-oompa! wheezed the instrument.

Shuffle-shuffle-kick, danced the bear.

Tap-tap-tap, went Jack's foot, as he set down the cake to dance with his new friends.

G-U-U-U-L-P!

"**Hey,**" cried Jack, "that bear ate the princess's cake!"

PATOOIE!"

"But not the strawberry," said the gypsy. "Samson hates fruit."

Jack looked down at his gift, and for several seconds he was unable to speak. Finally, he said, "At least I still have this—the reddest, juiciest, most succulent strawberry in the land."

STOP AND CHECK

Summarize What happened to the cake? Tell the events in order.

401

And holding the strawberry proudly before him, Jack continued on to the castle.

Across the drawbridge . . .

Through the fortress walls . . .

. . . Straight into the courtyard.

What a sight! There, smack in the center of all the merry festivities, sat the princess on her velvet throne, a long line of guests stretched before her. One by one, they presented her with their gifts, each more fabulous than the last.

But even the most **magnificent** treasures did not seem to interest Her Highness. "More rubies?" she said with a bored yawn. "How tiresome. Another tiara? How dull."

Joining the line, Jack glanced down at his **humble** gift.

"And just what have you brought the princess?" a guard asked from behind him.

"A strawberry," said Jack. "The reddest, juiciest, most succulent one in the land." He held it out for the guard to see.

"That is a fine piece of fruit," agreed the guard. "But I cannot allow you to give it to the princess."

"Why not?" asked Jack.

"Because she is allergic to strawberries," said the guard. "One taste and she swells up like a balloon."

"No!" gasped Jack.

"Yes," said the guard. "I'm sorry, but you'll have to give it to me."

Reluctantly, Jack handed over the strawberry.

"Mmmmm."

Now Jack found himself at the front of the line.

The princess turned her gaze to him. "And what have *you* brought me?" she asked.

Jack gulped. He blushed. He shuffled his feet.
"Well?"

Jack took a deep breath and knelt down before her.

"Your Highness," he began, "let me explain what happened."

And he told the princess about trading for the ingredients to bake a golden-sweet cake just for her. He told her about the swirling storm of blackbirds, the wild-haired troll, and the dark, dark wood. He told her about the old gypsy woman and her concertina, and the bear who loved to dance but hated fruit.

"And in the end," said Jack, "I still had the succulent strawberry, but ..." The boy sighed. "You're allergic to strawberries."

He waited for her to yawn.

"So the guard ate it," he concluded.

The princess laughed and clapped her hands in delight.

"A story!"

she exclaimed. "And an adventure story at that! What a fine gift."

STOP AND CHECK

Reread How did the princess feel about Jack's gift? Reread to find out.

Then the princess rose from her throne and proclaimed, "Time for birthday cake. And my new friend Jack shall have the honor of cutting it."

About the Author and Illustrator

When **Candace Fleming** was a little girl, she liked to tell tall tales about her three-legged cat and a family trip to Paris. Candace continued to tell great stories when she was an adult. In fact, she is now the author of more than twenty-five books for young people, including fiction, nonfiction, and biographies.

G. Brian Karas had his first art lessons when he was five. His sister taught him to draw Pilgrims. He has been passionate about books and drawing since then. Brian has illustrated more than fifty books for children. He has also written books, including a book about the Atlantic Ocean.

Author's Purpose

What is the theme, or lesson, of this story? What details help you figure it out?

Respond to the Text

Summarize

What are the important events in the story about Jack? The details from your Point of View chart may help you summarize.

Details

↓

Point of View

Write

How does the author use text and illustrations to show how Jack accomplishes his goal? Use these sentence frames to organize your text evidence.

The author describes how Jack . . .
Illustrations help me see . . .
This helps me know that Jack . . .

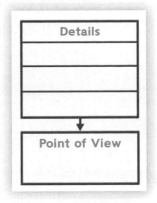

Make Connections

 How does Jack get what he needs to bake the Princess's cake? **ESSENTIAL QUESTION**

Why is it important to give thoughtful gifts? **TEXT TO WORLD**

Compare Texts

Read to find out the ways people get the things they need.

Money
Then and Now

What makes money valuable? If you think about it, a dollar bill is only a piece of paper. You cannot eat, wear, or live in a dollar bill. So why do people want it? People work hard to earn money. Money is considered valuable because it is hard to get.

FRESH
YELLOW-
ORANGE
PEPPERS
$=2.49 LB

SWEET-JUICY
CORN
4 for 5.00
1 for 1.40

SUNGOLD
CHERRY
TOMATO
$3.00

Bartering

Long ago, there was no money. If your family raised chickens, you might need to go to a marketplace to get milk. How would you pay for it? The chickens you owned were your only source of income, or way to earn money. You would not have traded a chicken for milk. The chicken was too valuable. Instead, you traded eggs for the milk. This is called bartering. People **barter** because it is a simple way to get what they need.

A History of Money

Money has changed a lot through the years. People have used many different forms of money to pay for the things they needed. For example, in China, cowrie shells were used as **payment**. The shells were lightweight, sturdy, and easy to carry. Some Native American people used strings of beads made from white shells. These shells were called wampum and they were used to trade with the colonists who came to America from Europe. People also used small lumps of silver and gold. Those lumps of metal were eventually formed into coins.

The problem with carrying around a bag of coins was that it could be heavy. As a result, people began using paper money. Paper money originally represented the gold or silver a person had saved in the bank. Today, we can tell the value of paper money by reading the numbers printed on it. People also use credit or debit cards. The cards are used to buy things, but no actual paper money is exchanged.

411

Earn and Spend

People earn money by working hard. They might have a job or invent something new. They might even start their own business. You might not be old enough to have a job, but there are many ways you can earn money. Lots of kids help their neighbors by raking leaves or walking dogs to earn cash. Some parents even give their kids an allowance in exchange for helping around the house.

What do you do with the money you earn? Well, you have a few choices. The easiest one is to spend the money you make on things you want or need. Spending money is easy. Learning to save money can be challenging.

Save and Donate

Saving money is important so that when you need it, you will have it. Many people put the money they want to save into a savings account at the bank. Then the bank pays interest, or money for every month the money stays at the bank.

Some people save some of their money, but want to help others, too. Donating money means giving it to someone who needs it to do something good. Maybe you want to help groups who work with dogs and cats. Maybe you want to help people who are working to clean up the oceans. Making a donation helps pay for the things these people do.

A lemonade stand is one way to earn money.

Bartering is still used today. Kids still trade snacks for baseball cards, but most people use the money they earn to get the things they need. So be smart about the way you spend, save, and donate. Make a budget.

How to Make a Budget

A budget is a plan for managing your money. Here's an easy way to make one.

1. Get three clean jars with lids. Label the jars: "Save," "Spend," and "Donate."

2. When you get money, decide how much you want to save. Place it in the "Save" jar. Always put money into this jar first.

3. Next, decide how much you want to donate. Place that money in the "Donate" jar.

4. The money you have left is the money you can spend. Put it in the "Spend" jar and decide how to use it.

Have fun managing your money. When the "Save" jar gets full, it might be time to go to the bank, open a savings account, and buy that new bike you were saving for.

? Make Connections

How do people get what they need? ESSENTIAL QUESTION

Think about the selections you have read. What are some ways people have gotten the things they need? TEXT TO TEXT

It's All in the
WIND

This wind farm in
Texas provides electricity
to many communities.

? Essential Question

What are different kinds
of energy?

Read about how people are using
the wind as a source of energy.

Go Digital!

People have been using boats with sails that capture the wind's power since ancient times.

Why are people using wind power?

People have been using wind as an energy **source** since ancient times. Sailors were the first to use wind power. Strong winds caused ships with sails to glide quickly across the water. Then people decided to use the wind to do other hard jobs, such as grinding grain or pumping water. As a result, they invented windmills. Windmills are machines that capture the wind's power.

STOP AND CHECK

Ask and Answer Questions
In what ways have people used the power of the wind?

Wind Is Energy

Most of the energy we use today comes from coal, natural gas, and oil. These are called fossil fuels. Wind is another kind of energy. Wind turbines use the power of nature to generate electricity and make things run. When warm air rises, cooler air moves in to take its place. These actions cause wind to form. As the wind rises above Earth, it blows faster. The faster the wind blows, the more energy it creates. This is the energy that powers windmills.

When a strong wind blows on the blades of a windmill, it causes them to spin around. The blades are connected to a long rod. When the blades spin, they turn the rod. The turning rod **produces** energy that can be used to do work.

Laurence Heyworth/Montagu Images/Alamy Stock Photo

415

Turbine Power

Today, wind turbines are a common way to turn wind into energy. They look like giant windmills. They are lined up in rows on wind farms. Some turbines are as tall as skyscrapers.

The turbines catch strong winds high above the ground. The wind causes the blades on the turbine to turn. As the blades spin, they produce energy. Inside the turbine, machinery turns the energy from the spinning blades into electricity. Then the electricity flows through wires from the turbine to bring power to homes and towns.

This offshore windfarm was built to catch stronger winds. It uses turbines.

Against the Wind

POINT COUNTERPOINT

Critics of wind energy worry that wind turbines harm wildlife. Birds and bats can accidentally fly into the tall turbines. Building new turbines can disrupt habitats for plants and animals on the ground. Some also think that wind turbines are eyesores that ruin the natural beauty of the landscape.

Some people also worry about the costs of wind energy. Turbines need to be built in locations with strong winds. This means wind farms are sometimes constructed offshore, or in the water. It can cost a lot of money to build in such a difficult place. Even after a turbine is built, workers must be paid to maintain them.

Critics of wind energy often prefer other sources, like solar power, or cheaper sources of energy, like fossil fuels.

How a Wind Turbine Works

This diagram shows how a wind turbine turns wind power into electricity.

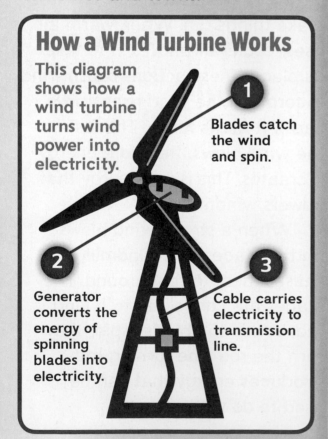

1 Blades catch the wind and spin.

2 Generator converts the energy of spinning blades into electricity.

3 Cable carries electricity to transmission line.

(b) Illustration: National Energy Education Development Project (t) Rudmer Zwerver/Shutterstock.com

A Breath of Fresh Air

Wind energy does have positives, however. **Natural** resources like coal, natural gas, and oil are running out. They cannot be **replaced**. But wind is a **renewable** resource. There will always be a supply.

Wind is also free and clean. Wind turbines are expensive to build, but the wind that powers them doesn't cost anything. And wind doesn't create harmful **pollution**.

Fossil fuels are not free. It costs money to pull coal, oil, and gas from deep underground. And burning fossil fuels pollute our air and water. Using more wind energy can help us clean up our environment.

Wind Gets Stronger

Every year, more companies are placing wind machines near communities. Recently, 3,000 wind machines were put in place in one year. These new machines are five times larger than the ones made ten years ago, and they produce fifteen times more energy. Clean energy with wind power is here to stay.

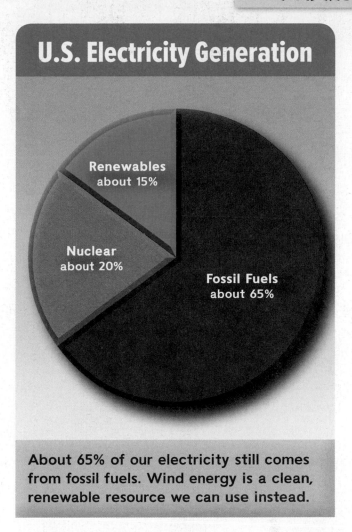

U.S. Electricity Generation

Renewables
about 15%

Nuclear
about 20%

Fossil Fuels
about 65%

About 65% of our electricity still comes from fossil fuels. Wind energy is a clean, renewable resource we can use instead.

Respond to the Text

Use important details from the selection to summarize. **SUMMARIZE**

How does the author show that wind energy is important? **WRITE**

Why are more people around the world using wind power? **TEXT TO WORLD**

TIME
FOR KIDS®

Compare Texts

Read to find out how people around the world are getting energy from the sun.

Power for All

Every day, students in many countries are in a race against the Sun. Many don't have electricity. For this reason, they must do their homework during daylight hours or use dangerous oil lamps or candlelight at night.

In Tsumkwe (CHOOM-kwee), a small town in Namibia, Africa, villagers were lucky. Until recently, they got all their electricity from a generator powered by oil. However, there were problems with the generator. It cost a lot of money. And it only produced electricity for three hours each day.

Namibia is a country on the southwest coast of Africa.

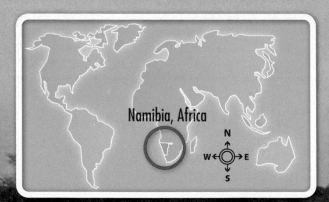

Namibia, Africa

N
W ← ⊙ → E
S

These solar panels provide enough power to run the town of Tsumkwe.

juwi

Alternative Power Comes to the Rescue!

Then life in Tsumkwe changed. A company from Germany built a solar power system in the village. The new system supplies electricity to 100 homes. As a result, now the villagers can have electricity 24 hours a day.

The people in Tsumkwe are not the only ones struggling to get electricity. Almost two billion people around the world still do not have electric power. That means hospitals have a hard time taking care of sick people. Most people in these countries must depend on energy from costly oil to light their way.

However, life is getting better in countries without good power sources. Energy companies are starting to provide wind and solar power to these communities.

Wind and solar power can be cheaper than **traditional** fuel sources, such as coal and oil. They are cleaner. And they are safer to use. These alternative **energy** sources are a very small part of the power that is used in the world, but more people are using these sources every year.

TOP 5 ENERGY SAVERS
Here are five easy ways that you can save energy every day. Try them all!

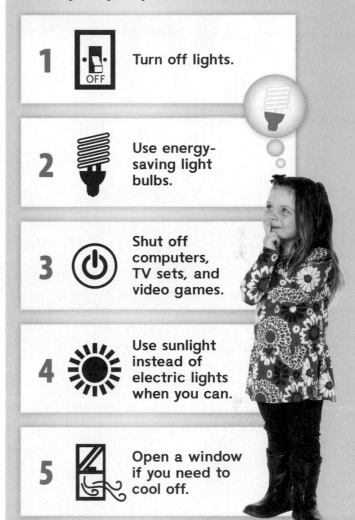

1 Turn off lights.

2 Use energy-saving light bulbs.

3 Shut off computers, TV sets, and video games.

4 Use sunlight instead of electric lights when you can.

5 Open a window if you need to cool off.

Make Connections

Why is it important to use different sources of energy? **ESSENTIAL QUESTION**

How is solar power like other forms of energy you have read about? **TEXT TO TEXT**

Wildfires

by Seymour Simon

Essential Question

How do teams work together?

Read about wildfires. Find out what causes them and how emergency teams respond when they happen.

Go Digital!

Wildfires are scary. Flames leap from one tree to another. Sometimes they move faster than a person can run. Wildfires can be disasters. They burn trees, destroy homes, and cost human lives.

But wildfires are not all harmful. They can help as well as hurt. Burning old trees lets small, young trees grow. Some trees, such as giant sequoias, need fires to release their seeds. Wildfires are not endings, but part of the cycle of the natural world.

How Fires Start

Heat causes fires. A flash of lightning can start a fire. So can an **accidental** spark from a campfire. A leaf starts burning. The heat sets fire to more leaves. The flaming leaves set fire to a branch. Then the whole tree is on fire. The heat sets fire to a nearby tree without even touching it. A huge, raging wildfire can be set ablaze by a flame from a **careless** match.

Fires also need fuel and oxygen to burn. Dry wood or dry grasses are the fuel of wildfires. Oxygen is an invisible gas in the air around us. Wet wood rarely burns because the water keeps oxygen from getting to the fire. That's why water is splashed on fires to put them out.

Ocean/Corbis

Lightning strikes a mountain in a wilderness area in Colorado.

Wildfires Are Not All Bad!

It's only partly true that "only you" can prevent forest fires. Few wildfires are started on **purpose**. Lightning starts most wildfires in the Western United States. Fires are natural in the wilderness. Complete wildfire **prevention** is not possible or wanted.

Wildfires create openings in a forest for new trees and shrubs. Parts of burned trees turn to ash. Rain and snow carry the minerals in the ash back into the soil. Flowering plants grow in full sunlight of the new forest clearings.

Cones from some pine trees release seeds only when they are heated. Even seeds in cones that fell fifty years earlier can grow after a fire. Some trees, such as the Western larch, have thick barks that guard them from heat. These trees often survive many wildfires.

Animals are not usually killed in wildfires. Most can run faster than the spreading flames. Birds and mammals eat the seeds they find in the clearings after a fire. Some plants grow quickly. They are food for animals that might otherwise starve.

Raymond Gehman/Corbis Documentary/Getty Images

Many scientists say that wildfires are natural. The only question is when they will happen. Communities must learn how to deal with them. In areas with houses, teams of firefighters need to **respond** right away. They must bring the fires under control as quickly as possible.

In wilderness areas, firefighters want to stamp out small fires quickly. Then leaves, dead branches and twigs pile up on the forest floor. This provides fuel that feeds fires. One way to prevent huge wildfires is to let small fires burn out naturally.

This firefighter protects people and property from harm.

Bob Peterson/UpperCut Images/Getty Images

STOP AND CHECK

Ask and Answer Questions Why does the author think that wildfires can be good? Reread pages 424-425 to find the answer.

These firefighters are clearing away bushes to make a fire break in Northern California.

California's Burning!

The spring and summer of 2008 were hot and dry in California. Almost no rain fell for three straight years. The spring was the driest on record for many places in the state. Trees and grasses were bone-dry. On June 20 and 21, thunderstorms and lightning rolled onshore along the coast. Lightning started more than 2,000 wildfires. The fires covered much of Northern California with a thick blanket of smoke. The sky turned yellow. The moon turned red.

Strong winds and high temperatures helped spread the flames. A heat wave began on July 7. Temperatures inland soared above 120° F. The National Weather Service gave fire danger warnings. By July 12, over 800,000 acres had burned. It was the largest bunch of wildfires in California history.

More than 20,000 firefighters battled the blazes. Some teams used fire trucks, fire engines, water tankers and bulldozers. Other teams used axes, picks and shovels. Many teams carried water, foam, hoses and pumps with them. They were fighting fires in places where there were no roads.

Special tankers and helicopters dropped water onto the fires. Teams of smoke jumpers parachuted from helicopters to help on the fire lines.

Fighting wildfires is very dangerous. It is hard to escape if the wind changes and the fires race toward you. The 2008 California wildfires caused the deaths of twenty-three people.

STOP AND CHECK

Ask and Answer Questions
How did firefighters respond to the wildfires in California? Reread this page to find the answer.

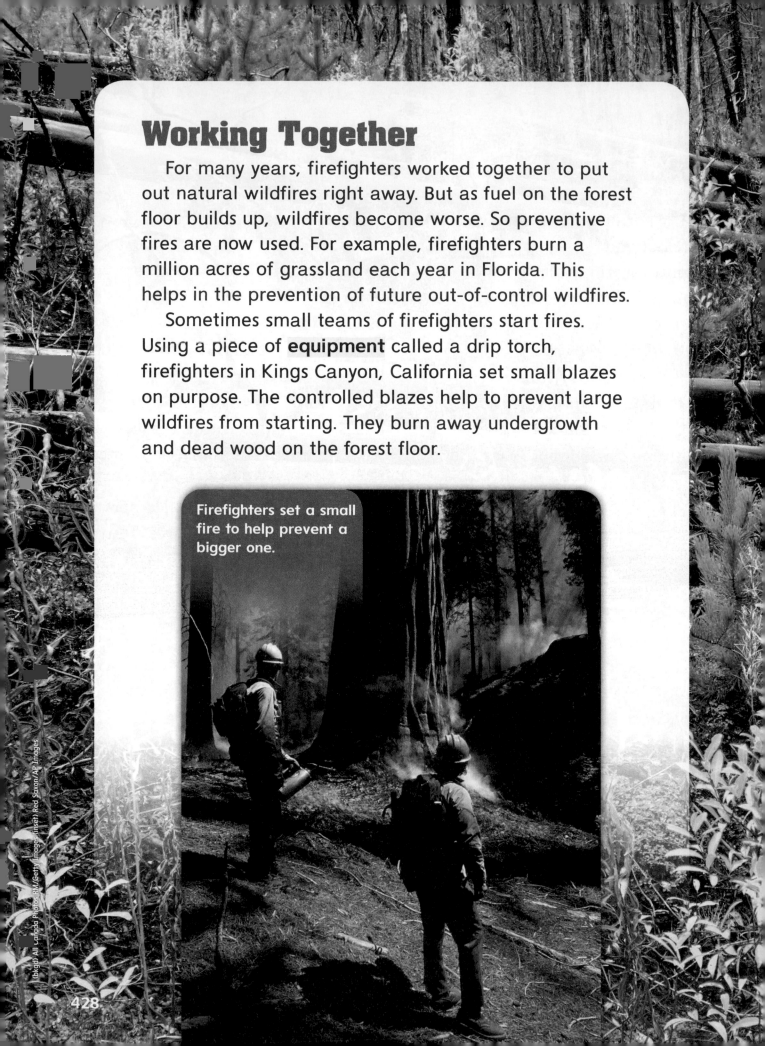

Working Together

For many years, firefighters worked together to put out natural wildfires right away. But as fuel on the forest floor builds up, wildfires become worse. So preventive fires are now used. For example, firefighters burn a million acres of grassland each year in Florida. This helps in the prevention of future out-of-control wildfires.

Sometimes small teams of firefighters start fires. Using a piece of **equipment** called a drip torch, firefighters in Kings Canyon, California set small blazes on purpose. The controlled blazes help to prevent large wildfires from starting. They burn away undergrowth and dead wood on the forest floor.

Firefighters set a small fire to help prevent a bigger one.

After a Wildfire

When wildfires burn out, they leave green and black patches in forests. The green areas are not burned. The black burned areas quickly start to turn green. Fire beetles lay their eggs in newly charred logs. Ants and centipedes are busy even while the ground is still warm. Plants soon appear from roots and seeds that were there before the fire.

Hawks spiral in the air. They hunt for small mammals in the open spaces. Woodpeckers drill for insects beneath the bark of blackened trees. The new grasses and wildflowers attract grazing animals. Small birds come from all over to catch insects in the fields.

A few years after the 2008 wildfires, burned areas grew new plants. Young pine trees grew as tall as a person. Before the fire, towering older trees blocked sunlight. Only a few kinds of plants could grow in the deep shade. The wildfires allowed young plants to grow.

Without wildfires, low-growing forest plants would die off completely. By about fifty years after a fire, the forest once again becomes mostly tall trees, such as pines. Smaller plants will die off on the shady forest floor. The cycle of burning and rebirth in nature continues.

After a fire in this national park in Canada, trees and plants begin to grow again.

Forests Are Reborn

Ten years after a wildfire, a forest is still renewing itself. Burned tree trunks lose their blackened bark and turn a mossy, silvery grey. Flowering meadows and small shrubs and trees grow in open fields in the forest. Burned areas slowly fade away.

The length of time between natural wildfires depends on location and weather. In much of the West, wildfires may burn a forest every two or three hundred years. However, in Florida's pine forests, wildfires occur every seven to ten years. In the cedar and spruce forests of Washington, a thousand years can pass between wildfires.

New trees and plants grow next to burned trees after a fire in Alberta, Canada.

Questions Still Remain

We still have much to learn about managing wildfires. Which fires should we fight immediately? Which fires should we allow to burn naturally? Are there places in a forest where it is too dangerous to live? We have learned one thing. Wildfires are not all bad or all good. Fires are just a part of the endless cycle of nature.

STOP AND CHECK

Summarize What happens after a wildfire? Summarize what you learned in the section "Forests Are Reborn."

About the Author

Seymour Simon loved nature from the time he was a kid growing up in New York City. He explored city parks and empty lots and observed insects, birds, and plants. During family vacations in the mountains, he spent even more time learning about nature. Seymour grew up to be a science teacher and an author. He has shared his love of nature with generations of students. Seymour has written more than 250 fiction and nonfiction science books for children.

Author's Purpose
Why do you think Seymour Simon wrote about wildfires?

Respond to the Text

Summarize

Summarize what you learned about wildfires. The details from your Point of View chart may help you summarize.

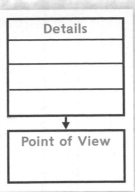

Details

Point of View

Write

How do the text features and the way Seymour Simon organizes information help you understand more about wildfires?

> Seymour Simon uses photographs and captions to . . .
> He also . . .
> This helps me to understand that wildfires . . .

Make Connections

Why do firefighters work in teams?
ESSENTIAL QUESTION

Why is firefighting an important job? **TEXT TO WORLD**

Compare Texts

Read how Windy Gale and her pet panther Gusty worked together to stop a hurricane.

Windy Gale
and the
Great Hurricane

Once, in Florida, a baby girl was born. That night was so windy that all the mountains blew away. Only the flat land we call the Everglades was left. Well, some of that wind must have blown into that baby girl. From the time she was knee-high to a tadpole, she could control the wind with her breath alone. That's why they called her Windy Gale.

One day when Windy was nine years old, a warning sounded on the radio. "A hurricane's a-comin'! We can't stop it! **Prevention** is out of the question, folks. You'll just have to stay inside and wait it out!"

Windy called Gusty, her pet Florida panther.

Windy said, "I don't believe for one windy minute that we should just wait out this storm! It'll hit Miami soon, and I need you to run me there fast!" She jumped on Gusty's back.

Gusty gave a roar. Then he ran so fast that he arrived a clear two minutes before he even left.

The hurricane was zooming up the Gulf. Windy knew just what to do to stop it. She took three BIG breaths, 1 . . . 2 . . . 3 . . . and sucked the wind right out of that hurricane. When she was done sucking, all that was left was a shy little breeze.

To thank Windy and Gusty, the mayor of Miami gave them both medals. He said, "This could have been one of the biggest **disasters** in the state of Florida. You are both heroes!"

Windy breathed a sigh of thanks and blew the hat right off the mayor's head!

Make Connections

Tell how Windy and her panther Gusty worked together to prevent the hurricane. ESSENTIAL QUESTION

How is this story like other stories about teamwork you have read? TEXT TO TEXT

BRAVO, TAVO!

by **Brian Meunier**
illustrated by **Perky Edgerton**

Essential Question

How can we reuse what we already have?

Read about how how Tavo finds a way to reuse an old pair of sneakers.

Go Digital!

Dribble-*flip,*
dribble-*boing...*

The ball bounced off the hoop.
Tavo had missed again.

He bent down to fix the duct
tape flapping around his patched
sneakers. The tape held the soles to
what **remained** of the canvas tops.
But Tavo wasn't easily **discouraged.**
He was excited, for he had the whole
summer to practice before the
regular basketball season started.

Tavo had seen the NBA games on the new satellite TV at the village store, and he wanted to play ball like one of those big American players.

He imagined that one day he, too, would have a great basketball name. A name like Air or Magic.

But for now, he was just Tavo. Gustavo the second . . . named after his father.

"If only I had new sneakers," Tavo said to himself as he tucked the ball under his arm and started up the path toward home. "Then I'd play better."

The ground crunched beneath his shoes, leaving trails of dust. The mountainside stretched before him, a patchwork of plowed fields separated by the remnants of ancient irrigation ditches called *zanjas*. It reminded him of the quilt on his bed, but in shades of brown. Tavo looked down at his frayed sneakers and kicked at the parched earth.

"If only I had new sneakers," he muttered again.

When he reached home, Tavo found his father poking around the old *zanja*, the ancient irrigation ditch, which ran along the edge of their field. Gustavo was always **tinkering** with something. Today he was putting up yet another scarecrow.

"Papa . . . look. Look at my sneakers. They are turning into sandals! I bet you can't fix them anymore," said Tavo.

"Tavo, I've told you this already," Gustavo replied wearily. "We can't afford new sneakers right now. Not until the rains come."

Sure, Tavo thought in **frustration**. *And* then . . . *I'll have to wait for the corn to grow. Then, to dry on the stalk. Then, to be harvested. Then, to be brought to the* molino *to be ground into flour. Then, to be sold in the market. The basketball season will be over by* then!

Tavo looked up at the sky as some dark thunderclouds rumbled with the promise of rain. One cloud slipped through the peaks and drifted out over the valley.

The two Gustavos watched silently as the cloud broke apart in the blazing sun, like a bursting piñata.

"Hopeless!" Gustavo said, throwing up his hands in exasperation. "There is only one thing left to do. I have a plan, and I'm going to present it at the meeting tonight."

The villagers had been called to an emergency meeting to discuss the drought. As the two Gustavos neared the village square, they could hear that the meeting had already begun. To Tavo's surprise, his father marched right up to the front and faced the crowd.

"We cannot wait for the rains to begin," he said. "Our ancestors knew the solution. The solution is in the *zanjas!* We must dig them up again, up into the mountains until we reach the ancient source of the water!"

"Gustavo," the mayor said, pausing for effect. "Go talk to your scarecrows!" The crowd burst into laughter. "If the *zanjas* worked so well in the past, why did our ancestors stop using them?" The mayor puffed up his chest and poked his finger in the air. "We must move forward, not backward!"

Gustavo abruptly turned and walked out. Tavo ran after him, his back burning with embarrassment.

441

Early the next morning, Tavo awoke with a start. His father was shaking his shoulder.

"Tavo, wake up."

Tavo rubbed his eyes and protested. "It is still dark outside!"

"Get up, Tavo. We have a lot of work to do."

"But Papa, I have practice today."

Gustavo handed Tavo a shovel. "Son, basketball comes later."

The two Gustavos started work at the edge of their field. All day long they shoveled out the silt that had filled in the ancient *zanja*. When night finally came, Tavo slumped into bed, every bone in his body aching.

They began all over again the next morning. Digging and digging and digging some more. Hours turned into days. Days turned into weeks as father and son slowly worked their way up the mountain.

STOP AND CHECK

Summarize What has happened so far in the story? Tell the important events in order.

443

There was one house high up in the mountain. It belonged to an old widow. Tavo had heard strange stories about her.

"Is it true what they say about her, that she is a *bruja*, a witch?" he asked his father nervously.

"Tavo," his father laughed. "Don't believe everything you hear. Señora Rosa is just a widow. People are always suspicious of anyone who is different."

"Señora Rosa?" Gustavo called out.

There was no answer, but in the yard they saw a patchwork quilt draped over a chair. A needle dangling from a silver thread swayed in the air.

As they left, Gustavo carved a channel to connect Señora Rosa's small garden to the main *zanja*. He turned toward Tavo with a mischievous smile. "Even witches need water."

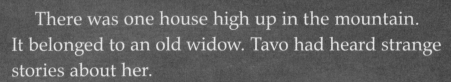

Higher and higher, they continued to dig. Weeks passed this way, and Tavo's muscles no longer ached from the hard work. One day, the two Gustavos worked their way up into a shadowy ravine near the top of the mountain. Under their feet the ground was soggy and green.

"We did it, Tavo! We found the spring!" Gustavo cried.

With triumph they cleared away the debris, and the water bubbled forth down the arid mountainside! **Jubilant,** they danced in its wake.

Down . . . down . . . down . . . splashing along.

Down . . . down . . . down . . . until the water reached their thirsty field.

As they whooped and hollered, Tavo felt the cool mud squishing between his toes. In his excitement, Tavo's ragged sneakers had slipped off his feet. And now they were lost somewhere in the muddy waters.

STOP AND CHECK

Summarize What happens when Tavo and his father find the spring? Tell the events in order.

447

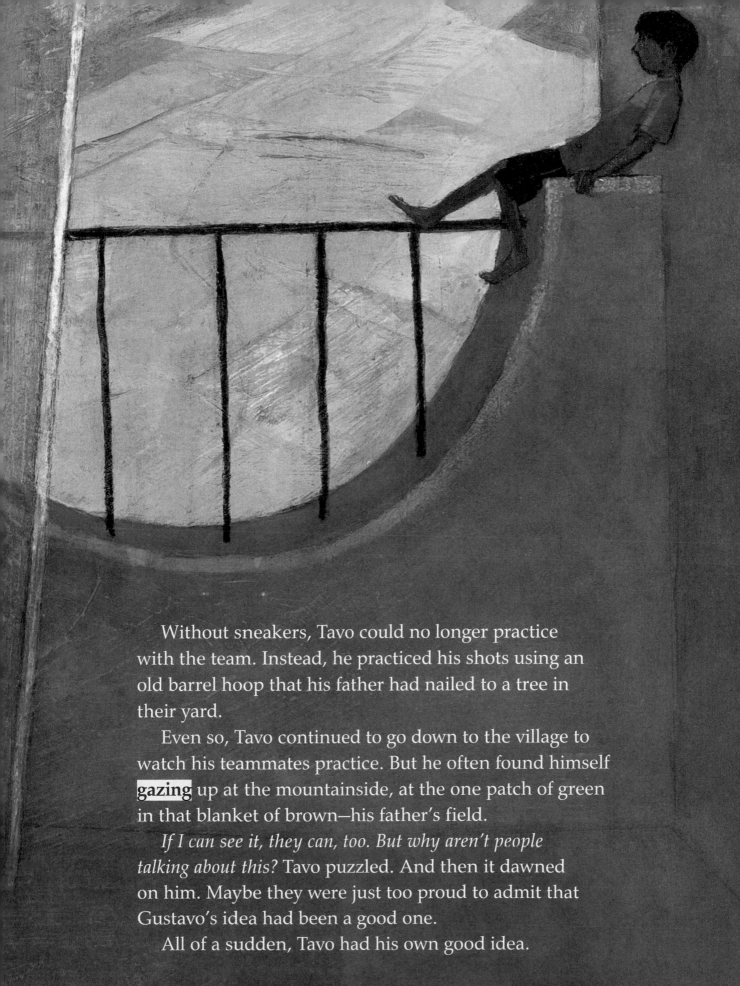

Without sneakers, Tavo could no longer practice with the team. Instead, he practiced his shots using an old barrel hoop that his father had nailed to a tree in their yard.

Even so, Tavo continued to go down to the village to watch his teammates practice. But he often found himself **gazing** up at the mountainside, at the one patch of green in that blanket of brown—his father's field.

If I can see it, they can, too. But why aren't people talking about this? Tavo puzzled. And then it dawned on him. Maybe they were just too proud to admit that Gustavo's idea had been a good one.

All of a sudden, Tavo had his own good idea.

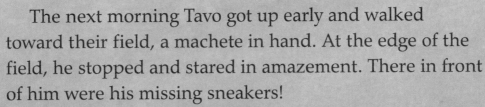

The next morning Tavo got up early and walked toward their field, a machete in hand. At the edge of the field, he stopped and stared in amazement. There in front of him were his missing sneakers!

The duct tape was gone, but so were the holes. His sneakers had been beautifully patched! He recognized the fabric and the silver thread.

"Señora Rosa!" he whispered aloud. He laced the sneakers on. And his feet began to tingle.

Tavo grabbed a cornstalk and cut it close to the ground. Then he raced down the mountain path, straight to the mayor's house. With the magic sneakers on his feet, he felt as if he could fly.

Though it was still early, Tavo eagerly knocked on the door. The mayor opened it, blinking sleepily in the morning light.

Tavo raised the stalk high. But he didn't say anything.

Then the mayor let out a sigh, his face softening.

"Yes, Tavo . . . yes. I see it. I believe it's time we all see your father's field."

For the next several weeks, Gustavo was much in demand helping the other villagers connect their own fields to the main *zanja*. And Tavo rejoined his teammates on the basketball court for the first game of the season.

From midcourt, Tavo could see his father, sitting in a place of honor next to the mayor.

Then the game began.

And what a game it was! One minute, Tavo's team was ahead, and the next minute, behind. At the end, the game was tied. It went into overtime. Then the ball was in Tavo's hands.

He planted himself, and crouched. He felt the tingling sensation in his feet shoot upward, through the muscles of his arms made so strong from shoveling. The ball soared toward the basket.

Sw-o-o-o-sh!

The villagers went wild.

"Tavo, Tavo! Bravo, Tavo!" They chanted in unison.

And he liked the sound of it. Tavo was a great basketball name!

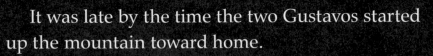

It was late by the time the two Gustavos started up the mountain toward home.

Gustavo looked over the moonlit fields high with corn. He stopped and put his hands on Tavo's shoulders.

"Son, it's time for new sneakers. What do you think?"

Tavo wiggled his toes. They still tingled with magic energy.

"No, Papa, these will do."

STOP AND CHECK

Reread Why doesn't Tavo want new shoes at the end of the story? Reread pages 454 and 455 to find the answer.

About the Author and Illustrator

Brian Meunier and his wife, Perky Edgerton, lived in a village in Oaxaca, Mexico. Their time there inspired them to write this story about Tavo and his shoes. Brian is also an artist and sculptor and teaches college students in Pennsylvania.

Perky Edgerton is a painter and a book illustrator. She worked on this story with her husband, Brian. The paintings she made for this story have a lot of energy, so they are a great fit for Brian's story.

Author's Purpose

What is the author's message in this story?

Respond to the Text

Summarize

Summarize the main events in *Bravo, Tavo!* The details from your Point of View chart may help you.

Details

↓

Point of View

Write

How does the author help you understand how Tavo's problems are connected to his father's problems? Use these sentence frames to organize your text evidence:

> The author uses descriptive words to...
> He uses dialogue to...
> This helps me understand that...

Make Connections

How does Tavo reuse what he already had?
ESSENTIAL QUESTION

Tell why it is important to reuse old things.
TEXT TO WORLD

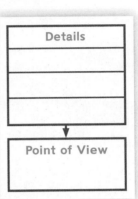

Trash into Art

One person's junk is another person's treasure. That is what some artists think. They look in garbage dumpsters or trash cans for old sheets of aluminum, plastic bottles, and computer parts. Alexander Calder, Miwa Koizumi (MI-wah koh-ee-ZOO-mee), and Marion C. Martinez are artists who have transformed junk into fantastic works of art!

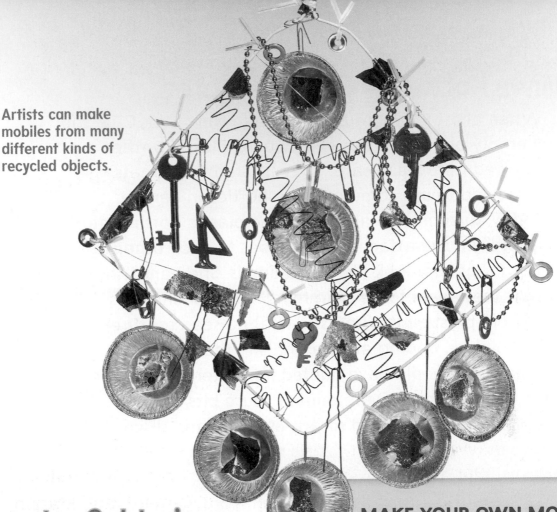

Artists can make mobiles from many different kinds of recycled objects.

Alexander Calder's Giant Mobiles

In the 1950s, the sculptor and artist Alexander Calder had a big problem. He wanted to build gigantic mobiles (MOH-beelz) from metal. A mobile is a moving sculpture. It hangs from a ceiling. It sways and moves when people touch it. Most metals were much too heavy to move the way Calder wanted.

Calder solved his problem by **recycling** aluminum from the bodies of old airplanes. The aluminum came in large sheets. It was easy to cut into interesting shapes. And it was light enough to move quickly. Calder reused the old metal to create his huge moving sculptures.

MAKE YOUR OWN MOBILE

Be an artist. Recycle some old materials to make a mobile.

Materials
wire hanger, string, scissors, old objects

1. Gather old objects that are light enough to hang from a string. Try old CDs, small plastic toys, parts of old plastic bottles, or paper cutouts.

2. Ask an adult to help you bend the hanger into the shape you want.

3. Keep the shape of the hook for hanging the mobile.

4. Cut different lengths of string.

5. Tie each object to one end of a string. Tie the other end of string to the hanger.

6. Hang the mobile up and give it a spin.

459

Miwa Koizumi's Sea Creatures

When artist Miwa Koizumi came to New York City, she saw empty plastic bottles everywhere. Plastic bottles overflowed from trash cans. They littered the streets. She decided to use some of these bottles in her art.

Today Koizumi cuts and melts the plastic bottles into shapes. Then she attaches the shapes to each other to create forms that look like sea animals. She hangs them so that they seem to be swimming. Koizumi changes bits of old plastic into fantastic floating sea creatures.

To Koizumi, finding art materials in the trash was only natural. People have hunted for materials to reuse since ancient times. Even animals reuse bits of junk. Birds build nests with old scraps of fabric and discarded materials. Why shouldn't artists search around outside for art materials?

Miwa Koizumi makes sculptures like these from old plastic bottles.

Marion C. Martinez's High-Tech Art

Almost twenty-five years ago, New Mexico artist Marion C. Martinez opened up her computer to fix it. She made a big discovery. The circuit boards and wires inside the machine were beautiful.

Martinez asked herself, "How can I use these amazing designs in my art?" Soon she began collecting computer circuit boards and other electronics from the trash. Martinez recycled these electronic parts. She made them into fabulous jewelry and wall sculptures. Now, the artist Marion Martinez is also helping the Earth by recycling. And she is turning computer parts into art. Now, that's real **conservation**!

Marion C. Martinez made this bear pin from old computer parts.

Every year, people throw away billions of plastic bottles. They toss out millions of tons of old electronics. They get rid of old machinery. Alex Calder, Miwa Koizumi, and Marion C. Martinez have helped recycle these bits of trash.

Make Connections

How do people reuse what they already have? ESSENTIAL QUESTION

What other articles and stories have you read about reusing old items? TEXT TO TEXT

Genre · Biography

Looking Up to ELLEN OCHOA

by Liane B. Onish

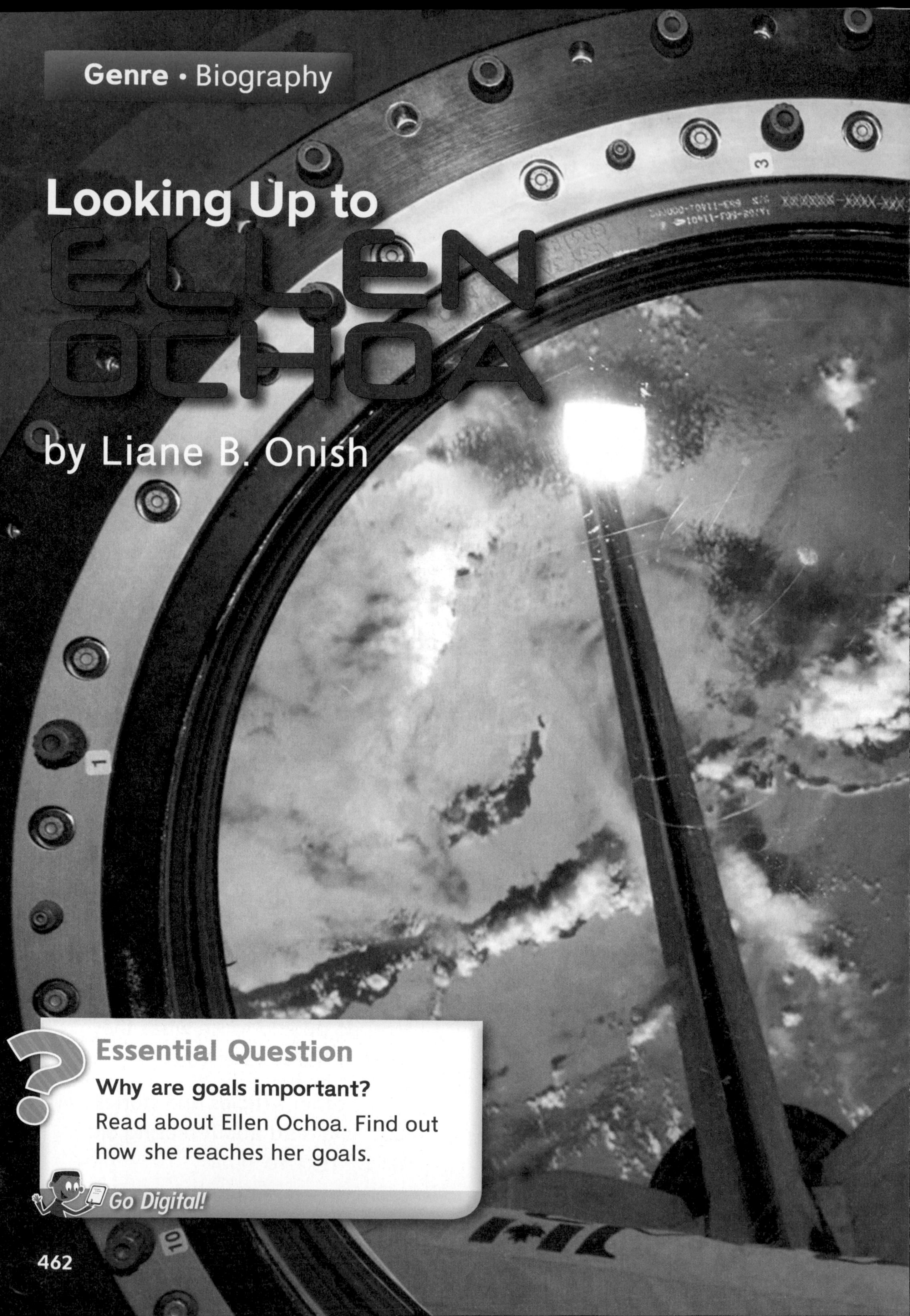

Essential Question

Why are goals important?

Read about Ellen Ochoa. Find out how she reaches her goals.

Go Digital!

Can you imagine what it would be like to look through the window of a spaceship into space? Ellen Ochoa can. As the first female Hispanic astronaut, Ellen knows exactly what that would be like. Her job has taken her into space four times, and now that she's back, she leads the Johnson Space Center in Houston, Texas. Her hard work and determination make her someone to look up to.

Ellen looks through the Earth observation window on the International Space Station.

NASA

Reaching for the Stars

Ellen Ochoa (uh-CHOH-ah) was born in California in 1958, the same year the space program began. Back then, only men became astronauts. Women were not allowed even to apply for the job. But in 1978, things changed. NASA began accepting women into their astronaut training program. Sally Ride was in that first class, and in June 1983, she became the first American woman to go into space.

It was Sally Ride's mission that inspired Ellen Ochoa to become an astronaut. But Ellen says that it was her mother who taught her how to get there. As a girl, Ellen learned that if she worked hard in school she could become whatever she dreamed of. While Ellen was studying at Stanford University, she decided to join the astronaut program. Most of the astronauts at that time were men. She wasn't a military pilot like many of them. Ellen wasn't chosen at first, but that didn't stop her. She wanted to go into space, and she knew this was a problem she could solve.

Ellen was a good math and science student.

"Don't be afraid to reach for the stars. I believe a good education can take you anywhere on Earth and beyond."
—Ellen Ochoa

WHAT IS NASA?

Do you know what NASA stands for? NASA is the National Aeronautics and Space Administration. It is a government organization that does more than send astronauts into space. Besides learning all they can about Earth and its neighbors, NASA scientists help teachers inspire and educate students who dream of going into space, just like Ellen.

Solving Problems

While at Stanford University, Ellen studied subjects related to space. She did **research** for several inventions that helped solve problems. One of her inventions helped guide robotic arms for work in space. Robotic arms work like human arms. They have parts that move like a shoulder, an elbow, and a wrist. They do jobs that are too hard or dangerous for people.

Many tasks in outer space require astronauts to use robotic arms. Ellen's experience with robotic arms helped her get into NASA's astronaut training program in 1990. But before Ellen could be an astronaut, she had one more problem to solve.

One of Ellen's inventions helps guide robotic arms.

STOP AND CHECK

Reread What accomplishment helped Ellen become an astronaut? Reread to find out.

NASA-MSFC

LAB1/C2-17

Training in Space

Once Ellen Ochoa was accepted into the astronaut training program, she had to get herself ready. It was not an easy task. Her strong background in math and science helped her do well in her new training classes. She also had to pass a physical exam.

During training, astronauts work on machines that get them used to working in space. One machine creates weightlessness conditions that astronauts feel in space.

"In training, things keep breaking, and problems have to be solved," Ellen says. "I was in training for three years before my first mission."

Ellen says weightlessness feels like swimming or scuba diving.

Space Work Is Teamwork

"An astronaut must be both a team player and a leader as well," Ellen says. She tells students, "You should get involved in activities where you work closely with other people. Working closely with others is an **essential** part of being an astronaut and solving problems in space."

First, there is the ground crew. They inspect and repair the shuttle before each mission. Next, Mission Control workers guide the astronauts through each moment of a mission and debrief them on procedures. They are responsible for knowing how equipment is working. They **communicate** with astronauts to check on how they feel.

STOP AND CHECK

Reread How did Ellen Ochoa train to be an astronaut? Reread to find out.

During a space flight, the teamwork continues. Ellen and the other astronauts work together to meet the goals of their mission. A space flight crew is like a sports team. The commander of the shuttle is the team captain. He or she makes the crucial decisions that have **serious** effects on a mission.

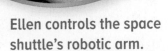

Ellen controls the space shuttle's robotic arm.

On her first mission in 1993, Ellen Ochoa was a mission **specialist**. Mission specialists are scientists who do experiments. Ellen used a robotic arm to send and get back a satellite that collected information about the Sun.

Then on her second mission in 1994, Ellen was the payload commander. The payload might be supplies or equipment, such as the robotic arm. She did satellite studies of the Sun's effect on Earth's climate, or weather.

The Mission Control Center in Houston supports NASA's spacecraft missions.

Astronauts have to work closely together in tight spaces.

To Space and Back

In 1999, Ellen was a mission specialist again on a space flight. She and the crew delivered supplies to the International Space Station. She "walked" in space for the first time during this mission.

Ellen has flown in space four times and spent almost 1,000 hours in orbit. On her last space flight in 2002, Ellen used the robotic arm to deliver supplies and help build new parts of the space station. But being on a space mission is not all work. Astronauts have free time to relax and do the things they enjoy on Earth. Some read or write. Some astronauts like to watch movies or listen to music. Ellen liked to play her flute in her spare time.

Before becoming an astronaut, Ellen was studying to be a professional musician.

An Interview with
ELLEN OCHOA

What is NASA training like?

In training, we prepare for anything that could happen on a space mission—anything that could go wrong.... Nothing has ever gone wrong on any of my missions, and our training helps us make sure that nothing will.... For my last mission, we trained for nine months before the actual flight.

Ellen Ochoa trained hard to become an astronaut.

How do you sleep on the space shuttle?

On my last mission... we slept in what can best be described as a sleeping bag with hooks. You would find a place to hook on to, and float in.

What advice would you give a third grader who wants to become an astronaut?

The opportunities I had were the result of having a good educational background. Strive for excellence and take what you are learning in school right now seriously. Have a **goal** and try to break your goal into small steps.

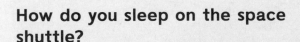

Women Who Counted

Long before NASA began letting women become astronauts, three African American women who loved math made a big contribution to America's space program. Their story was told in the book and film *Hidden Figures*.

Dorothy Vaughan, Mary Jackson, and Katherine Johnson worked for the National Advisory Committee for Aeronautics, or NACA. NACA was what the United States space program was called before NASA. Dorothy joined NACA in 1943, Mary joined in 1951, and Katherine joined in 1953. All three women studied math. They were hired to use their math skills to plan flight paths for early rockets and satellites.

Then, in 1958 when NASA was created, Dorothy, Mary, and Katherine continued to use math to help America's space program. They played a major role in NASA's success.

Thanks to these women and other people like them, NASA has launched countless satellites into space, roamed the surface of Mars, and used telescopes to learn about distant galaxies.

Like Ellen Ochoa, Dorothy, Mary, and Katherine worked hard to reach their goals.

Dorothy Vaughan

Mary Jackson

Katherine Johnson used her math skills when she worked for NASA.

(bkgd)NASA-MSFC; (r)Smith Collection/Gado/Archive Photos/Getty Images; (c)NASA Langley Research Center; (b)NASA

Ellen Ochoa encourages girls to reach for the stars at an annual event at the Johnson Space Center.

Ellen says it takes diligence, determination, and teamwork to be an astronaut.

Ellen Ochoa Today

Every day Ellen Ochoa uses what she learned as an astronaut to help her be successful. In 2007 Ellen became the deputy director of the Johnson Space Center. Then in 2013, she was promoted to director.

As director of the space center, Ellen believes that teamwork is the key to keeping the space program moving. She says that her training and experiences as an astronaut help her to do that. So whether Ellen is in a meeting, talking with students and teachers, or helping astronauts accomplish something is space, she encourages teamwork. For Ellen, working together is that important.

Ellen likes that every day she is reminded about what a special opportunity it was to be in space. She likes that there are five schools in the United States named after her. And she likes telling students and visitors to the space center how she solved the problem of becoming an astronaut and got to go into space.

"It was an amazing experience being up in space."
—Ellen Ochoa

STOP AND CHECK

Summarize How does Ellen feel about teamwork? Tell the details you learned in this selection.

(t)NASA/Bill Ingalls; (b)NASA

471

ABOUT THE AUTHOR

Liane B. Onish
is a writer and teacher
with a goal. She wants to help
kids learn in fun and exciting ways.
She has taught students in preschool
through fifth grade. She has worked as a
writer and editor for children's television
programs and educational publishing
companies. She now writes
children's books, magazines,
games, and classroom
materials.

Author's Purpose
Why do you think that the
author included the interview
with Ellen Ochoa?

RESPOND TO THE TEXT

Summarize

Summarize the important events in Ellen Ochoa's story. The details from your Problem and Solution chart may help you.

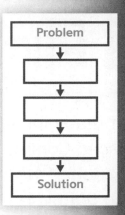

Write

How do the text features in Ellen Ochoa's biography help you understand how she reached her goals? Use these sentence frames to help organize your text evidence.

> The author uses photographs and captions to . . .
> The sidebars help me understand . . .
> I know Ellen Ochoa reached her goals because the author . . .

Make Connections

Tell how goals helped Ellen Ochoa to become an astronaut. ESSENTIAL QUESTION

Tell why it is important for people to set goals. TEXT TO WORLD

A Flight to Lunar City

"Get ready for landing," announced Commander Buckley.

"Fantastic!" whispered Maria, clinging tightly to her robot pooch. She could see the grey dusty surface of the Moon out the lunar lander's window.

Going to the Moon had been Maria's **goal** since she was five. The dream had **motivated** Maria to enter a science project in the National Space Contest. She had invented Robbie, the robot dog, as her science project. He was the perfect Moon pet. Maria and Robbie had won first prize—a trip to Lunar City, the first settlement on the Moon.

Now they were almost there! Robbie wriggled and squirmed. "Settle down!" Maria scolded. Sometimes Robbie was awfully wild, like a real puppy. Maria was thinking about adjusting his Personality Profile Program to make him a little calmer.

Suddenly there was a large bang. The lunar lander jerked forward and turned upside down. Then it rolled sideways. The lights on the ship dimmed. The emergency lights came on.

Illustration: Colin Mier

474

"The power is off!" gasped Commander Buckley. "We're stuck."

"Oh, no!" cried Maria.

"Woof!" yapped Robbie, as he squirmed and wiggled in Maria's arms.

"Hold on!" said Commander Buckley. She pushed buttons and touched the control screen. She tried to contact the landing station. Nothing worked. "This control stick is broken!" said Commander Buckley in a panic. "We can't move ahead." She tried to push the control stick into the right position for landing, but it would not budge.

Just then Robbie jumped out of Maria's arms and leaped across the landing ship. He jumped onto the stick with all four paws and growled fiercely. He tugged and chewed on it. "Stop!" cried Maria.

All at once, the control stick shifted into position. The lights came back on. The landing ship whooshed forward.

"Robbie, you did it!" laughed Commander Buckley. "Good dog!" She handed Robbie back to Maria. "Now we can land on the Moon."

Maria smiled proudly. Robbie was the best robot dog ever!

Make Connections

What was Maria's goal? What did she do to reach it? **ESSENTIAL QUESTION**

What other people with goals have you read about? How are they like Maria? How are they different? **TEXT TO TEXT**

Essential Question

How do you decide what is important?

Read about how King Midas discovers what he values most.

Go Digital!

476

KING MIDAS AND THE GOLDEN TOUCH

by Margaret H. Lippert

illustrated by Gail Armstrong

CHARACTERS

Storyteller

King Midas

Princess Marigold, King Midas's daughter

Nikolas, King Midas's servant

Rosie, a gardener's daughter

Rex, King Midas's horse

Mysterious Traveler

SCENE ONE

In the palace. Early morning.

Storyteller: The story of King Midas takes place long ago and far away, in the country of Greece. King Midas **possessed** more gold than anyone in the world. One morning, he is counting his gold in his treasure chamber.

King Midas *(tying the last bag of gold)*: So much gold. So much wealth. I love it!

Marigold: *(calling from off stage)* Papa! Where are you?

King Midas: *(calling)* Here, Marigold.

(Marigold enters.)

Marigold: Counting your gold again? You spend more time with your gold than with me.

King Midas: I'm locking it up because I'm leaving on a journey.

Marigold: I'll miss you, Papa.

King Midas: I'll miss you too, Marigold.

Marigold: More than your gold?

King Midas: *(laughing)* Of course! I have a roomful of gold, but only one Marigold! *(He looks out the window)* I see your friend Rosie is playing in the garden. Run along now. I'll say goodbye before I leave.

(Marigold exits.)

King Midas: *(calling)* Nikolas!

(Nikolas enters.)

Nikolas: Yes, your Majesty?

King Midas: Saddle my horse.

Nikolas: As you wish.

(Nikolas exits. King Midas puts the bags of gold into the trunk and locks it. He exits.)

SCENE TWO

Storyteller: A few minutes later, in the palace rose garden, Rosie is jumping rope.

Rosie: *(chanting in rhythm to her jumping)*
Roses are red, Violets are blue,
Sugar is sweet, And I AM TOO!
Roses are red, Violets are blue,
Sugar is sweet, And —

(Marigold runs in, twirling her jump rope.)

Marigold and **Rosie**: I AM TOO!

(They stop jumping and Marigold stoops down.)

Rosie: What are you doing?

Marigold: Hunting for a stone to give Papa.

Rosie: *(picking up a stone)* How about this one?

Marigold: I want to find one that looks like a heart.

(*Marigold picks up several stones and tosses them down again, then picks up a heart shaped stone and shows it to Rosie.*)

Marigold: I found one!

(*King Midas enters. Marigold runs to him and gives him the stone.*)

Marigold: Here, Papa. A heart, to remind you that I love you.

(*King Midas puts the stone in his pocket.*)

King Midas: Thank you, my darling.

(*Nikolas enters.*)

Nikolas: Rex is saddled, Your Majesty.

King Midas: (*to Marigold*) I must go now.

Marigold: Is it really **necessary**?

King Midas: Yes. (*He picks a rose and gives it to Marigold.*) But here is a gift for you. I will return in seven days, before it wilts.

Marigold: (*smelling the rose*) Mmmmm. I love the smell, almost as much as I love you.

King Midas: Farewell, my daughter.

Marigold: Farewell, Papa.

(*King Midas and Nikolas exit.*)

Marigold: (*to Rosie*) I'll put this rose in a vase by my bed. Come with me.

(*Marigold and Rosie exit.*)

SCENE THREE

Storyteller: One week later, early in the morning, King Midas rides Rex through a forest. He is returning home from his journey.

(Traveler moans offstage.)

King Midas: Hark! Someone is hurt.

(Traveler moans again.)

King Midas: *(stops and looks around.)* Am I dreaming?

(Traveler moans louder.)

Rex: *(Neighs)*

King Midas: *(patting Rex)* Calm down, Rex. Don't be **alarmed**.

(Traveler enters limping and falls to the ground.)

King Midas: What ails you, Traveler?

Traveler: My leg. I fell off my horse.

King Midas: You need help. My palace is just over the hill.

Traveler: My horse ran away.

King Midas: Then ride with me.

(King Midas and Traveler ride Rex together.)

Rex: *(Neighs.)*

King Midas: Good boy, Rex. We're almost home.

(They exit.)

SCENE FOUR

Storyteller: Soon they arrive back at the rose garden.

(*King Midas and Traveler dismount.*)

King Midas: Here we are. I'll call my servant.

Traveler: Wait. As a **reward** for your kindness to a poor Traveler, I will grant you a wish.

King Midas: You grant wishes?

Traveler: Make a wish, and see if it comes true.

King Midas: Well, I love gold! So I wish that everything I touch turns to gold!

Traveler: Your wish is granted.

King Midas: Really? I'll try it on the stone Marigold gave me! (*He takes the heart stone out of his pocket. It turns to gold.*)

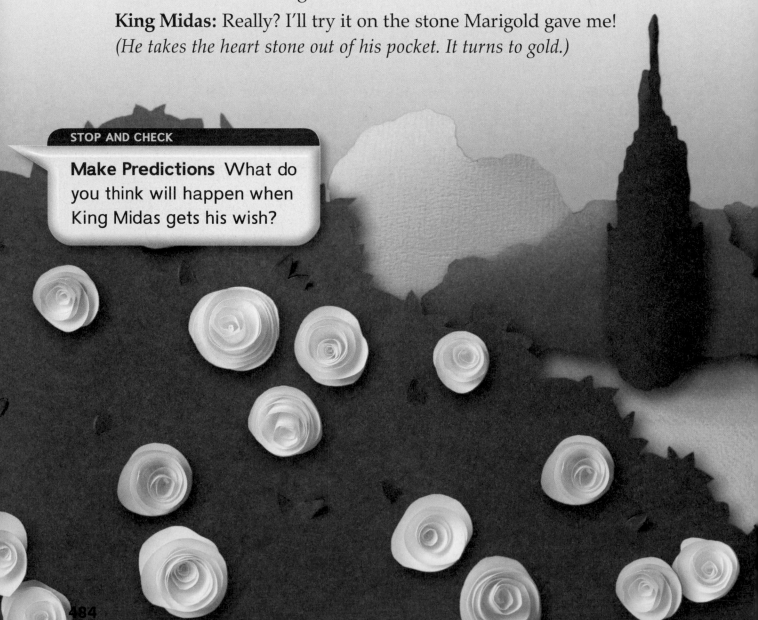

STOP AND CHECK

Make Predictions What do you think will happen when King Midas gets his wish?

484

King Midas: Incredible! This stone has turned to gold! *(He picks a rose. It turns to gold.)* Fantastic! This is gold too! What a perfect gift for Marigold!

Marigold: *(offstage)* Papa will be home today, Rosie. We can watch for him over the garden wall.

(Marigold and Rosie enter. King Midas holds the rose out to Marigold.)

King Midas: Look, my daughter. A gold rose for you!

(Marigold's happy smile turns to shocked surprise.)

Marigold: Oh Papa, how terrible. *(She smells it.)* It doesn't smell sweet.

485

King Midas: Terrible? No, it is WONDERFUL! I can turn everything to gold! *(He reaches out to take her hand. She freezes in place as if turned to gold.)* Oh no! My precious daughter has turned to gold!

Traveler: As you wished. You said, "I wish EVERYTHING I touch will turn to gold."

King Midas: But—

Traveler: No buts. You wished, and your wish came true. You were so **obsessed** with gold that all you wanted was more.

King Midas: *(He gives an anguished cry.)* But now all I want is Marigold, alive again. I wish I could undo my foolish wish.

Traveler: I can see by your **anguish** that now you realize true wealth is not gold, but life. So I will grant you one more wish.

King Midas: I wish that everything I have turned to gold becomes real again.

Traveler: Your wish is granted. Fill that watering can with water from the pond. Pour it on all you wish to be real again.

(King Midas fills the watering can and pours water over Marigold. She comes back to life.)

STOP AND CHECK

Confirm Predictions What happened when King Midas got his wish? Was your prediction correct?

487

King Midas: Oh how wonderful! You're alive again!

(King Midas takes her hands and joyfully swings her around.)

Marigold: What happened, Papa? Did I fall in the pond?

King Midas: *(laughing)* Oh no, my treasure. Come inside and dry off, and I will tell you the story.

Marigold: What story, Papa?

King Midas: The story of how I learned that my obsession with gold almost cost me what is truly precious. *(He takes the heart stone out of his pocket and pours water over it.)* I never noticed before how beautiful a real stone is. *(He pours water over the gold rose and smells it.)* I never appreciated how sweet a rose smells.

(Nikolas enters.)

Nikolas: Breakfast is ready, Your Majesty.

King Midas: *(to Traveler)* Come, join us at breakfast.

Traveler: Thank you, but I must be on my way. My leg is better and I have other wishes to grant. Farewell.

(He exits.)

King Midas: *(calling after him)* Farewell, and thank you!

Marigold: "Thank you?" For what, Papa?

King Midas: For showing me what is more valuable than gold. At breakfast I will tell you the story of my foolish wish, and how you got wet without falling into the pond!

(King Midas takes Marigold's hand, and Marigold takes Rosie's hand.)

Marigold: Rosie, come with me to hear Papa's story.

Storyteller: So ends the story of King Midas and the Golden Touch.

(All exit.)

STOP AND CHECK

Summarize What happened at the end of the story? Tell the important events in order.

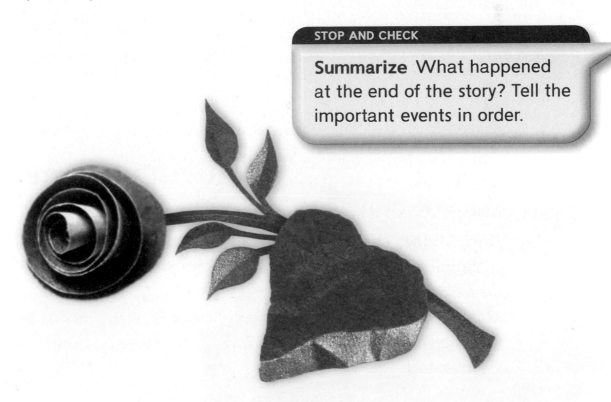

ABOUT THE AUTHOR AND ILLUSTRATOR

Margaret H. Lippert is a teacher, a storyteller, and an award-winning author of children's books. She has traveled around the world sharing stories. Margaret has written many books in which she retells folktales and stories from different cultures. She was excited to write a play about King Midas because his story is one of her favorite myths. She had fun naming the characters in the play. She says, "I thought a king who loved gold might name his daughter Marigold."

Gail Armstrong has been a paper sculptor for more than twenty years. She uses the traditional craft of paper folding, or origami, to create people, animals, flowers, and castles, then turns these paper sculptures into illustrations for books on a computer. Gail says, "I find it fascinating how something as ordinary as a piece of paper can be transformed with a simple cut or fold."

AUTHOR'S PURPOSE
What message was the author trying to tell in this play?

490

Respond to the Text

Summarize

What are the most important events in this story? Information from your Theme chart may help you summarize.

Detail
↓
Detail
↓
Detail
↓
Theme

Write

How does the author help you understand the theme of this play? Use these sentence frames to help you organize text evidence.

> The author uses sensory language to describe how King Midas . . .
> She also compares . . .
> This helps me understand the theme because . . .

Make Connections

What did King Midas value at the beginning of the play? How did his feelings change by the end?
ESSENTIAL QUESTION

Why is it important to value family and friends? TEXT TO WORLD

Genre · Realistic Fiction

Compare Texts
Read about a boy who learns to value something different.

Carlos's Gift

Carlos wanted a puppy in the worst way. He dreamed about puppies—big ones, little ones, spotted ones, frisky ones. Now it was his birthday, and Carlos had one thing on his mind. A puppy! When Mama handed him a flat, square box, Carlos almost started to cry.

It was a book about caring for dogs.

Papa smiled, "You need to learn how to care for a puppy before you get one."

Carlos read the book that night. He found a photograph of the exact kind of bulldog puppy that he craved. He eagerly showed Mama the next morning.

"That kind of dog is too expensive," said Mama. Noticing his crestfallen expression, she added, "Try earning some money. Ask our neighbors if they have jobs you can do."

Mama's suggestion made Carlos more optimistic. He could save up for the puppy of his dreams!

After two weeks, Carlos had saved twenty-six dollars. It seemed like a **treasure**, but it was not enough to buy a puppy. Then Papa pointed out a poster at the store: City Animal Shelter Needs Your Help!

"The shelter takes care of abandoned pets," Papa said. "Carlos, you can learn a lot by working there. Let's visit."

At the shelter, Miss Jones, the manager said,"We only take volunteers who work for free. All our money is devoted to helping animals."

"You'll learn a lot about dogs," Papa urged Carlos.

Carlos's shoulders drooped. How was he ever going to accumulate enough money for a puppy? Finally, he agreed to give it a try.

Carlos started working at the shelter on Saturday. His assignment was sweeping. Afterwards, the dogs scampered out to play. One dog named Pepper had a funny curly tail that never stopped wagging. She was fully grown but as playful as a puppy. When Pepper leaped in the pile of sticks and leaves that Carlos had just swept up, he laughed.

Carlos went to the shelter every weekend. He began to treasure his time with the dogs, especially Pepper. One day Carlos asked why Pepper was still at the shelter.

Miss Jones sighed, "We've had trouble finding a home for Pepper. Most people don't want such an energetic dog."

Carlos suddenly realized he didn't want a bulldog puppy. He wanted Pepper. "I wish I could buy her," he replied.

Miss Jones smiled, "You can't buy her, but you can adopt her. There's a fifteen-dollar fee, and your parents must complete a form proving that you can give Pepper a good home."

Both Mama and Papa agreed that Carlos had learned enough about dogs to adopt Pepper. Carlos was so thrilled that he ran all the way to the shelter to get Pepper.

Carlos used part of his hard-earned **wealth** to pay the fee. And he decided to donate the rest of his puppy fund to aid more shelter dogs. "I thought I wanted a bulldog puppy, but I got Pepper instead." Pepper barked with joy.

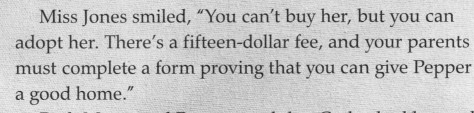

Make Connections

? What does Carlos value at the story's beginning? How have his feelings changed at the end of the story? ESSENTIAL QUESTION

What other stories have you read about how people changed their values? TEXT TO TEXT

Genre • Poetry

Essential Question

What makes you laugh?

Read this **humorous** poem about a lively classroom pet.

Go Digital!

Ollie's Escape

Ollie escaped in the classroom,
and that was an awful mistake.
It would have been folly
to try and catch Ollie,
since Ollie's a seven-foot snake.

He wiggled his way toward the teacher,
who jumped on her desk with a scream.
Faster and faster,
he squiggled right past her.
Old Ollie was picking up steam!

The rest of us ran for the closet
as Ollie slid right out the door.
We heard a loud squall
as he entered the hall.
He's a difficult snake to ignore.

He slithered his way to the office
as teachers jumped out of his way.
But Principal Poole
is the boss of the school.
We wondered just what he would say.

Illustration: Sholto Walker

It didn't take long for an answer.
In fact, he decided to scoot.
He burst through the door with a terrified roar
and a seven-foot snake in pursuit!

Ollie the snake was excited,
and we, of course, thought it was fun
to see teachers hiding
while Ollie was sliding
and Principal Poole on the run.

They ordered us out of the building,
and somebody called the police.
There were doctors and vets
and men with big nets
to make sure the problem would cease.

But Ollie, at last, was exhausted.
He snaked his way back to his den.
When they searched all around,
he was finally found—
curled up, asleep, in his pen.

—*Dave Crawley*

498

Respond to the Text

Summarize

Use important details from "Ollie's Escape" to summarize the poem. Information in your Point of View chart may help you.

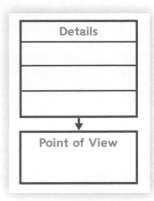

Details

Point of View

Write

How does the poet use words and phrases to help you understand how the characters in the poem feel about Ollie? Use these sentence frames to organize text evidence.

The poet uses sensory language to . . .
His words and phrases help me visualize . . .
This is important because it helps me understand . . .

Make Connections

What did the poet do to make you laugh?
ESSENTIAL QUESTION

What other kinds of things make people laugh?
TEXT TO WORLD

The Gentleman Bookworm

There once was a Gentleman Bookworm
Ate his words with a fork and a spoon.
    When friends crawled down
    From Book End Town,
He offered them *Goodnight, Moon*.

He fed them *The Wind in the Willows*
And a page out of *Charlotte's Web*.
    They were eating bizarre
    Where the Wild Things Are,
When one of the guestworms said,

500

''How sinfully rich and delicious!
Why should anyone bother to cook?
 You've done it, dear boy!
 Now sit down and enjoy
A bite of this poetry book!"

Having dined on the Table of Contents,
A worm, wiggling up to the host,
 Said, "When do we eat?"
 "Ah, *bon appétit!*"
Cried the Gentleman Bookworm. "A toast!

"Here's a bowl of my favorite verses
And a dish of ridiculous rhyme!
 But might I suggest . . . ?"
 Said the host to the guest,
"Chew them slowly. One line at a time!"

So the worm waved her postage-stamp napkin.
Curled up in a little round ball,
 She proceeded to swallow
 The poems that follow
Until she had swallowed them all.

—*J. Patrick Lewis*

Copyright © 1999 by J. Patrick Lewis. First appeared in The Bookworm's Feast, published by Dial. Reprinted by permission of Curtis Brown, Ltd.

Make Connections

? Why is a poem like "The Gentleman
Bookworm" good **entertainment?**
ESSENTIAL QUESTION

What other narrative poems have you
read? How are the poems similar?
How are they different? TEXT TO TEXT

Alligators and Crocodiles

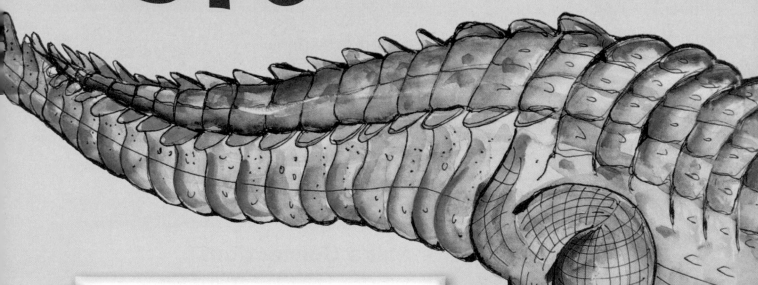

by Gail Gibbons

Something glides slowly through the water, barely making a ripple. It is well hidden and looks like a bumpy drifting log. Two eyes and a snout appear above the water. It is an alligator or a crocodile.

ALLIGATOR

CROCODILE

All reptiles are cold-blooded animals. In order to survive, they must keep their body temperature from getting too hot or too cold. They do this by moving to a cooler or warmer place.

Alligators and crocodiles are members of a group of reptiles called crocodilians (krok-uh-DILL-ee-ans). They are the closest living relatives of dinosaurs and the world's largest reptiles.

PALEONTOLOGISTS are scientists who learn about ancient life by studying fossils, the remains of a plant or animal that lived at least ten thousand years ago.

EXTINCT means no longer in existence.

According to paleontologists (pay-lee-on-TOL-o-jists), alligators, crocodiles, and dinosaurs lived on Earth about 230 million years ago. About 65 million years ago dinosaurs became extinct, but alligators and crocodiles continued to live.

WHERE ALLIGATORS AND CROCODILES LIVE

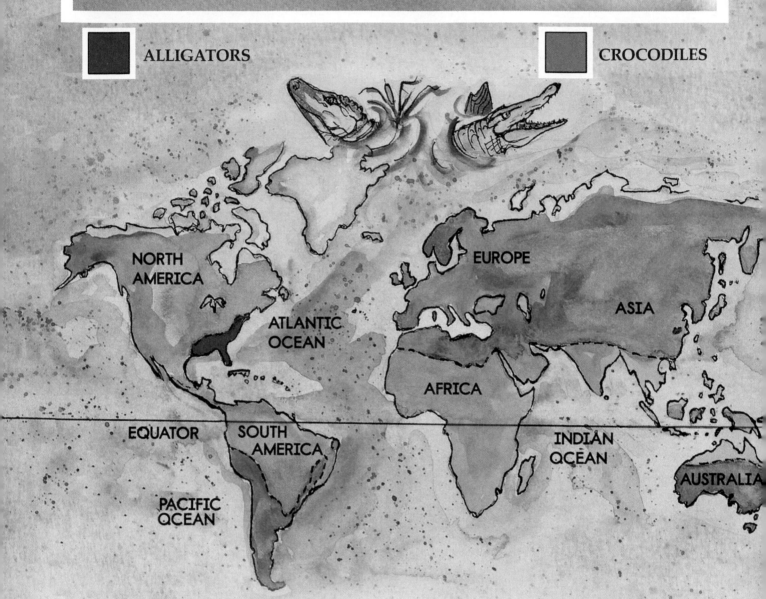

■ ALLIGATORS

■ CROCODILES

NORTH AMERICA

EUROPE

ATLANTIC OCEAN

ASIA

AFRICA

EQUATOR

SOUTH AMERICA

INDIAN OCEAN

PACIFIC OCEAN

AUSTRALIA

The word "crocodile" comes from the word *krokodeilos*, (kro-KO-day-los), which means "lizard" in Greek. The word "alligator" comes from *el lagarto* (L la-GAR-toe), which means "the lizard" in Spanish.

There are two different kinds of alligators and fourteen different kinds of crocodiles. The only area **inhabited** by both alligators and crocodiles is the southern tip of Florida and the Florida Keys.

WHERE AMERICAN ALLIGATORS AND CROCODILES LIVE IN THE UNITED STATES

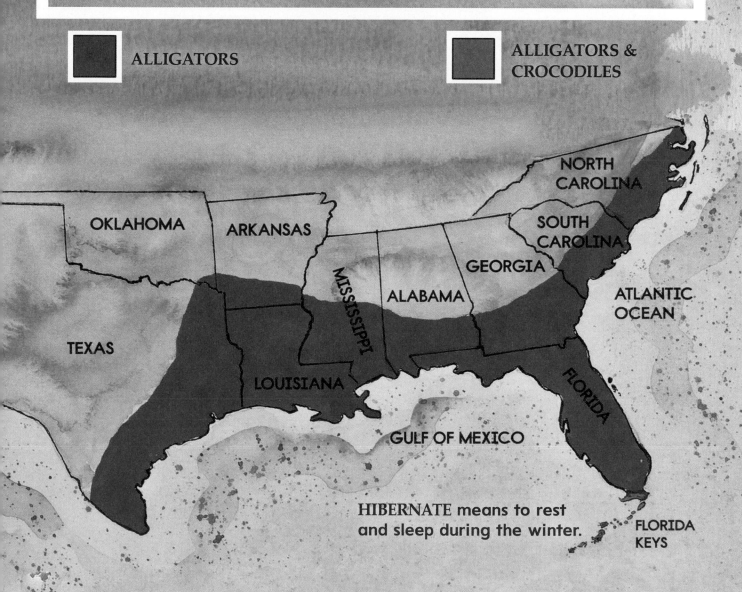

■ ALLIGATORS

■ ALLIGATORS & CROCODILES

NORTH CAROLINA

SOUTH CAROLINA

GEORGIA

OKLAHOMA

ARKANSAS

MISSISSIPPI

ALABAMA

ATLANTIC OCEAN

TEXAS

LOUISIANA

FLORIDA

GULF OF MEXICO

HIBERNATE means to rest and sleep during the winter.

FLORIDA KEYS

Alligators and crocodiles usually live in climates where the water and air temperatures are warm all year long. Some alligators live in cooler climates where they must hibernate if it gets too cold.

STOP AND CHECK

Reread Where do crocodiles and alligators live together? Reread page 508 to find the answer.

THE DIFFERENCES BETWEEN AN AMERICAN ALLIGATOR . . .

The HEAD, BACK, and TAIL are DARK GRAY or BLACK.

WIDE, ROUNDED SNOUT

NOSTRILS

WIDE HEAD

SENSORY PITS on head only

EAR SLITS

BACK

THICK, SKIN-COVERED BONY PLATES

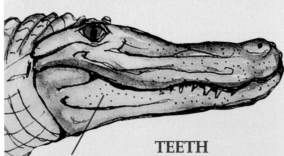

LONG, STRONG TAIL

LEG

KNEE

NECK

EYE

MOUTH

TONGUE

STOMACH

FOUR WEBBED TOES on each BACK FOOT

FIVE WEBBED TOES on each FRONT FOOT

AN AMERICAN ALLIGATOR'S MOUTH AND TEETH

STRONG JAWS

TEETH
Only TOP TEETH can be seen when jaws are closed.

LONG, STRONG TAIL

AN AMERICAN CROCODILE'S MOUTH AND TEETH

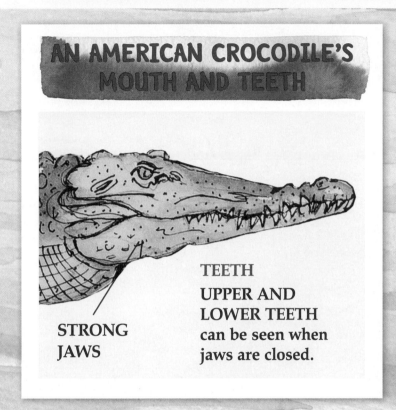

STRONG
JAWS

TEETH
UPPER AND
LOWER TEETH
can be seen when
jaws are closed.

NARROW HEAD

The HEAD, BACK, and TAIL
are TAN or GREENISH GRAY.

NARROW,
LONG SNOUT

THICK, SKIN-COVERED
BONY PLATES

SENSORY PITS
all over body

NOSTRILS

BACK

EAR SLITS

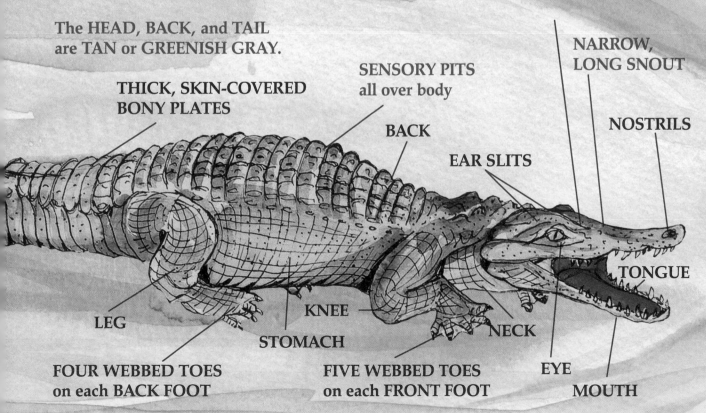

TONGUE

LEG

KNEE

STOMACH

NECK

EYE

FOUR WEBBED TOES
on each BACK FOOT

FIVE WEBBED TOES
on each FRONT FOOT

MOUTH

CARNIVORES are animals that eat meat.

Alligators and crocodiles each have about sixty pointed teeth. When they lose a tooth, a new tooth takes its place. They can grow about three thousand new teeth during their lives.

Alligators and crocodiles are carnivores. To catch their prey, they may stay perfectly still. When an animal comes near . . . SNAP! The animal is grabbed in a split second. Alligators and crocodiles may also swim slowly and quietly to their **unaware** prey and attack.

Cold-blooded animals do not eat as often as warm-blooded animals.

Young alligators and crocodiles usually feed on small prey such as fish, frogs, and birds, using their powerful jaws and sharp teeth. Larger, older alligators and crocodiles may eat big animals such as raccoons and deer. Often they grab their prey and hold its nose underwater until the animal drowns. Also, they may leap to catch their prey. They eat by ripping the animal apart and swallowing the pieces whole.

STOP AND CHECK

Reread What do alligators and crocodiles eat? Reread to find the answer.

ALLIGATORS AND CROCODILES LIVE IN THE WATER . . .

They can swim up to 6 miles (9.6 kilometers) an hour.

They can stay underwater for as long as two hours.

Alligators and crocodiles are good swimmers and spend most of their time in the water. They use their powerful, swishing tails to move forward. They are able to steer using their tails and back legs. By tucking in all four legs they are able to swim faster.

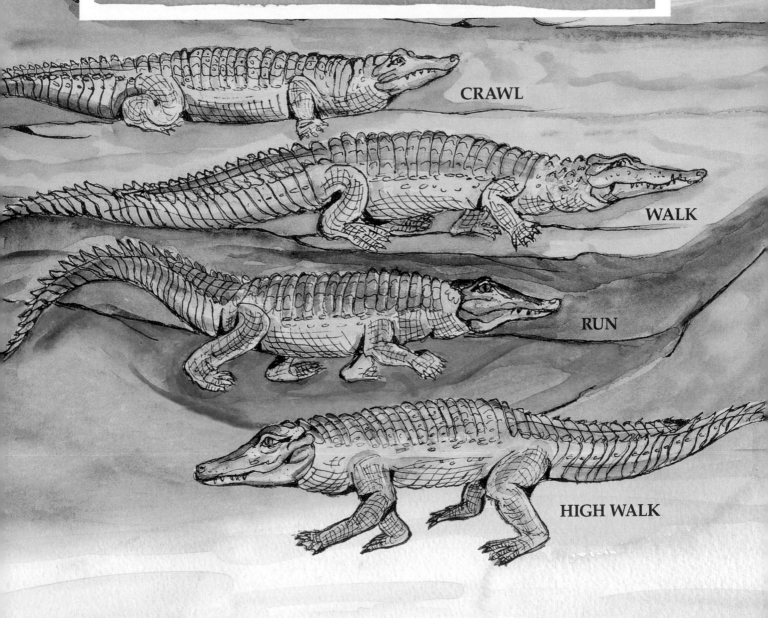

. . . AND ON THE LAND.

CRAWL

WALK

RUN

HIGH WALK

They can crawl, walk, and run.
Sometimes they walk with their bodies high
off the ground. This is called the "high walk."

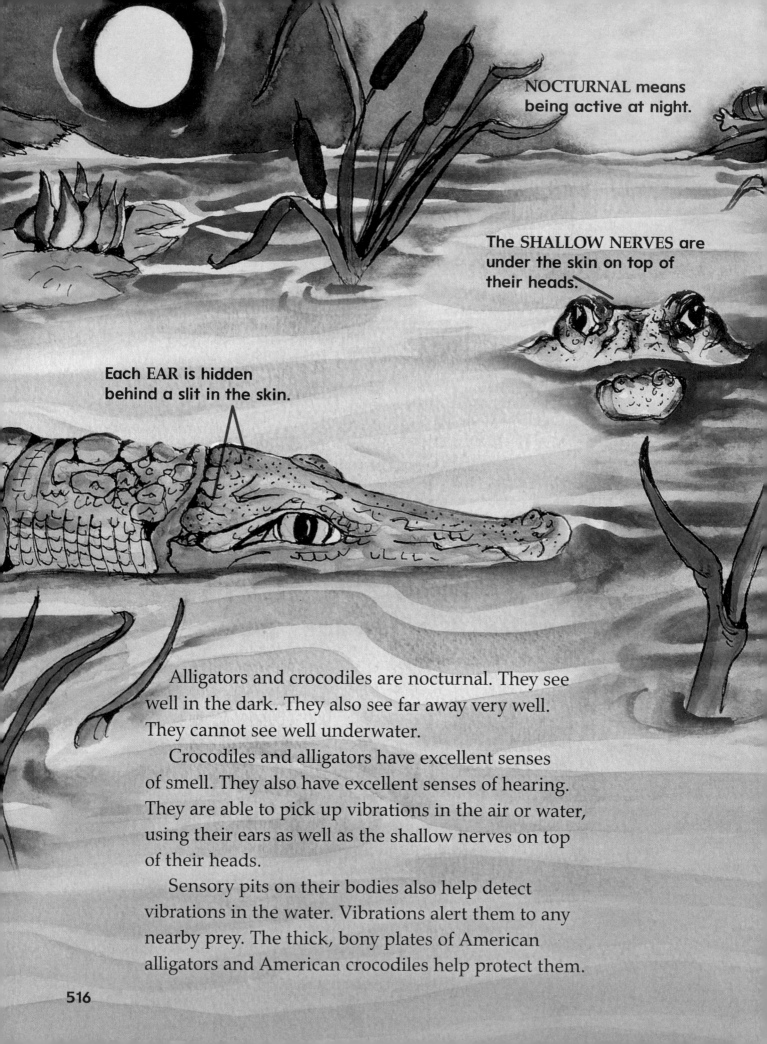

NOCTURNAL means being active at night.

The SHALLOW NERVES are under the skin on top of their heads.

Each EAR is hidden behind a slit in the skin.

Alligators and crocodiles are nocturnal. They see well in the dark. They also see far away very well. They cannot see well underwater.

Crocodiles and alligators have excellent senses of smell. They also have excellent senses of hearing. They are able to pick up vibrations in the air or water, using their ears as well as the shallow nerves on top of their heads.

Sensory pits on their bodies also help detect vibrations in the water. Vibrations alert them to any nearby prey. The thick, bony plates of American alligators and American crocodiles help protect them.

Alligators and crocodiles can make roaring, grumbling, and hissing sounds when they are protecting their territory. They will puff out their necks to show that they are ready to fight.

During mating season, males and females communicate by making grunts, barks, and low, rumbling sounds. Often they rub snouts, blow bubbles on the water's surface, and swim together in circles. Sometimes they will make sounds by slapping the surface of the water to attract a mate.

AN AMERICAN ALLIGATOR'S NEST

The female lays about forty-five eggs on a bed of leaves and grasses. She then completely covers them with a mound made of leaves, grasses, and mud. The mound is about 6 feet (1.8 meters) wide.

AN AMERICAN CROCODILE'S NEST

The female digs a hole in the ground and lays about fifty eggs. She covers each layer and the top with sand.

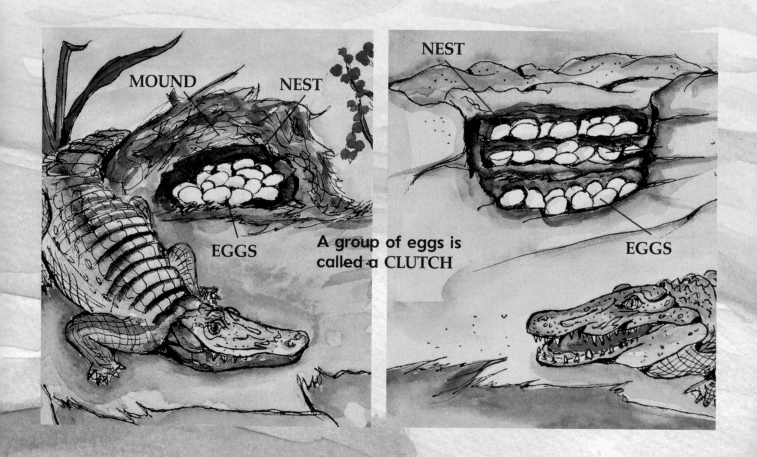

MOUND NEST

EGGS

A group of eggs is called a CLUTCH

NEST

EGGS

A few weeks later the females lay their eggs in nests, where the eggs will be kept warm and protected. Mother alligators and crocodiles are always on the alert, guarding their nests to protect their young from any egg-eating animals, such as skunks and raccoons.

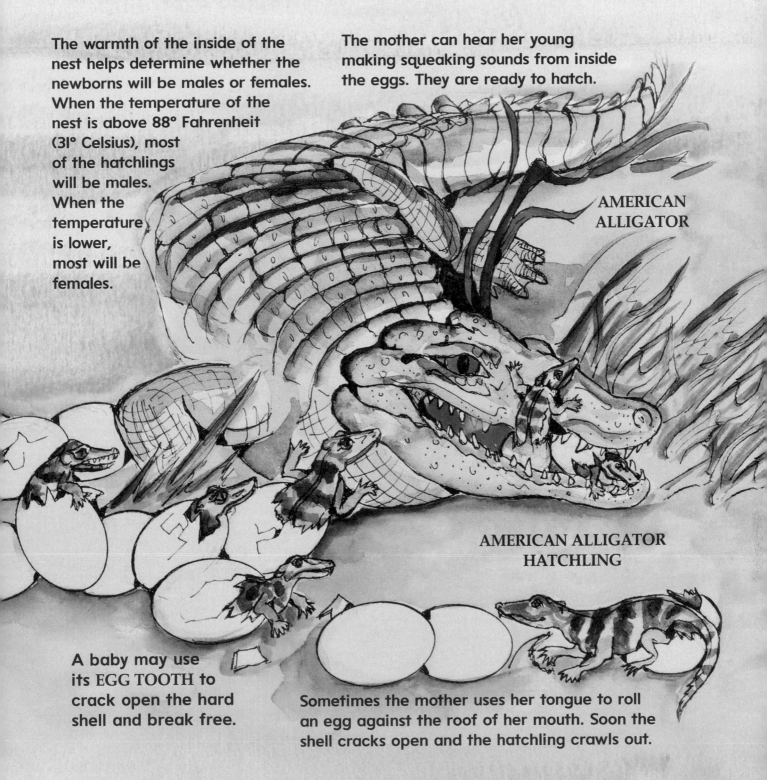

The warmth of the inside of the nest helps determine whether the newborns will be males or females. When the temperature of the nest is above 88° Fahrenheit (31° Celsius), most of the hatchlings will be males. When the temperature is lower, most will be females.

The mother can hear her young making squeaking sounds from inside the eggs. They are ready to hatch.

AMERICAN ALLIGATOR

AMERICAN ALLIGATOR HATCHLING

A baby may use its EGG TOOTH to crack open the hard shell and break free.

Sometimes the mother uses her tongue to roll an egg against the roof of her mouth. Soon the shell cracks open and the hatchling crawls out.

Usually it takes about sixty-five days before the alligator and crocodile eggs begin to hatch. Newborns are called hatchlings.

Most hatchlings are about 10 inches (25.4 centimeters) long. Within minutes of hatching, their mother takes them to the water.

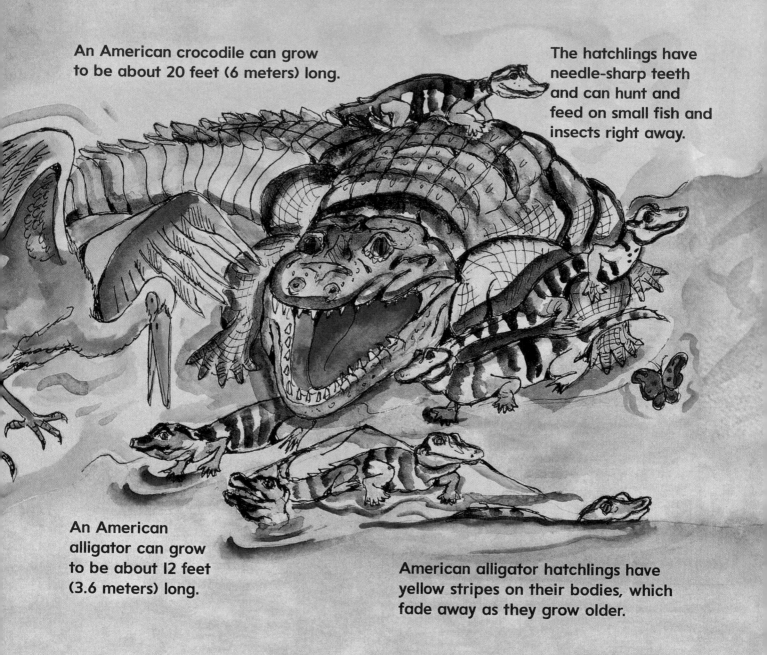

An American crocodile can grow to be about 20 feet (6 meters) long.

The hatchlings have needle-sharp teeth and can hunt and feed on small fish and insects right away.

An American alligator can grow to be about 12 feet (3.6 meters) long.

American alligator hatchlings have yellow stripes on their bodies, which fade away as they grow older.

The female alligator and crocodile stay close to their young for about a year. They protect them from harm before the young ones go off on their own. Young alligators and crocodiles grow about 1 foot (.3 meter) a year for their first six years. As they get older, they grow slower. They continue to grow throughout their lives.

Alligators and crocodiles use their strong legs, feet, and tails to dig holes in muddy marshlands. The holes fill with water. Other wildlife living nearby will also make use of these water holes.

American alligators and American crocodiles were hunted for hundreds of years for their meat and skins. Today it is **illegal** to hunt them, but humans are still their main enemy.

People have developed areas where these large reptiles once lived. There are fewer and fewer places where alligators and crocodiles can live in their natural environment.

STOP AND CHECK

Ask and Answer Questions Why are alligators and crocodiles endangered? Reread page 521 to find the answer.

ENDANGERED means
threatened with extinction.

Wildlife preserves have been created to
protect them.

Alligators and crocodiles have been around
for millions of years. Now they are **endangered**.
The lives of these **fascinating** creatures should
be **respected**.

523

About the Author and Illustrator

Gail Gibbons created her first picture book when she was four. She used yarn to hold the pages together. She studied art and went on to become an award-winning author and illustrator. Gail has written more than 170 nonfiction books about topics, such as dogs, dinosaurs, penguins, apples, knights, kites, and giant pandas. She lives mostly in Vermont, where she makes maple syrup in the spring. When she is not at home, you might find her in a tropical rain forest or at the top of a skyscraper! Gail travels around the world doing research for her books.

Author's Purpose

Why do you think the author wrote about alligators and crocodiles?

Respond to the Text

Summarize

Tell what you learned about alligators and crocodiles. The details from your Venn Diagram may help you summarize.

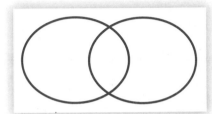

Write

Does Gail Gibbons do a good job organizing the information so that you understand how alligators and crocodiles are alike and different? Use these sentence frames to help organize text evidence.

Gail Gibbons uses text features to . . .
The illustrations and captions tell me . .
This helps me understand . . .

Make Connections

Why did learning about alligators and crocodiles teach you to respect them? ESSENTIAL QUESTION

In what ways are people helping alligators and other endangered animals? TEXT TO WORLD

Compare Texts

Read this folktale about how Old Croc learns to respect Monkey.

The Monkey and the Crocodile

an African folktale

Old Croc was the greatest hunter on the Congo River. All the **wildlife** that lived there feared him. The only animal he couldn't catch was Monkey. Each day he watched Monkey scamper *fast, fast,* across the rocks in the river to play with his friends on the other side.

One day, Old Croc came up with a plan. He would catch Monkey and have him for lunch. Old Croc hid in the river so his back stuck out of the water like a rock, and he waited for Monkey to cross. When Monkey stepped on his back, Old Croc grabbed his tail. "You're caught, Monkey! Now I will eat you," he growled.

Illustration: Carol Liddiment

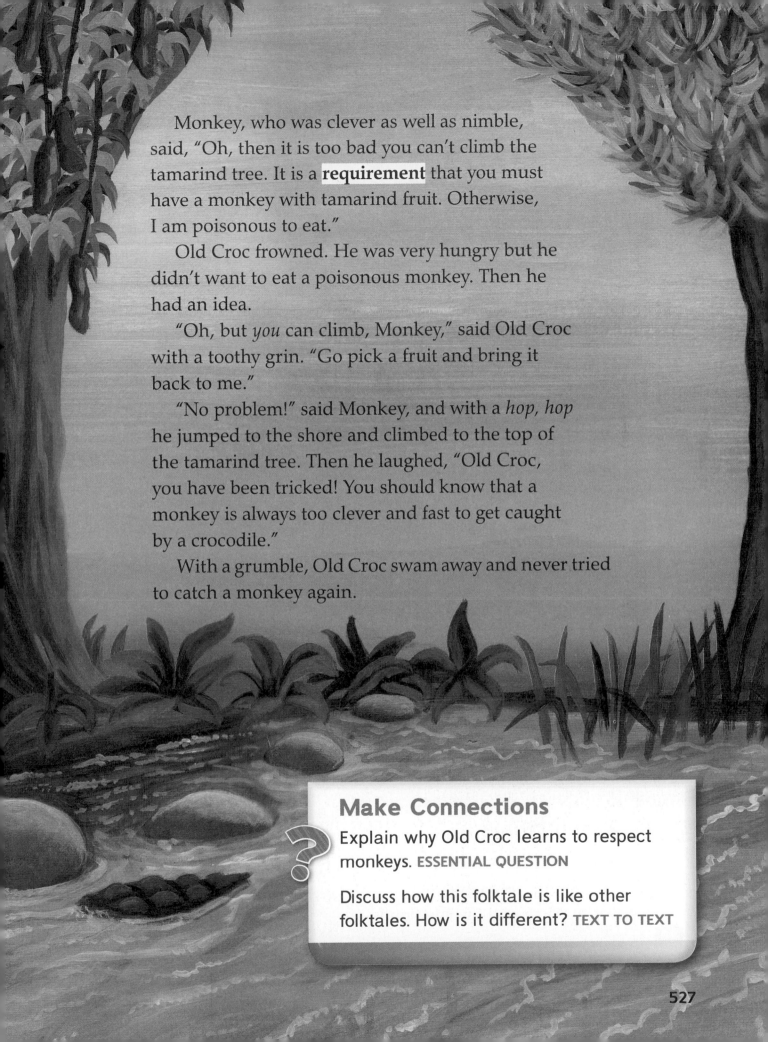

Monkey, who was clever as well as nimble, said, "Oh, then it is too bad you can't climb the tamarind tree. It is a **requirement** that you must have a monkey with tamarind fruit. Otherwise, I am poisonous to eat."

Old Croc frowned. He was very hungry but he didn't want to eat a poisonous monkey. Then he had an idea.

"Oh, but *you* can climb, Monkey," said Old Croc with a toothy grin. "Go pick a fruit and bring it back to me."

"No problem!" said Monkey, and with a *hop, hop* he jumped to the shore and climbed to the top of the tamarind tree. Then he laughed, "Old Croc, you have been tricked! You should know that a monkey is always too clever and fast to get caught by a crocodile."

With a grumble, Old Croc swam away and never tried to catch a monkey again.

Make Connections

Explain why Old Croc learns to respect monkeys. **ESSENTIAL QUESTION**

Discuss how this folktale is like other folktales. How is it different? **TEXT TO TEXT**

Nora's Ark

by Natalie Kinsey-Warnock

illustrated by Emily Arnold McCully

? Essential Question

How can weather affect us?

Read about a farm family that
survives a storm and terrible flood.

Go Digital!

When I was born, Grandma said I was so small I looked like a little bird. That's why I was named Wren. Grandma may look small, too, but she's made of granite, and she says I'm tough, just like she is. Good thing, or we never would have survived the 1927 Flood.

Grandma and Grandpa lived on a little farm by a river in Vermont. They didn't have much money, but there was always plenty to eat—milk from Grandpa's cows, vegetables from Grandma's garden, apples and plums from the orchard, fish from the river, and maple syrup that Grandpa and Grandma made each spring.

Grandpa was building Grandma a new house. It sat on a hill and, when finished, it would have electricity, a wringer washing machine, and best of all, an indoor bathroom.

"I don't need a new house, Horace," Grandma said. "We've lived here forty years, raised eight children, and been as happy as a family could be. That new house is just gravy."

"What do you mean?" I asked her.

Grandma thought how she could explain it to me.

"You like potatoes, don't you, Wren?"

"Yes, ma'am," I told her. Grandma made the best mashed potatoes in the world, with lots of milk, butter, and pepper in them. You could make a meal out of just her potatoes.

"You like gravy on them?"

"I reckon." Grandma did make good gravy. "But your potatoes taste good without gravy, too," I told her.

"Exactly," Grandma said. "Gravy tastes good, but you don't need it, and I don't need that new house. I like living here."

But Grandpa kept right on building.

When it began to rain on November 2, 1927, no one along the river had any idea nine inches of rain would fall in two days. Life in Vermont was about to change forever.

The rain came down in torrents. It drummed so loudly on the roof we couldn't talk. Grandma spent the morning baking bread. By noon, she'd made twenty-seven loaves.

"Grandma, why'd you make so much bread?" I shouted.

Grandma watched the water stream down the windows.

"We might need it," she said, but I couldn't imagine how we'd eat twenty-seven loaves of bread.

When Grandpa came in for lunch, he poured a quart of water out of each boot.

"I've never seen the river rise so fast," he said. "I think we'd best get up to the new house."

For once, Grandma didn't **argue**. By the time she'd packed quilts, candles, her photo albums, and a sack of potatoes, the water was up to the porch.

Grandpa let all the cows and horses out of the barn.

"What will happen to them?" I asked.

"They'll get to higher ground and be all right," he said. "Don't worry, Wren." But I could tell he was the one who was worried.

I loaded all those loaves of bread into my old baby carriage, covered it with an oilcloth, and pushed it through the mud and rain to the new house.

"Guess I built this place just in time," Grandpa said.

"If I didn't know better, I'd think you caused this flood just so I'd have to move into the new house," Grandma said, but she seemed glad to be on higher ground, too.

We'd scarcely set foot inside when we heard pounding on the door.

The three Guthrie boys stood on the porch, burlap bags in each hand. The bags squirmed and squawked.

"Our barn's flooded. Can we keep the chickens here?"

They emptied the chickens onto the kitchen floor.

"Some of our heifers are **stranded** in the fields," one of the boys said. "We're gonna see if we can push them to higher ground."

"I'll go with you," Grandpa said.

"May I go, too?" I asked.

"No!" Grandpa and Grandma both said at once.

"Be careful," Grandma told him, and he and the boys disappeared through the rain.

Even with all those chickens, the house seemed empty with Grandpa gone.

Grandma saw me shiver and wrapped a quilt around me.

"It's getting colder," she said. "I wish I had my cookstove here." She held me close as we stood watching the rain.

"I wish Grandpa would come back," I said.

"Me, too," said Grandma.

We both shrieked when a huge head appeared in the window. It was Major, one of the Fergusons' horses.

I was even more **astonished** when Grandma opened the door and led him in.

"You're bringing Major into the house?"

"We don't have a stove," Grandma said. "He's big. He'll add heat to the place."

Major took up half the kitchen. The other half was taken up by loaves of bread and chickens.

We had chickens in the cupboards, chickens on the shelves and in the baby carriage, even chickens roosting on Major's back.

Our next visitors were Mrs. Lafleur and her daughter, Madeleine. Mrs. Lafleur didn't speak much English.

"Our house wash away," Mrs. Lafleur said. "We row boat here."

Madeleine looked around the kitchen, and her eyes opened wide.

"Des poulets dans le chariot de bébé?" she said. I guess she'd never seen chickens in a baby carriage before.

By nightfall, the house was full to bursting. Besides Mrs. Lafleur and Madeleine, Mr. and Mrs. Guthrie, the Fergusons, and the Craig family had moved in, twenty-three people in all. There were also three horses, a cow, five pigs, a duck, four cats, and one hundred chickens.

The river rose until the house became an
island, and we watched our neighbors' houses
wash down the river.

Mr. and Mrs. Guthrie had brought a side of salt pork with them, though we had no way to cook it. The Fergusons had saved their radio, a skillet, a bag of dried apples, and a three-legged cat. They were delighted to find Major alive and well and in our kitchen.

The Craigs had lost everything but the clothes on their backs.

"We're just glad we all got out alive," Mrs. Craig said, which only reminded Grandma and me that Grandpa had still not returned.

We had bread and dried apples for supper, and rainwater Madeleine and I scooped out of the Lafleurs' rowboat. The water had a few fish scales in it, but no one **complained**.

With no stove or beds, we all huddled together for warmth, sharing Grandma's quilts as best we could. We sang Scottish songs and "Row, Row, Row Your Boat" in a round, and Mrs. Lafleur taught us "À la Claire Fontaine," a tune that brought tears to our eyes even though we couldn't understand the words. Mrs. Guthrie told how her grandfather had fought at Gettysburg, and Mr. Craig kept us laughing with stories of his boyhood days in a logging camp in Maine. If it hadn't been for the thought of Grandpa out there somewhere, it would have almost seemed like a party.

STOP AND CHECK

Make Predictions What do you think will happen to Grandpa?

I knew Grandma was worried about Grandpa. I was worried, too. He should have been home by now.

I wanted to ask Peter Ferguson if he would come with me to look for Grandpa, but I knew if Grandma overheard she'd **forbid** me to go, so when the sky was getting light, I sneaked out and sprinted for the rowboat.

Grandma was just getting into it.

"What are you doing here?" she wanted to know.

"Same as you, I reckon. Going to look for Grandpa."

"It's too dangerous," Grandma said. "Go back to the house," but I shook my head.

Grandma looked at me hard.

"All right," she said. "We'll look for him together."

I pushed us off into water that was full of furniture and trees and dead animals. Grandma had to be careful where she rowed. It was raining so hard I had to keep bailing water out of the boat.

Nothing looked the same. Fields had become lakes. Just the roofs of houses stuck up above the water.

On one of those roofs we saw a dog.

"Why, I believe that's Sam Burroughs' collie," Grandma said, and she rowed toward the house. The collie barked when she saw us coming.

I held on to the roof to steady the boat.

"Come on, girl," I said, and the dog jumped into the boat beside me. She whined and licked my face.

The strangest sight was yet to come. We rounded a bend in the river and I squinted, sure that my eyes were fooling me. Then I heard Grandma's voice behind me.

"Wren, are these old eyes failing me, or is that a cow in a tree?" Grandma asked.

It was indeed. A red and white Ayrshire was wedged into the crook formed by two branches, and she was bawling piteously. Higher up in the branches was a man. He was hollering almost as loudly as the cow.

"I believe we've found your grandpa," Grandma said, **relief** flooding her face.

"I was on my way home when I got swept away by the water," Grandpa said. "I thought I was a goner, too, but when this cow floated by, I grabbed her tail and stayed afloat until she got hung up in this tree."

We pushed and pulled on that cow, but she was stuck fast and we finally had to leave her. Grandpa promised he'd come back and try to cut her free, but he was crying as we rowed away.

STOP AND CHECK

Confirm Predictions What happened to Grandpa? Was your prediction correct?

"Goodness," Grandma said. "All that fuss over a cow." But Grandpa wasn't crying over just one cow.

"All our cows drowned, Nora," he said. "The house, the barn, the horses, they're all gone."

Grandma wiped the tears from his cheeks.

"You're safe, and that's all that matters," she said.

"We'll have to start over," Grandpa said, and Grandma smiled.

"We can do that," she said.

Grandpa smiled back at her, and I knew then that, no matter what, everything would be all right.

The Craigs, Fergusons, Guthries, and Lafleurs were glad to see us. Madeleine even hugged me.

"She was afraid you'd drowned," Peter said. He blushed. "I was, too," he added.

When Grandpa saw all the animals in the kitchen, he burst out laughing.

"Nora, I thought I was building you a house, but I see it was really an ark."

It took three days for the water to go down enough so our neighbors could go see what was left of their farms.

Grandpa put his arm around Grandma.

"I'll finish this house the way you want it, Nora," he said. But he shook his head when the Fergusons led Major out.

"I don't know as I'll ever be able to get those hoofprints out of this floor," he said.

I've now lived in my grandparents' house for more than forty years, and those hoofprints are still in the floor. I never sanded them out because they remind me of what's important: family and friends and neighbors helping neighbors.

Like Grandma said, everything else is just gravy.

STOP AND CHECK

Summarize What happened after Wren and Grandma rescued Grandpa? Tell the events in order.

ABOUT THE AUTHOR AND ILLUSTRATOR

NATALIE KINSEY-WARNOCK'S family has lived in Vermont for nearly two hundred years. Family stories like "Norah's Ark" inspire her writing. She says, "Every family has stories that are too good to be forgotten. These stories need to be passed on to the next generation." Natalie has written more than twenty books for young people. Most are about life in Vermont.

EMILY ARNOLD McCULLY'S family inspired her to become an artist. She started drawing as a child. Her mother encouraged her to practice, so she drew everything she saw. She never stopped creating art. Emily has illustrated more than a hundred books for children. Emily hopes to inspire people's imaginations through her books.

AUTHOR'S PURPOSE
Why do you think the author wrote a story about a Vermont flood that happened long ago?

Respond to the Text

Summarize

How did the weather affect Wren and her grandparents? Use details from your Theme chart to help you summarize the events in the story.

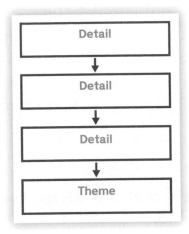

Detail

↓

Detail

↓

Detail

↓

Theme

Write

How does what the author says about Wren and her grandmother at the beginning of the story help you understand the message? Use these sentence frames to help organize your text evidence.

At the beginning of the story, the author . . .
She uses illustrations to . . .
This helps me understand . . .

Make Connections

What did people in the community do to survive bad weather and a flood? ESSENTIAL QUESTION

Explain why people are always watching the weather report. TEXT TO WORLD

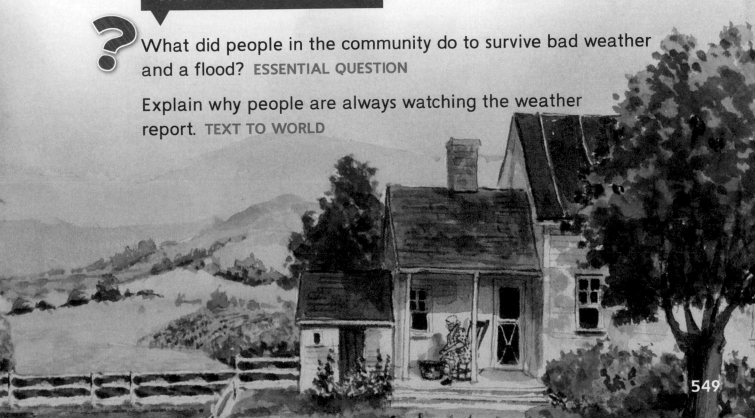

Compare Texts

Read about a contest between the Wind and the Sun to see who is stronger.

The Wind and the Sun

from the fable by Aesop

The Wind and the Sun both lived in the sky. Like most neighbors, they got along much of the time. However, sometimes they argued about who was strongest.

"I am stronger than you!" boasted the Wind one day. "I can topple trees and flatten homes. On a sunny day, I can spoil the weather **conditions** by blowing in clouds and rain."

The Sun smiled, "No! I am stronger. I provide daylight and the heat that keeps people warm."

"Let's have a contest to determine who is stronger," blustered the Wind. "See that farmer down there in his field? We'll each try to make him take off his coat. Whoever succeeds is the winner."

Illustration: Renata Gallio

"Okay, you go first," the Sun agreed.

The Wind took a big breath and blew and blew. He tried to blast away the farmer's coat with all his strength, but the farmer only pulled his coat tighter.

"*Brrr!* That's peculiar," said the farmer. "The weather **forecast** on the radio didn't predict a freezing wind for today."

Soon the Wind grew tired and stopped howling. "Your turn, Sun," he panted.

Sun nodded and smiled. He sent out his warmest rays.

The farmer began to sweat as he labored in the field. "Ah, it certainly has become a warm, sunny day," he sighed with relief as he removed his coat. And with that, the Sun won the contest.

Gentle persuasion works better than force.

Make Connections

Why is the Sun stronger than the Wind? ESSENTIAL QUESTION

Compare this story to other stories about the weather. TEXT TO TEXT

Glossary

This glossary can help you find the meanings of words in this book that you may not know. The words in the glossary are listed in alphabetical order.

Guide Words

Guide words at the top of each page tell you the first and last words on the page.

anticipation/barbeque

First word on the page

Last word on the page

Sample Entry

Each word is divided into syllables. The way to pronounce the word is given next. You can understand the pronunciation respelling by using the pronunciation key.

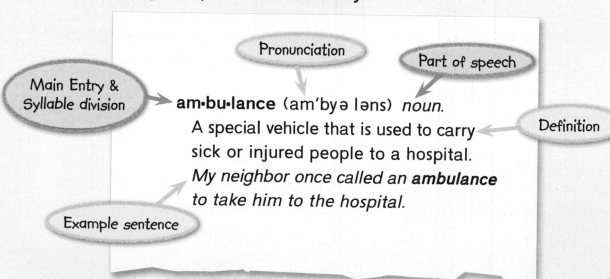

Pronunciation

Part of speech

Main Entry & Syllable division

am·bu·lance (am'byə ləns) *noun.*
A special vehicle that is used to carry sick or injured people to a hospital.
*My neighbor once called an **ambulance** to take him to the hospital.*

Definition

Example sentence

Pronunciation Key

You can understand the pronunciation respelling by using this **pronunciation key**. A shorter key appears at the bottom of every other page. When a word has more than one syllable, a dark accent mark (′) shows which syllable is stressed. In some words, a light accent mark (′) shows which syllable has a less heavy stress.

Phonetic Spelling	Examples	Phonetic Spelling	Examples
a	**a**t, b**a**d, pl**ai**d, l**au**gh	d	**d**ear, so**d**a, ba**d**
ā	**a**pe, p**ai**n, d**ay**, br**ea**k	f	**f**ive, de**f**end, lea**f**, o**ff**, cou**gh**, ele**ph**ant
ä	**fa**ther, c**a**lm		
âr	c**are**, p**air**, b**ear**, th**eir**, wh**ere**	g	**g**ame, a**g**o, fo**g**, e**gg**
e	**e**nd, p**e**t, s**ai**d, h**ea**ven, fri**e**nd	h	**h**at, a**h**ead
ē	**e**qual, m**e**, f**ee**t, t**ea**m, p**ie**ce, k**ey**	hw	**wh**ite, **wh**ether, **wh**ich
i	**i**t, b**i**g, g**i**ve, h**y**mn	j	**j**oke, en**j**oy, **g**em, pa**g**e, e**dge**
ī	**i**ce, f**i**ne, l**ie**, m**y**	k	**k**ite, ba**k**ery, see**k**, ta**ck**, **c**at
îr	**ear**, d**eer**, h**ere**, p**ier**ce	l	**l**id, sai**l**or, fee**l**, ba**ll**, a**ll**ow
o	**o**dd, h**o**t, w**a**tch	m	**m**an, fa**m**ily, drea**m**
ō	**o**ld, **oa**t, t**oe**, l**ow**	n	**n**ot, fi**n**al, pa**n**, **kn**ife, **gn**aw
ô	c**o**ffee, **a**ll, t**au**ght, l**aw**, f**ou**ght	ng	lo**ng**, si**ng**er
ôr	**or**der, f**or**k, h**or**se, st**or**y, p**our**	p	**p**ail, re**p**air, soa**p**, ha**pp**y
oi	**oi**l, t**oy**	r	**r**ide, pa**r**ent, wea**r**, mo**r**e, ma**rr**y
ou	**ou**t, n**ow**, b**ou**gh	s	**s**it, a**s**ide, pet**s**, **c**ent, pa**ss**
u	**u**p, m**u**d, l**o**ve, d**ou**ble	sh	**sh**oe, wa**sh**er, fi**sh**, mi**ssi**on, na**ti**on
ū	**u**se, m**u**le, c**ue**, f**eu**d, f**ew**	t	**t**ag, pre**t**end, fa**t**, dress**ed**
ü	r**u**le, tr**ue**, f**oo**d, fr**ui**t	th	**th**in, pan**th**er, bo**th**
ů	p**u**t, w**oo**d, sh**ou**ld, l**oo**k	<u>th</u>	**th**ese, mo**th**er, smoo**th**
ûr	b**ur**n, h**ur**ry, t**er**m, b**ir**d, w**or**d, c**our**age	v	**v**ery, fa**v**or, wa**v**e
		w	**w**et, **w**eather, re**w**ard
ə	**a**bout, tak**e**n, penc**i**l, lem**o**n, circ**u**s	y	**y**es, on**i**on
b	**b**at, a**b**ove, jo**b**	z	**z**oo, la**z**y, ja**zz**, ro**s**e, dog**s**, hou**s**es
ch	**ch**in, su**ch**, ma**tch**	zh	vi**si**on, trea**s**ure, sei**z**ure

Aa

ac·ci·den·tal (ak′si den′təl) *adjective*. Not expected or planned. *Be sure to blow out the candle to prevent an accidental fire.*

ached (ākt) *verb*. Had a dull and steady pain. *My tooth ached, so I went to the dentist.*

a·chieve·ment (əchēv′mənt) *noun*. Something that is accomplished. *Climbing a mountain is an achievement.*

ad·mires (ad mīrz′) *verb*. Thinks well of. *The student admires his teacher.*

ad·mit (ad mit′) *verb*. To confess. *I had to admit that I lost my ticket.*

ad·ven·tur·ous (ad ven′chər əs) *adjective*. Willing to experience something scary or unusual. *The adventurous family went skydiving.*

a·gree·a·ble (əgrē′əbəl) *adjective*. Nice; pleasant. *The flowers in the room had an agreeable smell.*

a·larmed (əlärmd′) *verb*. Made fearful or afraid. *The big dog alarmed the child.*

a·lert (əlûrt′) *verb*. Warn about a danger. *The principal will alert the police if the problem continues.*

a·maze·ment (əmāz′mənt) *noun*. Great surprise or wonder. *The people watching the whales swim by were filled with amazement.*

a·mount (əmount′) *noun*. Quantity; how much. *What is the amount of money you spent this week?*

an·guish (ang′gwish) *noun*. Serious suffering of mind or body. *The boy felt anguish when his dog died.*

an·nounced (ənounsd′) *verb*. Made something known officially. *The broadcaster announced the winner at the end of the game.*

a·pol·o·gized (əpol′ əjīzd′) *verb*. Said one is sorry; made an apology. *Emma apologized for yelling.*

ap·pre·ci·ate (əprē′shē āt′) *verb*. To understand the value of. *Henry appreciates a good game of chess.*

ar·gue (är′gū) *verb*. To disagree and show a difference of opinion. *It is disrespectful to argue with your parents.*

ar·rived (ərīvd′) *verb*. Came to a place. *The family arrived at their vacation home safely.*

a·ro·ma (ərō′mə) *noun*. A pleasant smell or fragrance. *The aroma of homemade bread filled our home.*

as·ton·ished (əston′ishd) *adjective*. Greatly surprised. *I was astonished to learn that I had won the contest.*

as·tron·o·my (ə stron'ə mē) *noun.* The study of the Sun, Moon, stars, and planets. *I want to study **astronomy** to learn about the Sun and stars.*

at·tempt (ə tempt') *noun.* A try. *We made an **attempt** to climb the hill.*

at·ten·tion (ə tən'shən) *noun.* The act of watching, listening or concentrating. *The clown held the children's **attention** through her skit.*

au·di·ence (ô'dē əns) *noun.* A group of people gathered to hear or see something. *The **audience** applauded loudly after the show.*

awk·ward (ôk'wərd) *adjective.* Not graceful; clumsy. *The baby's first steps were **awkward**.*

Bb

bar·ter (bär'tər) *verb.* To trade things for other things without the use of money. *The early settlers had to **barter** to get supplies.*

boomed (bümd) *verb.* Increased quickly. *The population in many Western towns **boomed** after the new railroad was built.*

bounce (bouns) *verb.* To spring back up after hitting something. *I can **bounce** the rubber ball off the wall.*

brav·er·y (brā'və rē) *noun.* Being able to face danger without being afraid; courage. *The soldiers showed their **bravery** by going to battle.*

Cc

can·di·date (kan'di dāt') *noun.* A person who seeks a position. *Our mayor wants to be a **candidate** for president.*

care·less (kâr'lis) *adjective.* Not paying close attention. *The **careless** child tripped over her scooter.*

care·tak·ers (kâr'tā'kərz) *plural noun.* People who take care of others. *The nurses are the main **caretakers** at the hospital.*

carved (kärvd) *verb.* Cut something into shape. *She **carved** the furniture out of wood.*

cel·e·brate (sel'ə brāt') *verb.* To honor a special day or event. *People in the United States **celebrate** Thanksgiving every November.*

---

at; āpe; fär; câre; end; mē; it; īce; pîerce; hot; ōld; sông; fôrk; oil; out; up; ūse; rüle; pùll; tûrn; chin; sing; shop; thin; this; hw in white; zh in treasure.

The symbol ə stands for the unstressed vowel sound in about, taken, pencil, lemon, and circus.

cit·i·zen·ship (sit′ə zen ship′) *noun.* The ways a member of a country should behave. *Helping your neighbors is part of good citizenship.*

class·mate (klas′māt′) *noun.* A member of the same class in school. *I invited my classmate to the party.*

clues (klüz) *plural noun.* Hints that help you solve a problem. *The detective used clues to solve the case.*

com·mu·ni·cate (kə mu′ni kāt′) *verb.* To share feelings, thoughts, or information with people. *To communicate his ideas, Doug wrote in his blog.*

com·mu·ni·ty (kə mu′ni tē) *noun.* A group of people who live together in the same place. *Our community voted to build a new library.*

com·pe·ti·tion (kom′pi tish′ ən) *noun.* The act of trying to win or gain something. *The class had a competition for best school spirit.*

com·plained (kəm plānd′) *verb.* Talked about something that was wrong or annoying. *Ken complained that no one was listening to his speech.*

con·cen·trate (kon′ sen trāt′) *verb.* To pay close attention. *It is hard to concentrate in a noisy place.*

con·di·tions (kən dish′ənz) *plural noun.* Ways a person or thing are. *The weather conditions were perfect for flying our kites.*

con·fi·dence (kon′fi dəns) *noun.* Belief in oneself. *When you have confidence in yourself, you have a good chance to achieve your goals.*

con·ser·va·tion (kon′sər vā′shən) *noun.* The protection of natural resources. *Our town helped in the conservation of our park.*

con·si·dered (kən sid′ərd) *verb.* Thought about carefully before making a decision. *After Kim considered her choices, she decided to take the job at the bank.*

con·tin·ue (kən tin′ū) *verb.* To go on without stopping. *Continue reading until you finish the story.*

con·trib·ute (kən trib′ ūt) *verb.* To give something to others. *Volunteers contribute their time to help the animal shelter.*

con·trolled (kən trōld′) *verb.* Used power to make something happen. *The driver controlled the car as she drove through the ice storm.*

con·vince (kən vins′) *verb.* To cause a person to believe or do something. *I tried to convince my sister to let me borrow her sweater.*

co·op·er·a·tion (kō op′ə rā′shən) *noun.* The act of working together. *People in the community showed great cooperation when they worked together to clean up the park.*

cour·age (kûr′ij) *noun*. The strength to face danger; bravery. *The firefighters show great **courage** every day.*

cou·ra·geous (kə rā′jəs) *adjective*. Showing bravery in the face of fear or danger. *The **courageous** police officer arrested the robber.*

cre·at·ed (krē āt′ id) *verb*. Caused something to exist or happen. *The artist **created** a sculpture for the museum.*

cre·a·tion (krē ā′shən) *noun*. Something that has been made. *The artist's **creation** was shown in the gallery.*

Dd

dar·ing (dâr′ing) *adjective*. Being courageous or bold. *The **daring** explorer went looking for new lands.*

de·ci·sion (di sizh′ən) *noun*. The result of making up one's mind. *She did well because of her **decision** to study hard for the test.*

de·scen·dants (di sen′dənts) *plural noun*. People who are relatives of someone who lived in the past. *They are **descendants** of the town's early settlers.*

de·sign (di zīn′) *verb*. To make a plan, drawing, or outline of, or make a pattern for. *They will **design** the costumes for our play.*

di·rec·tion (di rek′shən) *noun*. The way or route towards a specific point. *We walked in the **direction** of the park.*

dis·ap·pear (dis′ə pîr′) *verb*. To go out of sight. *We watched the plane **disappear** behind a cloud.*

dis·ap·point·ment (dis′ə point′mənt) *noun*. A feeling of sadness. *The children showed their **disappointment** when the party was cancelled.*

di·sas·ters (di zas′ tərz) *plural noun*. Events that cause much harm or suffering. *Hurricanes, earthquakes, blizzards, and tornadoes are examples of natural **disasters**.*

dis·be·lief (dis′ bi lēf′) *noun*. Not believing. *The audience stared in **disbelief** as the bear rode the bicycle around the ring.*

dis·cour·aged (dis kûr′ ijd) *adjective*. Not having hope or confidence to do something. *The team felt **discouraged** after losing the game.*

---

at; āpe; fär; câre; end; mē; it; īce; pîerce; hot; ōld; sông; fôrk; oil; out; up; ūse; rüle; půll; tûrn; chin; sing; shop; thin; this; hw in white; zh in treasure.

The symbol ə stands for the unstressed vowel sound in about, taken, pencil, lemon, and circus.

dis·cov·er·y (dis kuv′ə rē) *noun*. Seeing or finding out something for the first time. *The **discovery** of electricity led to many inventions.*

dis·may (dis mā′) *noun*. A feeling of fear or being discouraged in the face of danger. *I felt **dismay** when I missed the school bus.*

do·nat·ed (dō′ nā′ tid) *verb*. Gave; contributed. *The children **donated** their money to the pet shelter.*

Ee

ed·u·cat·ed (ej′ə kā′tid) *adjective*. Having knowledge. *The **educated** manager knew how to solve the problem.*

ef·fec·tive (i fek′ tiv) *adjective*. Works in the correct way. *The medicine was **effective** in stopping my cough.*

ef·fort (ef′ ərt) *noun*. Hard work. *It took much **effort** to finish all my homework.*

e·lect (i lekt′) *verb*. Choose by voting. *We will **elect** a new class president this week.*

em·bar·ras·sed (em bar′ əsd) *adjective*. Feeling shy or ashamed. *I felt **embarrassed** when I tripped and fell.*

em·i·gra·tion (em′ i grā′ shən) *noun*. Moving away from your country or home to settle in another place. *The new railroad speeded up the **emigration** of people out of eastern cities.*

en·cour·aged (en kûr′ijd) *verb*. Gave help or hope. *The teacher **encouraged** her students to study.*

en·dan·gered (en dān′ jərd) *adjective*. Close to no longer existing or being extinct. *Many plants and animals are becoming **endangered** when their habitats are destroyed.*

en·er·gy (en′ər jē) *noun*. The ability to do work. *A runner must have a lot of **energy** to take part in a marathon.*

en·vi·ron·ment (en vī′rən mənt) *noun*. The natural surroundings of a person, animal or plant. *An animal depends on its **environment** to survive.*

e·quip·ment (i kwip′ mənt) *noun*. Supplies provided for a particular use. *Don't forget to pack the camping **equipment** in the car!*

es·sen·tial (i sen′ shəl) *adjective*. Important or necessary. *It is **essential** to eat a good breakfast every day.*

es·ti·mate (es′ tə mit) *noun*. An educated guess. *What is your **estimate** for how long the trip will take?*

ex·am·ine (eg zam′ in) *verb*. To look at closely; check. *The doctor will **examine** me during my check-up.*

ex·am·ple (eg zam′ pəl) *noun.*
Something that is used to show what
other similar things are like. *The teacher
gave us an **example** of the project we
had to do.*

ex·cel·lent (ek′ sə lənt) *adjective.*
Very good; outstanding. *Julia won
a prize for her **excellent** essay.*

ex·pect (ek spekt′) *verb.* To think that
something will happen. *We **expect** that
school will be closed tomorrow because
of the snowstorm.*

ex·treme·ly (ek strēm′ lē) *adverb.* Very.
*The baby developed an **extremely** high
fever overnight.*

Ff

fab·u·lous (fab′ yə ləs) *adjective.*
Unbelievable; amazing. *The circus
performers put on a **fabulous** show!*

fas·ci·na·ting (fas′ ə nat′ing)
adjective. Very interesting. *The speaker
held the audience's attention with a
fascinating speech.*

fea·tures (fē′ chers) *plural noun.* A part
or quality of something. *All birds share
many **features**, such as feathers.*

fla·vor·ful (flā′ vər fəl) *adjective.* Full
of pleasant taste. *A tray of **flavorful**
brownies was eaten in minutes.*

flight (flīt) *noun.* An object's movement
through the air. *The Wright brothers'
first airplane **flight** was in Kitty Hawk,
North Carolina.*

for·bid (fər bid′) *verb.* Not allow
someone to do something. *I **forbid** you
to use my computer.*

fore·cast (fôr′kast′) *noun.* A prediction
about the weather. *The weather
forecast predicted rain.*

frus·tra·tion (frus′ trā′ shən) *noun.*
The feeling of being annoyed or upset.
*Our mother showed her **frustration**
when she yelled at us.*

fu·ri·ous·ly (fyur′ ē əs lē) *adverb.*
Frantically; with anger. *The dog barked
furiously at the stranger.*

Gg

gaz·ing (gāz′ ing) *verb.* Looking at
something for a long time. *Mina enjoyed
gazing up at the stars.*

---

at; āpe; fär; câre; end; mē; it; īce; pîerce; hot; ōld;
sông; fôrk; oil; out; up; ūse; rüle; pùll; tûrn; chin;
sing; shop; thin; <u>th</u>is; hw in white; zh in treasure.

The symbol ə stands for the unstressed vowel
sound in about, taken, pencil, lemon, and circus.

globe (glōb) *noun.* A round ball with a map of the world on it. *Find the country where you live on the globe.*

goal (gōl) *noun.* Something that a person aims for or tries to get. *My goal is to graduate from college.*

gov·ern·ment (guv'ərn mənt) *noun.* The group of people in charge of managing a country, state, or other place. *The government makes our laws.*

grace·ful (grās' fəl) *adjective.* Beautiful or pleasing in design, movement, or style. *The graceful dancer gave a wonderful performance.*

grand (grand) *adjective.* Large and splendid. *The old castle looks like it would be a grand place to live in.*

Hh

harm·ful (härm'fəl) *adjective.* Causing injury or hurt. *It could be very harmful to ride a bike without wearing a helmet.*

health·ful (helth' fəl) *adjective.* Something good for a person's health. *Eating lots of fruits and vegetables is a healthful habit.*

hor·ri·fied (hôr' ə fīd') *adjective.* Shocked and upset. *They felt horrified when they saw the damage the storm had caused.*

hum·ble (hum' bəl) *adjective.* Not big or important. *This neighborhood is made up of many humble homes and small apartment buildings.*

Ii

i·den·ti·cal (ī den' ti kəl) *adjective.* Exactly the same. *The identical twins looked and even dressed alike.*

il·le·gal (i lē' gəl) *adjective.* Against rules or laws. *If you break the law, you are doing something illegal.*

i·ma·gine (i maj' in) *verb.* To picture a person or thing in the mind. *Close your eyes and imagine you are on vacation.*

im·i·tate (im'i tāt) *verb.* To behave just as another person does. *My little sister is always trying to imitate everything I do.*

im·mi·grate (im' i grāt') *verb.* To come to live in a country where one was not born. *The family will immigrate to the United States from Poland.*

im·pos·si·ble (im pos'ə bəl) *adjective.* Unable to happen or be done. *It was impossible to study in the noisy room.*

im·proved (im prüvd') *verb.* Became better; made something better. *My tennis has improved very much since I began practicing.*

in·de·pen·dent (in′di pen′dənt)
adjective. Free from control or rule of
others. *An independent country is free
to make its own laws.*

in·hab·it·ed (in hab′it id) *verb*. Lived in.
*A brown bear and its cubs inhabited the
large den in the forest.*

in·spect·ed (in spek′ tid) *verb*. Looked
at closely and carefully. *The mechanic
inspected the car for safety problems.*

in·spired (in spīrd′) *verb*. Caused to take
action. *My teacher's kind words inspired
me to keep studying.*

in·ter·fere (in′tər fîr′) *verb*. To disturb or
interrupt. *The girl did not want to interfere
when her mother was speaking.*

in·ter·rupt·ed (in′ tərup′tid) *verb*.
Stopped the speaking or acting of a
person. *I couldn't hear the rest of the
story because you interrupted us.*

in·ven·tor (in vən′ tər) *noun*. A person
who invents something. *Alexander
Graham Bell was the inventor of the
telephone.*

in·ves·ti·ga·tion (in ves′ti gā′shən) *noun*.
The act of looking carefully in order
to find facts. *The police completed the
investigation of the crime.*

in·volve (in volv′) *verb*. To take part
in an activity; to include or have as a
necessary part. *The coach will involve
all his players in the final game.*

Jj

ju·bi·lant (jü′bə lənt) *adjective*. Feeling
or showing great joy or happiness. *The
team was jubilant over their victory.*

Ll

land·mark (land′ märk′) *noun*. An
important building or place. *The Statue
of Liberty is a national landmark in New
York City.*

launch (lônch) *verb*. To start in motion;
to send off. *What time will the rocket ship
launch into space?*

lead·er (lē′dər) *noun*. Someone who
shows the way; a person who leads.
Eric is a group leader in the Boy Scouts.

lus·cious (lush′əs) *adjective*. Having a
rich, sweet taste. *The luscious cake took
all day to bake.*

---

at; āpe; fär; câre; end; mē; it; īce; pîerce; hot; ōld;
sông; fôrk; oil; out; up; ūse; rüle; pùll; tûrn; chin;
sing; shop; thin; this; hw in white; zh in treasure.

The symbol ə stands for the unstressed vowel
sound in about, taken, pencil, lemon, and circus.

Mm

mag·nif·i·cent (mag nif'ə sənt) *adjective.* Very grand and splendid. *The queen looked* **magnificent** *in her fancy gown.*

mas·sive (mas' iv) *adjective.* Of great size; very big. *The* **massive** *ship dwarfed the tug boat in the port.*

ma·te·ri·al (mə tîr' ē əl) *noun.* What something is made of. *The table was made from a dark, heavy* **material.**

mo·del (mod'əl) *noun.* A small-sized copy of something. *My father and I made a model of an airplane.*

mo·ment (mō'mənt) *noun.* A short period of time. *I will answer your question in just one* **moment.**

mon·u·ment (mon'yə mənt) *noun.* A building or statue that is made to honor a person or event. *The Lincoln Memorial in Washington, D.C. is a* **monument** *to Abraham Lincoln.*

mo·tion (mō' shən) *noun.* Movement. *The rolling* **motion** *of the boat made me sick to my stomach.*

mo·ti·vate (mō' tə vāt) *verb.* To cause to happen. *I hope the gym trainer will* **motivate** *me to exercise.*

Nn

na·tion·al (nash'ə nəl) *adjective.* Belonging to a nation. *The president runs the* **national** *government.*

nat·u·ral (nach' ər əl) *adjective.* Found in nature; not made by people. *The environmentalist used* **natural** *resources in her experiment.*

nec·es·sar·y (nes'ə ser' ē) *adjective.* Required to be done. *It is* **necessary** *for athletes to practice every day.*

nerv·ous (nûr'vəs) *adjective.* Not able to relax; fearful. *The strange noises made the teens* **nervous** *to be home alone.*

Oo

ob·serve (əb zûrv') *verb.* See or notice something. *Did you* **observe** *that robin building a nest?*

ob·serv·er (əb zûr'vər) *noun.* A person who watches or notices something. *The volunteer acted as an* **observer** *at the election site.*

ob·sessed (əb sesd') *adjective.* Thinking of something constantly. *My neighbor became* **obsessed** *with collecting baseball cards.*

of·fered (ô'fərd) *verb.* Showed a desire to give something. *I* **offered** *to help set the table for dinner.*

op·por·tu·ni·ty (op'ə r tü' ni tē) *noun*. A good chance to do something. *The student got the **opportunity** to go to college.*

Pp

par·ti·ci·pate (pär tis' əpāt') *verb*. Take part or join with others. *My cousins want to **participate** in the family reunion activities.*

pas·sen·gers (pas'ən jərz) *plural noun*. People who travel by different types of transportation. *The **passengers** on the train gave the conductor their tickets.*

pay·ment (pā'mənt) *noun*. The act of paying for something. *You have to make a **payment** to the store.*

pho·to·graphs (fō'tə grafs') *plural noun*. Pictures that are made by a camera. *The couple took many **photographs** at the wedding.*

pi·o·neers (pī'ə nîrz') *plural noun*. People who were among the first to explore and settle in a region. *The **pioneers** faced many hardships while they traveled.*

pol·lu·tion (pə lü'shen) *noun*. Harmful materials that dirty or harm the environment. *Smog, or dirty air, is a cause of air **pollution**.*

pop·u·lar (pop'yə lər) *adjective*. Being accepted and liked by people. *Emily is very **popular** and always has a lot of friends.*

pop·u·la·tion (pop'yə lā' shən) *noun*. The number of people who live in a place. *The **population** of the city has grown over the years.*

pos·sess (pə zəs') *verb*. To own or have. *They **possess** several keys to the house.*

prac·tic·ing (prak' tis ing) *verb*. Doing an action over and over to gain skill. *You will learn to play the piano better by **practicing**.*

pre·cious (presh'ə s) *adjective*. Having great value. *My dog is very **precious** to me.*

pre·fer (pri fûr') *verb*. To like better. *I **prefer** basketball to baseball.*

pre·ven·tion (pri ven'shə n) *noun*. The act of keeping something from happening. *Putting out campfires helps in the **prevention** of forest fires.*

---

at; āpe; fär; câre; end; mē; it; īce; pîerce; hot; ōld; sông; fôrk; oil; out; up; ūse; rüle; pull; tûrn; chin; sing; shop; thin; this; hw in white; zh in treasure.

The symbol ə stands for the unstressed vowel sound in about, taken, pencil, lemon, and circus.

pride (prīd) *noun.* A feeling that one has worth and importance. *The student felt **pride** at his good grades.*

pro•duce (prə düs′) *verb.* To make something. *Chickens **produce** the eggs we eat on the farm.*

pro•fes•sion•al (prə fesh′ə nəl) *adjective.* Working for money doing a job. *That baseball team has **professional** players.*

pro•posed (prə pōzd′) *verb.* Suggested something for consideration. *We **proposed** taking the subway to the city to save money.*

pro•nounce (prə nouns′) *verb.* To make a sound of a letter or word. *As the child reads a new word, she has to **pronounce** every letter slowly.*

pro•tec•tion (prə tek′shən) *noun.* The act of keeping safe. *A turtle's shell offers it **protection** from harm.*

pur•pose (pûr′pəs) *noun.* A reason for which something is done. *The **purpose** of studying is to learn.*

Qq

qual•i•ty (kwol′i tē) *noun.* How good or bad something is. *That market sells fruits and vegetables of the highest **quality**.*

Rr

re•al•ized (rē′ə līzd′) *verb.* Understood something. *I **realized** the hike was going to be very hard when I started.*

rec•og•nize (rek′əg nīz′) *verb.* To know and remember from before. *Since I have not seen my old friend in years, I did not **recognize** her at first.*

re•cy•cle (rē sī′kel) *verb.* To fix up to be used again. *My community plans to **recycle** cans, bottles, and paper.*

re•fused (ri fūzd′) *verb.* Said no; rejected. *My mother **refused** to celebrate her birthday.*

re•lat•ed (ri lā′tid) *adjective.* Within the same family. *We are **related** on my father's side of the family.*

rel•a•tives (rel′ə tivz) *plural noun.* Animals or people who belong to the same family. *Uncle John and Aunt Martha are my favorite **relatives**.*

re•lief (ri lēf′) *noun.* The ending of worrying over something. *We felt **relief** when the test was finished.*

re•luc•tant•ly (ri luk′tent lē) *adverb.* Not willing. *The child **reluctantly** gave her toys to her sister.*

re•mained (ri mānd′) *verb.* Stayed behind. *I **remained** at home while my family went out.*

re•mind (ri mīnd′) *verb.* To cause someone to remember. *Please **remind** me to take my umbrella.*

re•new•able (ri nü′ə bəl) *adjective.* Able to be made new again. *Trees are an example of a **renewable** resource.*

re•place (ri plās′) *verb.* To fill in the place of. *When you use up all of the milk in the carton, please **replace** it.*

re•quire•ments (ri kwīr′mə nts) *noun.* Things that are needed or necessary. *Our main **requirements** are food, clothing, and shelter.*

re•search (ri′sûrch) *noun.* A study done to find information. *The student did **research** about butterflies.*

re•sources (rē′ sôrs′ə z) *noun.* Things that are used for help or support. *Forests and oceans are natural **resources**.*

re•spect•ed (ri spekt′id) *verb.* To be given honor or high importance. *The mayor is **respected** in the city.*

re•spond (ri spond′) *verb.* Said something in reply; Reacted. *My friend did not **respond** to my call.*

re•ward (ri wôrd′) *noun.* Something given in return for something well done. *The swimmer got a gold medal as a **reward** for winning the race .*

Ss

sat•is•fied (sat′is fīd) *adjective.* Pleased or delighted. *The student was **satisfied** with his good grades.*

scared (skârd) *adjective.* Afraid or frightened. *The children were **scared** to enter the big, empty house.*

se•ri•ous (sîr′ē ə s) *adjective.* Important; not joking. *Tim was **serious** when he said he was sick.*

shel•ter (shel′tə r) *noun.* Something that protects. *During the winter, a bear's **shelter** is its cave.*

sim•i•lar (sim′ə lə r) *adjective.* Having many but not all qualities that are the same; alike. *My holiday dress was **similar** to Julia's.*

sim•ple (sim′pə l) *adjective.* Easy to understand or do. *Dan showed me his **simple** recipe for salsa.*

---

at; āpe; fär; câre; end; mē; it; īce; pîerce; hot; ōld; sông; fôrk; oil; out; up; ūse; rüle; pùll; tûrn; chin; sing; shop; thin; this; hw in white; zh in treasure.

The symbol ə stands for the unstressed vowel sound in about, taken, pencil, lemon, and circus.

so·lar sys·tem (sō′lər sis′təm) *noun.* The Sun and all the planets and objects that revolve around it. *Earth is part of the **solar system**.*

so·lu·tion (sə lü′shən) *noun.* The answer to a problem. *Have you found the **solution** to the problem?*

source (sôrs) *noun.* Where something comes from or begins. *A mountain lake is the **source** of that river.*

spe·cial·ist (spə sh′ə list) *noun.* A person who knows a lot about something. *I had to see a **specialist** for the pain in my knee.*

splen·did (splen′ did) *adjective.* Very beautiful or magnificent. *The queen wore a **splendid** dress to the ball.*

strand·ed (strand′ id) *verb.* Left in a difficult or helpless position. *We were **stranded** on the island.*

sub·sti·tute (sub′sti tüt′) *noun.* To put in place of another. *We used honey as a **substitute** for sugar in the cookies.*

suc·cess (sək ses′) *noun.* A result that was hoped for. *My mom was pleased with the **success** of my performance.*

sup·port (sə pôrt′) *verb.* To provide for. *My mother will **support** us by working at the post office.*

sur·face (sûr′fis) *noun.* The outside of a thing. *The astronauts explored the **surface** of the Moon.*

sur·vive (sər vīv′) *verb.* To stay alive. *We were lucky to **survive** the storm!*

sym·bol (sim′bəl) *noun.* Something that represents something else. *The **symbol** for addition is the plus sign.*

Tt

tal·ents (tal′ənts) *noun.* Natural abilities. *Kayla has many **talents** besides singing.*

tem·per·a·ture (tem′pər ə chər) *noun.* The degree of heat or cold. *The **temperature** fell below freezing.*

tem·po·rar·y (tem′pə rer′ ē) *adjective.* Lasting or used for a short time. *Some people get **temporary** jobs during the holiday season.*

threat·ened (thret′ ənd) *verb.* Caused danger or harm. *The lack of rain **threatened** the farmer's crops.*

tim·id (tim′ id) *adjective.* Easily frightened; lacking courage. *The **timid** kitten was afraid of mice.*

tin·ker·ing (ting′ kər ing) *verb.* Making small changes to fix something. *My uncle was outside **tinkering** with his car when we arrived.*

traces (trā′ sez) *plural noun.* Small bits or signs left behind showing something was there. *We found **traces** of the trail as we hiked.*

tra·di·tion (trə dish′ən) *noun.* A belief, custom or way of doing things that is passed down. *It is a **tradition** to have a parade on the Fourth of July.*

tra·di·tion·al (trə dish′ə nəl) *adjective.* According to customs. *Rice is a **traditional** food in Japan.*

trans·por·ta·tion (trans′pər tā′shən) *noun.* A system for moving people or goods from place to place. *The bus is the form of **transportation** we use the most.*

treas·ure (trezh′ər) *noun.* Something that has great value or importance. *The king kept his **treasure** in a locked room.*

tum·ble (tum′bəl) *verb.* To fall in a helpless or clumsy way. *The little puppies might **tumble** down the stairs.*

Uu

un·a·ware (un′ə wâr′) *adjective.* Not realizing or knowing. *The child was **unaware** of the danger of lightning.*

un·fair·ness (un fâr′ nes) *noun.* The act of being not fair or right. *The teacher showed **unfairness** when she picked her favorite student as the winner.*

u·nique (ū nēk′) *adjective.* Being the only one of its kind. *Each family member has a **unique** personality.*

Vv

val·u·a·ble (val′ū ə bəl) *adjective.* Worth a lot of money. *Ira collected **valuable** coins from all over.*

va·ri·e·ty (və rī′i tē) *noun.* A lot of things that are alike but different in some ways. *The restaurant offered a **variety** of choices on its menu.*

ve·hi·cles (vē′ə kəls) *plural noun.* Means of carrying or transporting people or goods. *Cars, trains, airplanes and buses are types of **vehicles** that people use every day.*

Ww

warmth (wôrmth) *noun.* The state or quality of being warm; heat. *The **warmth** of the thick blanket made me feel cozy.*

---

at; **ā**pe; f**ä**r; c**â**re; **e**nd; m**ē**; **i**t; **ī**ce; p**î**erce; h**o**t; **ō**ld; s**ô**ng; f**ô**rk; **oi**l; **ou**t; **u**p; **ū**se; r**ü**le; p**ù**ll; t**û**rn; **ch**in; s**i**ng; **sh**op; **th**in; **th**is; **hw** in **wh**ite; **zh** in trea**s**ure.

The symbol ə stands for the unstressed vowel sound in **a**bout, tak**e**n, penc**i**l, lem**o**n, and circ**u**s.

watch•ful (woch′ fəl) *adjective*. Being alert or attentive. *The **watchful** mother kept an eye on her son.*

wa•ver (wā′ vər) *verb*. To be uncertain; show doubt. *I **waver** when I have too many choices.*

wealth (welth) *noun*. A great amount of money or riches. *The king and queen have great **wealth**.*

weird (wîrd) *adjective*. Odd or strange. ***Weird** sounds came from the empty, old house.*

whis•pered (wis′ pərd) *verb*. To speak softly. *Derek **whispered** the secret to me.*

wild•life (wīld′līf′) *noun*. Wild animals that live in a specific area. *Lions, cheetahs, and elephants are examples of **wildlife** in Africa.*